Eternal Virtues

Spiritual Attributes of
Pramukh Swami Maharaj

Eternal Virtues

Spiritual Attributes of
Pramukh Swami Maharaj

Gujarati Text: Sadhu Aksharvatsaldas
Translation by: Yogi Trivedi

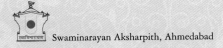
Swaminarayan Aksharpith, Ahmedabad

Eternal Virtues

Spiritual Attributes of Pramukh Swami Maharaj

1st Edition: December 2008
2nd Edition: February 2011

Copies: 10,000 (Total: 15,000)

Price: ₹100/- (Reduced from ₹125/- by courtesy of Swaminarayan Aksharpith)

ISBN: 978-81-7526-438-0

Published & Printed by

Swaminarayan Aksharpith

Shahibaug Road, Ahmedabad 4.

Website: www.baps.org

Bhagwan Swaminarayan

Dedication

Dedicated at the lotus feet of Bhagwan Swaminarayan,

Aksharbrahman Gunatitanand Swami,

Brahmaswarup Bhagatji Maharaj,

Brahmaswarup Shastriji Maharaj and

Brahmaswarup Yogiji Maharaj

who exemplify these eternal, divine virtues,

and for gifting us with

Guruhari Pramukh Swami Maharaj,

an ideal disciple, sadhu and guru...

GLORY OF A SADHU BY PREMANAND SWAMI

Eva Santni balihāri re, jene gune rijhyā Girdhāri re…
Kām, krodh, lobh manmā na āne,
  sonu ne dhul te samm kari jāne;
    Hā re jene Gitāji gāy chhe pukāri re…1
Hari vinā bijo ghāt na lāge,
  lobh laharno lesh na lāge;
    Hā re nāri na shake nayan bān māri re…2
Brahmavidyā jene dradh kari sādhi,
  pind brahmāndni taji re upādhi;
    Hā re bhutprāni tanā hitkāri re…3
Brahmaswarupmā rahe nitya nahāyā,
  pragat Hari gunmā chittada harāyā;
    Hā re Premsakhi evā Sant upar vāri re…4

I repeatedly praise such a Sadhu, by whose virtues God is pleased…
He never entertains thoughts of lust, anger, greed in his mind,
  and regards gold and dust as equal;
                The Gita sings his praises profoundly… 1
He thinks of nothing except God,
  and remains untouched by greed;
                A female cannot cast her enticing gaze upon him…2
He has firmly attained *brahmavidya*,
  and has shed the burdens and attachments of the body and universe;
                He does good for all forms of life…3
He believes himself to be Brahmaswarup,
  and his mind is constantly focused on the virtues of God;
                Premanand is overwhelmed by such a Sadhu…4

सत्यं शौचं दया क्षान्तिस्त्यागः सन्तोष आर्जवम्।
शमो दमस्तपः साम्यं तितिक्षोपरतिः श्रुतम् ॥

ज्ञानं विरक्तिरैश्वर्यं शौर्यं तेजो बलं स्मृतिः।
स्वातंत्र्यं कौशलं कान्तिर्धैर्यं मार्दवमेव च ॥

प्रागल्भ्यं प्रश्रयः शीलं सह ओजो बलं भगः।
गाम्भीर्यं स्थैर्यमास्तिक्यं कीर्तिर्मानोऽनहंकृतिः ॥

Satyam shaucham dayā kshāntistyāgaha santosha ārjavam।
Shamo damastapaha sāmyam titikshoparatihi shrutam॥
Jnānam viraktiraishvaryam shauryam tejo balam smrutihi।
Svātantryam kaushalam kāntirdhairyam mārdavameva cha॥
Prāgalbhyam prashrayaha shilam saha ojo balam bhagaha।
Gāmbhiryam sthairyamāstikyam kirtirmānonahamkrutihi॥

Truth, purity, compassion, forgiveness,
renunciation, contentment, simplicity;
Mental control, sensory control, austerity, equality,
tolerance, worldly disinterest, scriptural obedience.

Experiential knowledge, detachment, power, courage,
illustrious personality, vigour, remembrance;
Independence, skill, beauty, patience, kindheartedness.

Maturity, love, integrity, endurance,
radiance, strength, lordship;
Profundity, mental stability, faith in God,
fame, worthy of reverence, humility.

- Shrimad Bhagvat 1.16.26-28

Contents

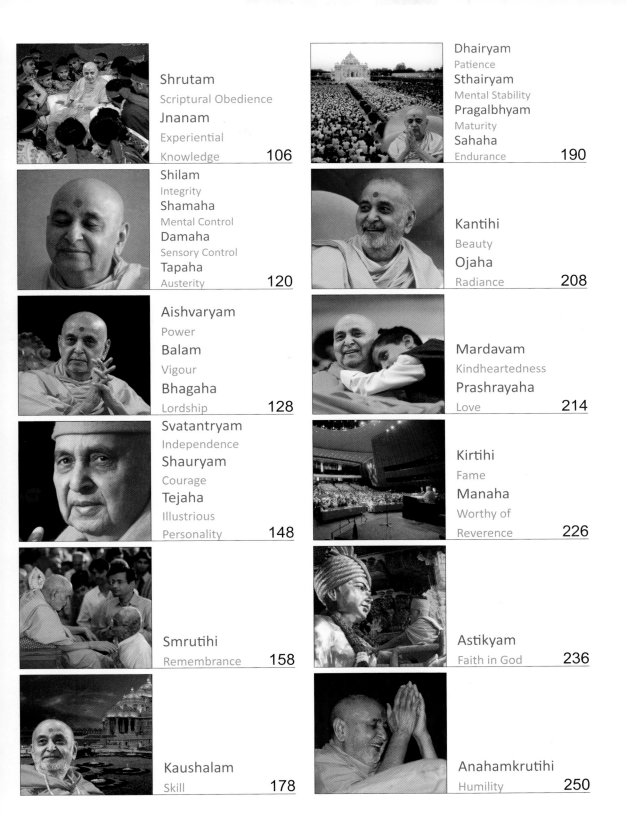

Preface

With the passage of time you come to appreciate what you had previously overlooked. I have heard it said many times but have come to realize it recently. It was in 1988 that I first experienced the saintliness of Pramukh Swami Maharaj (Swamishri). Though I didn't make much of it then, that small incident has since become the guiding light of my life.

Swamishri was having dinner in a modest white-coloured house behind the BAPS Shri Swaminarayan Mandir in Flushing, New York. A few sadhus and devotees were sitting around him enjoying his darshan. I started reciting a story about Bhagwan Swaminarayan's childhood. Swamishri was listening attentively. While I was half way through my story, Swamishri received a phone call from India. The sadhus and devotees began to talk among themselves. I was heartbroken. No one was listening to my story. I left the dining room and ran into a smaller room at the front of the house. A five-year-old carries his emotions on his face! I was no different. Anandmuni Swami was the first to notice. He followed me to the room and asked me as to what was wrong. I told him that I felt that I was being ignored, and I started crying hysterically. Anandmuni Swami took me to Swamishri, whose response was short and beyond my expectation "Sorry! I am sorry I didn't listen to you. Continue. I promise to pay attention this time…" And Swamishri listened to me intently while he finished his meal.

I was overjoyed. I had won! I made Swamishri realize his 'mistake' and apologize! Little did I realize then that this apology would be etched forever in my heart.

Though I was too young to understand the extent of Swamishri's humility, this incident profoundly changed my life. Swamishri's selfless persona humbled me. This was one of his many liberating virtues. As the years passed, I was fortunate enough to appreciate and experience many of his virtues at firsthand.

Based on Pujya Aksharvatsal Swami's original Gujarati, *Jena Gune Rijhya Girdhari,* this publication, *Eternal Virtues,* is a humble attempt to bring forth the 39 liberating qualities of God and the Gunatit Sadhu described in the Shrimad Bhagvat. It provides a deeper understanding of a true Sadhu and his rapport with God. This book does not claim that Pramukh Swami Maharaj is God. It does not compare him to God, nor does it equate him with God. It merely describes the life of a true sadhu – based on 39 virtues.

With Pramukh Swami Maharaj's blessings and Pujya Ishwarcharan Swami's guidance I was able to complete this book in less than a month. Their constant support and motivation have helped me scale new heights. It has forever changed my understanding of God and his Gunatit Sadhu – truly a blessing.

Translating from one language into another is more than merely translating words. It is translating a culture, traditions, rituals, a lifestyle and a thought process. There are many parts of the book that are a direct translation. Others have been completely rewritten to suit the readers of English.

The greatest challenge faced was to find suitable equivalents for Gujarati and Sanskrit terms. I found it rarely possible to use only one English word to fully denote its Sanskrit counterpart. Therefore, I have defined the Gujarati and Sanskrit words using a set of English words. Also, I have kept important Sanskrit or Gujarati words in the text for authenticity and relevance. These words are included in the glossary.

The title of each chapter is based on the Sanskrit word for each of the virtues. However, in the text, the popularly used Gujarati words have been retained. The Appendix serves as a guide on how to pronounce these words.

The text takes a detailed look at Swamishri's life. The incidents are not in chronological order, but have been classified with reference to the 39 virtues of God and his holy Sadhu as enumerated in the Shrimad Bhagvat. His life and work seem beyond human comprehension. It would be a loss not to appreciate Pramukh Swami Maharaj's rapport with God. God lives and works through him.

Every individual involved in the incidents mentioned in this book has experienced this through his selfless love, understanding and tolerant ways. I hope all who read this book will feel the same way.

This second edition of *Eternal Virtues* incorporates some improvements to the first edition.

Yogi Trivedi
BAPS Shri Swaminarayan Mandir
Toronto, Ontario, Canada

Introduction

In every aspect of life there is a set of parameters to aspire for. Whether the subject is animate or inanimate, it is these ideals which set the standard. These can be applied to the whole spectrum of life: in the pursuit of perfection, from common everyday objects like potato chips, medicines, cars, houses, and so on to rare objects. This principle is equally, if not more, relevant in the realm of living objects. We often hear about the characteristics of an ideal child, parent, teacher, doctor, entrepreneur, footballer, leader... the list is endless.

The ideals that define a particular object may change as man's knowledge develops. However, the ideals in the spiritual sphere are eternal and everlasting. So, they have long been established and are unchangeable. The only thing remaining is to understand and apply them to attain spiritual perfection.

In the Shrimad Bhagvat, written by Veda Vyasji, the 39 virtues of God are described by Mother Earth in a conversation with Dharma (1.16.26-8). The shastras also specify that a sadhu whose life exemplifies these virtues is an ideal sadhu, worthy of reverence on par with God.

Bhagwan Swaminarayan (1781-1830 CE) incarnated on this earth and was worshipped as Purna Purushottam Narayan, Supreme God. His life exemplified the 39 virtues described in the Shrimad Bhagvat.

Bhagwan Swaminarayan placed total emphasis on internalizing these virtues for achieving spiritual progress. And to guide aspirants on this path, he established a succession of ideal sadhus who exemplify these 39 virtues in their lives.

Bhagwan Swaminarayan describes the ideal, holy sadhu who has these virtues as Gunatit, Param Bhagvat, Param Ekantik, Brahmaswarup and also refers to him as the manifest form of

Bhagwan Swaminarayan and Aksharbrahman Gunatitanand Swami

Aksharbrahman or Akshar or Akshardham. These terms describe the same virtuous personality.

Such a sadhu is in constant rapport with God and is the manifest form of God on earth, through whom God guides and inspires countless spiritual aspirants.

The sole purpose of Bhagwan Swaminarayan's manifestation on earth was to help each *atma* attain the *brahmarup* state and in that spiritually elevated state, offer devotion to Purushottam.

Thus, in Vachanamrut, Vartal 19, Bhagwan Swaminarayan states, "Whenever a *jiva* attains a human body in Bharat-khand, God's avatars or God's sadhus will certainly also be present on earth at that time. If that *jiva* can recognize them, then he becomes a devotee of God."

The challenge, then, is for all aspirants to identify God or his Gunatit Sadhu and follow their guidelines to attain spiritual perfection.

Bhagwan Swaminarayan's vision was clear: whatever else one does, one's spiritual development is gauged by the understanding and application of these virtues. And only by surrendering to one who has perfected these virtues can such perfection be attained. On numerous occasions Bhagwan Swaminarayan identified Aksharbrahman Gunatitanand Swami (1785-1866 CE) as the first in this succession of Gunatit Sadhus, who also continued to stress this essential point.

In 1828 CE, Bhagwan Swaminarayan consecrated a grand mandir in Junagadh. While appointing Aksharbrahman Gunatitanand Swami as the Mahant, Bhagwan Swaminarayan said to the Nawab of Junagadh, "I appoint my abode Gunatitanand Swami, who is as virtuous as I, as the Mahant."

These sterling qualities were plainly evident in the life of Gunatitanand Swami. He even inspired many sadhus and devotees to attain such spiritual perfection.

Brahmaswarup Bhagatji Maharaj

Gunatitanand Swami revealed Bhagatji Maharaj (1829-1897 CE) as his successor. He, too, received great acclaim for his saintly virtues and under his guidance many experienced the bliss of God.

Bhagatji Maharaj identified Shastriji Maharaj (1865-1951 CE) as the next in Bhagwan Swaminarayan's tradition of Gunatit Sadhus. Shastriji Maharaj was widely respected and among the 2,000 sadhus in Vartal none matched him in saintliness or scriptural wisdom. Shastriji Maharaj established the Bochasanwasi Shri Akshar Purushottam Swaminarayan Sanstha (BAPS) in 1907 and his saintly virtues served as the bedrock for the Sanstha's phenomenal growth.

In turn, Shastriji Maharaj revealed Yogiji Maharaj (1892-1971 CE) as his successor. Describing the greatness of Yogiji Maharaj, Shastriji Maharaj would often say, "If Veda Vyasji has omitted any virtues of a sadhu from the shastras, they can be found in Yogiji Maharaj."

Yogiji Maharaj then identified Pramukh Swami Maharaj (b. 1921 CE) as the next Gunatit Satpurush and praised his saintliness before all.

Pramukh Swami Maharaj was born on 7 December 1921 (Magshar *sud* 8, V.S. 1978) in the village of Chansad, near Vadodara, in Gujarat. His childhood name was Shantilal, and his parents were Motibhai and Diwaliba. From a young age, Shantilal's serene and spiritual nature was apparent. His service and devotion to God, and understanding of the shastras were remarkable. He also obediently completed his duties at home and school and on the family farm.

Shantilal excelled in studies and sports — especially cricket and swimming. But the focus of his life was God and guru Shastriji Maharaj. In fact, Shastriji Maharaj had already taken the permission of Shantilal's parents to initiate him into the sadhu-fold. Shantilal was merely awaiting his guru's order to renounce the world. When that moment arrived, the circumstances were quite unusual.

Brahmaswarup Shastriji Maharaj

Shantilal was almost 18 years old. He was one of the better cricket players in the village and so he was entrusted with the responsibility of using the princely sum of Rs. 500 to buy equipment for the village team. As he prepared to leave, Shantilal received a letter. It was from guru Shastriji Maharaj, instructing Shantilal to leave immediately and join him to become a sadhu. There was no hesitation. No second thoughts. Shantilal showed the letter to his parents and, with their blessings, left home for good. The task of purchasing the cricket kit was passed on to others.

Shastriji Maharaj first initiated Shantilal into the *parshad*-order on 22 November 1939 (Kartik *sud* 11, V.S. 1996), at Babubhai Kothari's house in Amli Vali Pol, Ahmedabad. Subsequently, on 10 January 1940 (Posh *sud* 1, V.S. 1996), Shastriji Maharaj initiated him into the sadhu-order. This auspicious ceremony took place at the Akshar Deri in Gondal. Giving him his new name, Shastriji Maharaj said, "He is the form of Narayan, so he shall be called Narayanswarupdas."

Through his innate saintly nature, and sincere service and devotion, the young Narayanswarup Swami earned the trust and respect of guru Shastriji Maharaj. At the age of 24, Shastriji Maharaj appointed him as the Kothari of the BAPS Mandir in Sarangpur. Narayanswarup Swami continued to serve with humility and dedication.

Shastriji Maharaj took great pride in the young Narayanswarup Swami. The late Prabhashankar Pandya often described one such incident that he had witnessed:

"Shastriji Maharaj was in Atladra. Arjunbhai Mistry was discussing the design of the front gate of the Sarangpur mandir. Motibhai was standing right next to him. Shastriji Maharaj pointed at Motibhai and asked Arjunbhai if he knew him. Before he could answer, he introduced him as the father of Narayanswarup Swami. Shastriji

Pramukh Swami with
Shastriji Maharaj

Maharaj said, 'He has given me his virtuous son. I am forever indebted to him.' "

On 21 May 1950, Shastriji Maharaj appointed the 28-year-old Narayanswarup Swami as President (Pramukh) of the BAPS. Even at that young age, now fondly called Pramukh Swami, he shouldered all the Sanstha's rapidly expanding administrative responsibilities.

Shastriji Maharaj left for Akshardham in May 1951 and for the next 20 years, Pramukh Swami served sincerely under his guru Yogiji Maharaj.

In January 1971, Yogiji Maharaj passed away to Akshardham and Pramukh Swami became the spiritual guru of BAPS. Having sincerely served for over three decades at the feet of his two great gurus, Pramukh Swami was ready to lead the BAPS into a new era. Without compromising his saintly ideals, Pramukh Swami Maharaj, or Swamishri, has been guiding the growth of BAPS ever since.

Over the last four decades, Swamishri has inspired a multitude of educational, environmental, healthcare, social care, disaster relief, tribal welfare, women's uplift, cultural and spiritual activities.

He has shown how to blend spirituality and worldly responsibilities, which serves as a benchmark for others to follow.

Despite his multifarious responsibilities, Swamishri's focus is on God, Bhagwan Swaminarayan. It has always been and shall always remain so. That is why he is able to live such a pure life and still accomplish so much.

In November 2005, Dr Subramanium, Swamishri's bypass surgeon, visited Swaminarayan Akshardham in New Delhi. He was very impressed by the architecture and exhibitions. Afterwards he met Swamishri and questioned, "Swamishri, what is your next project?" Swamishri instantly replied, "Our main and permanent project is to worship God. Everything else is a by-product."

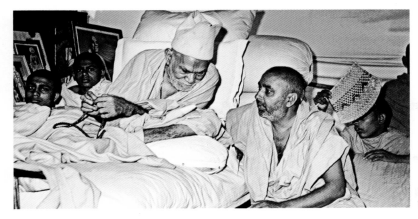

Pramukh Swami with
Yogiji Maharaj

This, in essence, is Swamishri. His greatest asset is his constant rapport with Bhagwan Swaminarayan. This book will delve into the life of Pramukh Swami Maharaj and give a glimpse of how he is able to maintain that unbroken link with God.

This is a book about virtues and values. The virtues which distinguish God and his holy Gunatit Sadhu from the rest of humanity. Of all the Gunatit gurus in Bhagwan Swaminarayan's succession, the life of Pramukh Swami Maharaj has been most extensively recorded. This book describes how each of the 39 virtues described in the Shrimad Bhagvat by Veda Vyasji are evident in Pramukh Swami Maharaj's life.

The incidents presented here barely touch the surface of the vast ocean of virtues Swamishri possesses. But it is a beginning. It will certainly give genuine spiritual aspirants an insight into the saintly attributes that all have to perfect to experience the bliss of God.

◆

Satyam
सत्यम्

The search for the ultimate Truth is eternal.
Philosophers and theologians have arrived at
different definitions of this Truth.
The ancient Hindu shastras regard
it as of paramount importance.
The Chandogya Upanishad says,
"Tat satyam sa ātmā," *meaning,*
"*The God who resides in us is the ultimate Truth*" *(6.8.7).*
The Mundak Upanishad says,
"Satyam param dhimahi. Satyameva jayate," *meaning,*
"*God is the only Truth and the Truth always prevails*" *(3.1.6).*
The Sadhu who has realized the ultimate
Truth is also the form of that ultimate Truth.

In September 1998, just a few weeks after his heart bypass surgery, Pramukh Swami Maharaj was in Edison, New Jersey. Pulitzer Prize winner and the Executive Editor of the *Philadelphia Inquirer*, Ronald Patel, was interviewing Swamishri about his recent medical experiences.

The interview ended a lot sooner than he had planned. He asked Swamishri, "What was the first thought that came to your conscious mind after your quintuple bypass surgery?"

Without a moment's hesitation Swamishri said, "God." Astonished by Swamishri's quick and confident response, Ronald Patel looked unconvinced. He asked, "After regaining consciousness, didn't you feel disappointed that you were back on earth and not in the presence of God?"

"No, God is always with us."

Swamishri's casual, yet assured and lucid response was enough to satisfy Ronald Patel.

After his brief interview with Swamishri, Ronald Patel addressed

"Truth is one. It appears in various forms."

the assembly of devotees, "I had planned to ask Swamishri many questions. After all, that is my job. I am a journalist. Every time I asked Swamishri a question expecting a nifty or dodgy response, I was surprised by the simplicity and ease with which he answered the question. I have interviewed many politicians and spiritual leaders, but none that compares to Pramukh Swami Maharaj. His answers do not have a hidden agenda. They are not manipulative. Instead, they are pure, consistent and divine. They share a sense of sincerity and selflessness."

On 11 February 1991, Swamishri was in Rajkot meeting devotees on his way back to his room after the evening satsang assembly. An unfamiliar youth stopped him and said, "I want to ask you a question."

Swamishri stopped and smiled.

"Ask."

"Have you ever seen God?" the youth asked.

"I have. Hence, I can experience his bliss and speak of him."

"So, you know God?"

"Yes, I know God."

Swamishri's ease and composure was enough to convince the youth.

Jitu Sompura, a reporter for the *Janmabhumi-Pravasi*, a Gujarati daily newspaper, came to ask Swamishri a few questions in Borsad on 28 February 1985.

"Do you recall the first time you experienced God?"

Swamishri replied, "I have experienced God from the very beginning."

Swamishri is the purest form of truth because he experiences God continuously. He has realized God's true greatness. He is in constant rapport with God and, therefore, he is in a constant state of divine bliss and satisfaction.

This constant state of bliss and satisfaction enables him to live truthfully in his thoughts, words and actions. There is no deceit in one who has recognized the ultimate Truth. That is why he always speaks the truth, lives up to his word and acts accordingly. In Swamishri's life the truth is evident in many forms. There is a natural genuineness and honesty in all he says and does.

Sanjay Ramanbhai Patel, a youth from Toronto, Canada, describes his experience of truth in the presence of Pramukh Swami Maharaj in his own words:

"Swamishri walked in and sat down for his morning puja. People were still arriving for his darshan and the din of their conversations filled the hall. Amid all this, devotees started singing bhajans accompanied by a few musical instruments. Simply put, there was noise all around. To my surprise, Swamishri calmly applied the *tilak-chandlo* on his forehead, closed his eyes and was absorbed in deep meditation. His state of tranquillity was obvious from his face. I was dumbfounded. Despite all the commotion, Swamishri had entered a state of serenity, as if there was no one around him. Just the two of them — he and his God! His devotion was charged with a sense of truth and divinity. This experience changed me forever."

Swamishri's actions speak louder than his words, working solely for the benefit of those around him and not for praise or recognition. There is no false portrayal. For him, there is no need to show, boast or package. He is what he is. It is due to his sincerity and faith that Swamishri has been able to touch the hearts of millions.

The Cultural Festival of India brought the magnificent sights and sounds of India to Europe in 1985. Thousands gathered in London to witness the 30 days of traditional festivities. Shri Manek Dalal, then Chairman of the Bharatiya Vidya Bhavan, decided not to visit the festival despite repeatedly hearing great things about it. Mr Dalal had a bias against Hindu sadhus. He felt that they often misused their spiritual authority for fraudulent personal gains.

However, he was soon surprised.

A few weeks after the festival had ended, Swamishri was visiting the Bharatiya Vidya Bhavan for a spiritual conference, where a small gathering had also been organized. Mr Dalal was walking past and decided to sit in the assembly. After listening to just a few minutes of Swamishri's speech, Mr Dalal felt that there was something different about this sadhu. Swamishri spoke with his natural sincerity and truthfulness. Mr Dalal was quick to correct his misperceptions, "I have heard many sadhus and mahatmas speak, but none are so genuine and simple. There is no manipulation in his speech." Swamishri's transparent persona changed Mr Dalal's outlook towards sadhus.

One cannot be truthful and selfish. One cannot be truthful and deceptive. Swamishri lives for the truth. He does not believe in creating a false image or portraying a persona that doesn't exist.

Shortly after Yogiji Maharaj had passed away to Akshardham, and Swamishri started to serve as the spiritual guru of BAPS, Swamishri's personal attendant, Devcharan Swami, commented on his quiet and introspective personality, "Now that you are in Yogiji Maharaj's place, you should act like him. Like Yogiji Maharaj, you should bless devotees by giving them *dhabbaas*, clap your hands and sway during bhajans. This way people will love you as they loved Yogiji Maharaj."

Eternal Virtues

Swamishri was quick to respond, "That was Yogiji Maharaj's way of doing things. That's not my style. It doesn't make sense for me to copy him. This is what I am. I am not good at impersonating other people and the fact that they love Yogiji Maharaj is great."

Swamishri's truthfulness is highlighted by his transparency and straightforwardness. Once in Bochasan, he had told the sadhus seated in front of him. "If there is one thing I dislike, it is deceit and manipulation."

Thousands of local devotees and people flock to get a glimpse of Swamishri when he is in a particular city or town. Hundreds also line up to meet him and receive his blessings everyday. After one such exhausting day, Janmangal Swami decided to have a laugh with Swamishri. He said, "Didn't you get tired of blessing five thousand devotees? Putting your hand on each one is a physically straining task. We should consider fabricating a wooden hand, attaching it to a motor and blessing every devotee that comes to meet you with it! The devotees won't be able to tell that it's automatically powered..."

Swamishri interrupted, "Why would you want to deceive them? I don't keep fake things. I only stock real things."

Though the incident seems trivial, it brings out a few of Swamishri's most important personality traits – honesty and transparency.

Only one who has nothing to hide can afford to be completely transparent. Swamishri's life is like an open book. Every moment is lived in someone's presence. Eating, sleeping, reading, writing, during the day, and even at night, there is not a single moment when he is alone. There is no need for it either.

Swamishri was attending a meeting in Gondal. As the meeting continued, Swamishri kept on scribbling a few important dates on a small notepad. Vishwavihari Swami noticed and asked Swamishri, "What are you writing in that private diary?"

Swamishri replied, "My whole life is open to the public. There are no secrets. If you have secrets, you always fear them being revealed. I live my life openly with God as my witness."

Truth is eternal and unchanging.

The secret behind Swamishri's commitment to the eternal truth lies in his loyalty to the principles and moral code laid down by Bhagwan Swaminarayan. With his direction, BAPS has soared to Himalayan heights in the past 50 years, but never at the expense of its principles.

Mahant Swami has witnessed the past 50 years of growth and

notes that Swamishri's consistency has stood the test of time, "Many political and spiritual leaders change their principles and belief systems every year, sometimes every six months! Pramukh Swami Maharaj has been the President of this Sanstha for over 50 years and yet his ideals and principles remain unchanged. That is a measure of his truthfulness and spiritual altitude."

Sage Valmiki describes Bhagwan Ramchandra as being, *"Rāmo dhvirnābhibhāshate"*. That is, Bhagwan Ramchandra's actions and principles were always truthful. There was never a need for double standards; his actions and principles were always consistent.

The same can be seen in Swamishri's life. If at times, someone tries to fabricate a story to prove a point, Swamishri is quick to reply, "I don't recall that ever happening."

The Inspector General of Police of Bihar State, Rakesh Asthana, came to meet Swamishri in Vadodara on 16 August 2006. Swamishri blessed him and instructed him to always support the truth, "God is pleased with those that side with the truth. We don't bear ill-will for anybody, but the truth must be established. The truth can be bitter, but in the long-run it is always beneficial. You may have to endure at first, but the truth always prevails."

In his *Yogasutra,* Maharshi Patanjali speaks of one who is truthful, "For one who has established the truth through his life, his every word and action comes true."

The Chhandogya Upanishad (8.1.5) states that every wish and desire of Aksharbrahman represents the truth.

Swamishri's words and wishes bear fruition because he lives such a truthful life.

The last few months leading up to the Birth Bicentenary Celebrations of Gunatitanand Swami in 1985 were very tense and chaotic. There was an impending famine in Gujarat and students were organizing agitations to protest changes in the education system. It was already the third month of the monsoon season and there wasn't a cloud in the sky. Many community leaders wanted the festival to be postponed. Swamishri had asked everyone to pray and said, "The festival will be celebrated as planned. It will rain. God is merciful; he will listen to our prayers." To everyone's surprise, it rained, removing any fear of famine; and the students' issues were also resolved.

After the land for Swaminarayan Akshardham in New Delhi had been officially acquired, Swamishri said, "We want to build the foundations in such a way that there will be no problem for a thousand years." However, India's renowned structural engineer,

Shri B.V. Chaudhari, and other experts had their doubts, "Pramukh Swami's wish to build a foundation to last a thousand years in the sandy, earthquake-prone zone on the banks of a river did not seem possible and was beyond our capacity." Yet Pramukh Swami Maharaj insisted that the task would be accomplished. Today, as the monument stands glistening on the banks of the River Yamuna, designers Shri Mahesh Desai and Shri B.V. Chaudhari are still wondering how it was accomplished. They comment, "It seems like a miracle. There is no way we could have found an answer by ourselves. It is due to divine intervention. Now we are confident that this remarkable edifice will glow for centuries to come."

A similar observation was noticed while shooting for the *Neelkanth Yatra* large format film that is part of the cultural exhibitions at Swaminarayan Akshardham, New Delhi, and its global version is called *Mystic India*.

The shooting was scheduled to begin in the Himalayas on 3 March 2003. Once the shooting crew from America and other members of the shoot arrived in Nepal they realized the difficulties that had to be overcome. First, it had been raining for many days with no sight of the sun. More importantly, there was no snow on the mountains at Muktinath. Clearly visible were the dull black stones with no snow or ice and hence – no shine. The locals were the first to point out that there was never any snow on those mountains at that time of year. Without sunshine and snow the shooting would not be possible.

The organizing team of BAPS volunteers telephoned Swamishri, who was then at Gondal. After listening to them, he said, "God will help finish the filming. Be patient." Another day passed, and yet there was no sign of sun or snow. They also searched for other suitable locations to shoot, but without success. Again, the organizers called up Swamishri, "How will we be able to shoot tomorrow?" Swamishri told them, "Go ahead with the shooting tomorrow. It will be all right."

The next morning, the crew and organizers saw to their delight that the mountains were covered in snow. The rain had stopped and the sun was shining brilliantly.

Buoyed up by this dramatic, overnight change the crew was able to gather an hour of footage in just one day.

Award-winning cinematographer, Reed Smoot, who witnessed the entire situation unfold, commented, "Along with the 16 voluntary departments working for BAPS, there is a seventeenth one. Nature. Prayers help manage this department. Pramukh Swami Maharaj's prayers!"

Many would dismiss these occurrences as mere coincidence, but the power of Swamishri's prayers lies in his unflinching commitment to and faith in Truth. His honesty and transparency bring power to his words —call it divine power.

Veda Vyasji defines the ultimate truth. "One who unconditionally does good to all living beings is the ultimate truth" (Mahabharat, Shanti Parva, 316.13). Swamishri often says, "I have never even thought of hurting anyone or any being." He lives by the credo, "In the joy of others, lies our own." His prayers resonate with peace and hope for all living beings.

On 6 April 1984, the day before Swamishri was going to meet the Pope in the Vatican, a journalist from the Reuters news agency, Frank Pullela, asked him, "What will you discuss with the Pope when you meet him? Others often discuss politics."

Swamishri replied, "We do not want to talk about politics, but about how the world can become nobler and happier, and how God can be worshipped by all."

In 1994, when reporters in the Czech Republic asked the reason for his visit, Swamishri replied, "We have come here to honour the invitation extended by Professor Fric. We have come to pray for the success of this country and that friendship develops between everyone."

This was not a reply just to please the media. A few days later, Swamishri visited the historic St. Bartholomew's Cathedral. As everyone was observing the grandeur and marvelling at its cross-vaulted ceiling, Swamishri was praying, reciting the Swaminarayan mantra and saying, "May God bless this country and its people. May their faith in God be strengthened. And may God bless the priests here."

The sight of a Hindu sadhu praying for them seemed to slow down and impress every European tourist that walked by.

On 4 September 1999, Swamishri uttered a similar prayer at the Wailing Wall in Jerusalem, "May good prevail upon those that come here."

For the benefit of others, Swamishri has selflessly endured many difficulties.

In Atladra, Janmangal Swami jokingly remarked, "So many people come to meet you. If you charge a fee then the rush will be less."

Swamishri said, "I do not wish well for just a few people. I wish well for all living beings. So I do not expect anything in return."

Only one who is in continuous rapport with God can act selflessly for the good of others. In his bhajan, Brahmanand Swami describes such an ideal sadhu as being '*param hitkari*', meaning, he wishes for the highest good for all – by removing the attachment others have for their body and engaging them in the divine form of God.

In 1988, Swamishri was getting ready to leave Pravinbhai Bhavsar's house in Paris. Pleased with their devout service, Swamishri said to the devotees, "You have all served wholeheartedly. What else can I give you in return? I have God, so I will give him to you."

Many have experienced this divine blessing, including Dr V. Subramanium, the renowned cardiothoracic surgeon at the Lenox Hill Hospital in New York. He had performed Swamishri's heart bypass operation in July 1998. Then, on 6 September 1998, Swamishri attended his first public assembly after the operation. Westchester County Hall was filled with thousands of devotees, each enthralled to have the darshan of their beloved guru. It was an opportunity to honour everyone who had helped during Swamishri's operation and recovery. When Dr Subramanium's name was announced, the devotees applauded with great delight and vigour. Dr Subramanium walked from his seat on the stage and prostrated at Swamishri's feet on the stage floor.

Everyone on the stage and in the audience was astonished by this humble gesture from a self-proclaimed atheist. Addressing the gathering, Dr Subramanium, revealed, "On 7 July 1998, Bhagwan Swaminarayan graced my operation theatre at Lenox Hill Hospital. Everyday after the surgery when I went to meet Swamishri, it felt as if I was going for the darshan of God. It felt as if each glimpse of his purified me a little more."

Swamishri loves all living beings and this is why he gives them the greatest gift possible – God. Swamishri's presence has helped many others like Dr Subramanium experience God. That in itself is an experience of the eternal truth.

Swamishri often quotes the Vachanamrut and says, "God is the eternal Truth. God's words are the eternal Truth. The Gunatit Sadhu who beholds God – Aksharbrahman – is also the eternal Truth, and all who have faith in that Sadhu attain the eternal Truth."

This is *satyam*.   ◆

Shaucham

शौचम्

Shaucham means to be clean, spotless, pure.
The ancient Hindu shastras prescribe five forms of purity:
in mind, action, character, speech and the physical body.
The Gunatit Sadhu, who has realized God,
exemplifies all the five forms of purity.
Pramukh Swami Maharaj's life radiates the
fragrance of this quintet of purity.

A pure mind is one that is free of malice or hatred. Pramukh Swami Maharaj's pure mind is without animosity and deceit.

To perform good deeds without expectations reflects purity of action. Pramukh Swami Maharaj has been performing good deeds for nearly 90 years without expecting anything in return, except the blessings of God.

Whatever the circumstances, to live by God's moral laws is the mark of a pure character. Pramukh Swami Maharaj has resolutely followed the moral code given by Bhagwan Swaminarayan.

Purity of speech is to speak that which is truthful, pleasant and beneficial. Pramukh Swami Maharaj's words have comforted, guided and inspired millions worldwide.

Hygiene and cleanliness are the hallmarks of physical purity. Pramukh Swami Maharaj always stresses the importance of a hygienic and healthy lifestyle.

Adi Shankaracharya has grouped these five forms of purity into two main categories: internal and external. External purity pertains to one's body and the surrounding environment. Internal purity is that of one's mind and soul.

Throughout his life Swamishri has worked tirelessly to promote such internal and external purity among all: purity of body, mind, actions and thoughts; and purity in the individual, family, home, mandir, community, nation and the world at large.

Swamishri has encouraged internal and external purity in people from all walks of life, including the tribal villagers seen here.

Swamishri states, "To become pure within, one must first begin with outer purity." Swamishri's life is full of incidents which illustrate this belief.

This is an incident from the 1960s. Thousands of devotees had gathered in the small town of Sarangpur to celebrate the Jaljhilani Ekadashi festival. After the festival was over, the devotees left for their homes and the volunteers were taking rest in the afternoon. Swamishri too decided to rest as well.

After a while, Dharmajivan Swami, who was sleeping near Swamishri in the assembly hall, noticed that he had gone somewhere. So, he got up and started looking for him. His search led him to the common toilets at the rear of the mandir campus.

To his surprise, Swamishri was cleaning the overflowing toilets. He was carrying a bucket full of excreta and taking it to the dumpsite, pausing momentarily between rounds to sweep the toilets.

Dharmajivan Swami quickly ran to Swamishri and tried to forcibly take the bucket and broom from him. Swamishri simply remarked, "Don't make a noise. You will wake up the other sadhus who are resting. Now, two is better than one. If you want me to finish this sooner, get me some water so that I can clean the toilets."

The President of the BAPS Swaminarayan Sanstha happily performed the most menial and repulsive of services.

After the Kalash Jayanti Celebrations in Gadhada in May 1961, Swamishri joined volunteers in cleaning the dining areas. Also, he had been just as eager in picking up the used *datan* sticks outside a bathroom in Dharmaj on the morning of his birthday celebration in 1971.

Once, as Swamishri was passing through the mandir corridor in Bochasan, he stopped to look at the condition of a bathroom. As he peeked in, he smelled a strong stench indicating that the bathroom hadn't been cleaned for some time. Swamishri walked in, locked it from the inside and started scrubbing away. The sadhus and devotees assumed that Swamishri was using the urinal. It was only after he came outside that they realized that he had single-handedly cleaned the whole bathroom. The incidents show that he has an inclination for cleanliness and hygiene, and to clean up whenever an opportunity arises.

Swamishri was staying at a devotee's new house in Anand. The house had just been constructed and still had paint and cement stains on the tiles in the bathroom. Swamishri went in for a shower and decided to clean the tiles himself. Narayancharan Swami stopped him and said, "We are only here for a day and a half. Why bother with all that extra effort?"

Yet Swamishri was adamant, "We should leave the place in better condition than we had found it. The devotee was kind enough to let us stay at his place. He might not have had the time to clean up. We should help him. It is our *seva*."

Swamishri often says, "Our home and mandir should be clean, so that God would like to stay there. How can you expect God to stay where there is filth? Keeping the mandir clean inspires everyone to keep their homes clean. If everyone kept their homes and neighbourhoods clean, it would make the whole country a cleaner place."

Swamishri's insistence on cleanliness and hygiene has inspired many devotees to adopt and promote a similar lifestyle.

Dr Rajiv Vyas lives in Cherry Hill, NJ. A practising physician, Dr Vyas has a staff of over 38 physicians and 800 healthcare employees under him. Yet, he begins his day by visiting the BAPS Shri Swaminarayan Mandir in Cherry Hill. After darshan, he goes to the public toilets in the mandir and cleans them each morning before going to work.

In Surat, a group of affluent youths clean the general toilets every Sunday.

Dr Rohit Patel, Dr Dipak Patel, Anup Morzariya and other youths have been washing dishes and cooking utensils on Saturdays in London mandir for over 22 years.

These youths and devotees have pleased Swamishri with their efforts to clean and tidy their homes, mandirs and surroundings. Swamishri has blessed them, many times saying, "Since you have worked so hard to clean and purify the outside, God will purify your hearts and souls."

Swamishri's efforts to promote cleanliness have helped create a spiritually pure and physically tidy environment in all BAPS

Mandirs around the globe. To this day, he makes it a point to check the bathrooms and other facilities at even the smaller mandirs as well as the mega-mandirs like Swaminarayan Akshardham in Gandhinagar and New Delhi. He inspects every nook and corner of the mandir, in particular, the kitchens, dairy room, storage area, public conveniences and the *garbhagruha*, for dirt or clutter. At the students' hostel in Vidyanagar, Swamishri occasionally makes impromptu checks on the students' rooms. Frantically, the students try to clean them, but Swamishri's sharp and trained eyes quickly analyze their efforts. He sweetly reprimands those that are not clean and praises those that are.

During his stay at Sarangpur in October 1997, Swamishri was inspecting the mandir grounds. He entered one of the bathrooms and immediately called the head organizers of the housekeeping department to bless them, "This is very clean. It should be like this all the time and everywhere. Very good."

Even during large festivals, when the arrangements for the thousands of people who attend ultimately rest on Swamishri's shoulders, he undertakes unannounced inspections of the festival grounds to ensure that the proper level of cleanliness and hygiene is constantly maintained. He specially insists that the kitchen and dining areas be kept spotlessly clean. *Kothari* and *bhandari* sadhus and volunteers are first to hear from Swamishri about keeping the mandirs and kitchens under their charge clean.

Swamishri was visiting New York in 2004, where he met Subhodhbhai Amin. Swamishri was speaking to him and his Jewish partner about their dairy business and the conversation veered round to matters of cleanliness. Swamishri said, "Whenever you make any yogurt, *paneer* or even when you process milk, make sure that hygiene is a priority. Ensure that all the utensils and machinery are scrubbed before you start producing any dairy products. You are from Vahelal and a descendent of Vakhatba. You come from a family that is very particular about its purity; it only makes sense for you to do this."

Swamishri's devotion to Bhagwan Swaminarayan is reflected through his insistence on cleanliness in Thakorji's *thal*, ornaments and the shrine itself. He even stresses the importance of personal hygiene to the cooks that prepare Thakorji's *thal*.

Swamishri has visited over 250,000 homes and each *padhramani* echoes the same message, "You do not need a large home, but a home that is tidy and clean. Things that belong in the kitchen should never be left in the living room and vice versa. It is important for us to practise these ideals so that our children learn them. Cleanliness and spirituality are the keys to a happy home."

These experiences highlight Swamishri's insistence on external purity. The following incidents highlight Swamishri's internal purity and life free of deceit and prejudice. He tirelessly inspires even those who come only into fleeting contact with him to attain internal purity of the mind and soul.

Swamishri insists that community leaders, politicians and other public figures be pure in character and reputation.

Speaking to a local town representative he said, "You have to lead by example. It is your duty to make this town a better place to live in. You can only do it by living a spotless life so that it makes an impact on the society."

Once in Atladra, Swamishri walked by a few youths who were cleaning the filters of an old air-conditioning unit. He stopped and said to them, "The filters of this A.C. unit became filled with dirt so it had to be removed for cleaning. Similarly, when life becomes spoilt by bad habits it is degraded. So you have to inspect your character for impurities and cleanse it."

Swamishri has transformed the lives of thousands of people around the world and they provide testimony of his contributions in purifying society.

A tribal devotee from the village of Uber described his first darshan of Swamishri, which changed his life, "I first had your darshan in Atladra. I didn't think it was ever going to happen, but it did. It was like a miracle. With your blessings, my entire family has stopped eating meat, smoking and drinking. We have been able to bring our tempers under control. It has been eight months now and I can say that we feel 100 percent purified! My adulterous behaviour has also gone. I feel privileged to have received your blessings."

On 18 July 1996, a youth came to meet Swamishri in Dallas, Texas. In 1994, he had promised Swamishri that he would quit drinking and eating meat. He fell at Swamishri's feet and described his success, "Swami, though it seemed impossible, your blessings made my wife's dream a reality. I have given up eating meat and all other addictions. In fact, I don't even get angry any more. I never thought it would be possible, but you made it happen."

These are just a few of the countless transformations people have had as a result of their association with Swamishri.

Only one who is clean, pure and spotless can transform the lives of others. Thousands of individuals have developed inner purity through Swamishri's blessings and many more are in the process of achieving it.   ◆

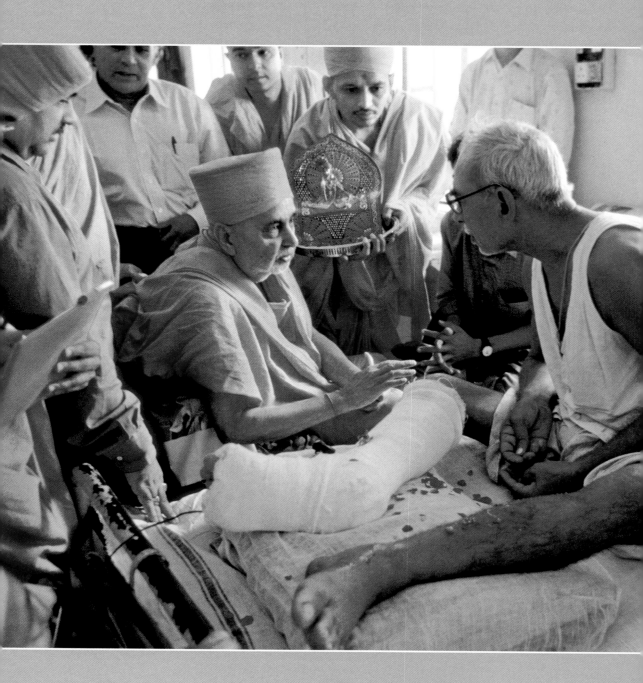

Daya दया

Daya is compassion.
Compassion is listed as one of the foremost qualities of
a true sadhu in the 11th chapter of the Shrimad Bhagvat.
Shri Tulsidasji says in the Ramacharitamanas that
a true sadhu has a tender heart that melts on hearing
the sorrows and difficulties of those around him.
Pramukh Swami Maharaj has an amazing
level of personal resilience, but his heart melts with
compassion on seeing the suffering of others.

Aksharbrahman Gunatitanand Swami says, "God is the root of compassion. It is from him that all compassion is born."

A closer look at Bhagwan Swaminarayan's life reveals just how true this observation is. The day he was appointed as the spiritual heir by Ramanand Swami, the 21-year-old Sahajanand Swami asked for two boons from him for the welfare of his disciples: "If your *satsangi* is destined to suffer the distress inflicted by the sting of one scorpion, may the distress of the stings of millions and millions of scorpions befall each and every pore of my body, but no pain should afflict your *satsangi*. Moreover, if the begging bowl is written in the destiny of your *satsangi*, may that begging bowl come to me, but on no account should your *satsangi* suffer from the lack of food or clothing. Please grant me these two boons."

The *paramhansas* who compiled the Vachanamrut describe Bhagwan Swaminarayan's compassionate ways: "Upon hearing about a devotee in despair or difficulty, he would utter 'Rama, Rama, Rama'. At other times he would give food, clothing and shelter to those in need. He could never tolerate another person being beaten or offended and would call out to intervene."

Such compassion is also clearly visible in Pramukh Swami Maharaj. His love for all living beings is the basis of his empathy for all. For him to feel the pain and suffering of others is as natural as breathing.

Caring for livestock during a drought. Cattle Camp in Raisan, Gujarat, 2001.

Swamishri's care and concern for all living beings are evident from his active support for the victims of natural calamities, his involvement in anti-addiction drives and campaigns to promote vegetarianism, his mediation in resolving domestic quarrels and even social unrest. He has inspired tens of thousands of volunteers to help lessen the troubles of those around them.

In 1990 the monsoon had nearly passed in Gujarat, and not a single drop of rain had quenched the dry earth. Swamishri was in London at the time and was alerted on the grave drought situation. Swamishri's response? Sleeping less at night. Swamishri would wake up in the middle of the night, sit up in his bed and pray to Bhagwan Swaminarayan for the much-needed rain. One night his attendant sadhu realized that Swamishri was awake at about 2.00 a.m. He observed him for a while and then asked him why he was awake. Swamishri told him about his nightly prayer sessions. From then onwards, the attendant sadhu too joined in the prayers every night.

Not one to normally highlight such things, Swamishri wrote in a letter from London, "The monsoon has almost gone. It is natural that you are worried, but have faith in God. I am praying daily in the Akshar Deri. Shriji Maharaj, Gunatitanand Swami, Shastriji Maharaj and Yogi Bapa will all shower their compassion. There is still time."

Swamishri has always shown his love and kindness whenever he found or heard people suffering.

In 1979, due to severe rains the Machhu Dam in Morbi gave way. There was widespread destruction. Swamishri mobilized over 1,500 sadhus and volunteers to rush there and help. A volunteer still recalls the sorrow visible on Swamishri's face as he surveyed the muddy streets of Morbi strewn with bodies.

During the severe famine in Gujarat in 1987, Swamishri was visiting Ratanpura, a small town near Rajkot. The town had a

Eternal Virtues

government-operated cattle camp. The camp had about 5,000 famished calves. As Swamishri approached the camp, a group of calves gathered around him and followed him. The volunteer explained that the calves hadn't eaten for three days. Swamishri's eyes welled up with tears as he heard this. He remained silent. When he reached Gondal, he immediately summoned Jnanprasad Swami and said, "The way those calves in Ratanpura were running after us was unbearable for me. So, arrange to send some trucks full of fodder for them immediately."

In the days to follow Swamishri was not himself. He would stop his routine activity and would become lost in deep thought. He would say, "I can't think of anything else right now. I really feel for the people and livestock that are suffering because of the drought. In everything that I do, I think of the rain."

Pramukh Swami Maharaj's concern gave birth to a project that was to change the lives of hundreds of farmers and thousands of cattle in Gujarat.

Watching helplessly as their livestock was perishing, the farmers decided to sell their cattle. Swamishri stopped the farmers from doing so. He organized cattle camps to take care of the animals until their owners could provide for them. Swamishri realized that these animals were the source of livelihood for their owners. The animals were nourished and looked after for a year till their owners were able to take care of them.

Pravinsinh of Vadheda couldn't help but cry after seeing his cattle being cared for so well.

Kasambhai, a Muslim resident of Madhupur Gir, was touched by Swamishri's kindness, "I feel that Pramukh Swami Maharaj is my Khuda."

Swamishri's kindness and compassion knows no bounds. His work bridges the barriers of caste, creed, culture and geographical boundaries. During the Maharashtra Earthquake of 1993, Swamishri adopted and rebuilt two villages – Samudral and Kondjigadh. The people of Orissa, who had lost everything in the 1999 supercyclone experienced similar support and warmth. Under the guidance of Swamishri extensive emergency relief work was undertaken by BAPS. Further, two villages were adopted and rebuilt along with various other long-term relief efforts. The people of Orissa said, "We feel the love and care of Bhagwan Jagannath through Pramukh Swami Maharaj."

Similar compassion was experienced by those affected by the

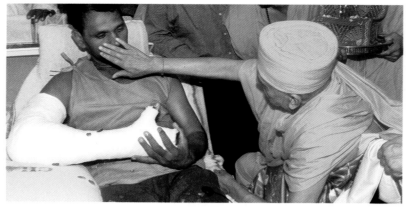

Comforting a wounded soldier in Ahmedabad, 2002.

South Asian Tsunami, the California Wildfires, Hurricanes Katrina and Rita and the 2006 Surat Floods through the services inspired for them by Swamishri.

He has travelled even to remote villages affected by such disasters and comforted the unfortunate victims.

At 8.46 a.m. on 26 January 2001 a devastating earthquake rattled Gujarat. It measured 7.6 on the Richter scale, demolishing buildings, infrastructure and killing thousands. While most people were still recovering from the initial shock of the earthquake, Pramukh Swami Maharaj had arranged warm meals for survivors by lunchtime. Swamishri mobilized the BAPS Sanstha's sadhus and volunteers to begin emergency relief work. He was so involved in organizing the relief efforts that he was on the phone the next morning even before taking a bath. For the whole year, Swamishri coordinated the Sanstha's earthquake relief work, often staying up till well past midnight to contact people in India and abroad to make the necessary arrangements.

At the BAPS relief camps in and around Bhuj, the epicentre of the earthquake, more than 40,000 people were fed warm and nutritious meals daily. Attending to the smallest of details, Swamishri called Vedagna Swami, the Kothari in Bochasan, regarding the grains being sent to Bhuj, "The grains that are being grinded for the relief kitchens have to be of the best quality. Make sure they are cleaned and sifted for small stones."

Swamishri visited the kitchen in Atladra where food packets for distribution were being prepared. After inspection he suggested that two green chillies be included in each packet, explaining, "People from the Kutch region enjoy spicy food. Also, they will taste good with the sweets."

The survivors of the earthquake will probably never know the care Swamishri took in organizing the relief work.

Swamishri personally walked through the rubble-strewn streets of earthquake-devastated villages in Kutch, showering his grace and compassion on the survivors. He blessed the injured and traumatized victims to lessen their pain and sorrow.

More than 500 villages were provided with aid and 15 villages and colonies were reconstructed. Today, these villages are considered among the finest in Gujarat, made possible by Swamishri's meticulous care.

Pramukh Swami Maharaj's compassion is selfless. There are no expectations, except one – to please God.

On 18 August 2006 Swamishri was in Bangalore in South India. From there he phoned the volunteers who had served in the aftermath of the floods in Surat, "You have put up with difficulties to help those in need. Bhagwan Swaminarayan will be pleased. Remember, this service is not done for recognition. It is to help humanity and to please God. Bhagwan Swaminarayan has instructed us to serve the needy. So, serve with care to ensure that the relief supplies reach the people. Please do not harbour any partiality when distributing the supplies. Give them to everyone. Keep everyone happy."

In London, on 30 April 2004, Swamishri finished meeting the devotees who had come for personal guidance at 10.00 p.m. He then read a long letter. When he finished, he sighed and revealing his inner anguish, said, "There is not one happy letter. Only letters describing pain and misery. Even in this country there is much conflict. Hearing about them causes much pain." Many have witnessed Swamishri's watery gaze even on merely hearing about the misery of others.

Swamishri's tolerance is immeasurable, but he does not tolerate any cruelty to animals.

He has been a strong advocate of vegetarianism around the world. He often says, "Every being has the right to live. Killing to survive is just not humane."

With this understanding, Swamishri has successfully convinced hundreds of thousands of people to adopt a vegetarian diet. Speaking to a youth that enjoyed hunting as a pastime, Swamishri expressed his value for life, "Just as we have the right to live, don't they? Do not commit such a grave sin. These poor animals live on grass. Do they harm anyone? If somebody hits us do we not feel pain? They also have feelings. Promise that you will never kill again. You will find the strength to abstain. You will experience peace and happiness."

The youth agreed, but while taking the pledge he murmured,

Serving earthquake victims, Bhuj, 2001.

"I will not be able to stay without hunting." Swamishri heard this and then, looking directly into the youth's eyes, patiently explained, "What do you mean? There's nothing you can't live without. Give up that thought. You will get strength from satsang. Hunting does not benefit you or the animals. The poor animals suffer and die. They also have a soul. God has given them an animal body and us a human body. You are a Kshatriya and so your duty is to protect. Killing is demonic, and the more you do it the more miserable you will become."

Out of his compassion towards those that have addictions, Swamishri has personally counselled and inspired hundreds of thousands of people to give up such harmful habits. No matter how busy he may be, but whenever Swamishri meets someone entangled in addictions, he always finds time to speak to them and convince them to give up bad habits. He repeatedly reminds people of their vows to eschew their vices and constantly follows up with them for years.

Swamishri was meeting devotees as he walked towards the assembly hall in Ahmedabad, when suddenly a youth bowed at Swamishri's feet. A sadhu started to introduce him, but Swamishri interrupted, "I know him. How are you Atul? Are you still on it?"

"On what?"

"Brown sugar, Atul. I haven't forgotten."

Atul couldn't look into Swamishri's eyes. Swamishri noticed his body language and said, "You are still addicted? I have told you so many times. How have you benefited from it? Everyone is telling you to give up. Is it because they want to harm you? You have to decide. How much do you take?"

"Around two hundred rupees worth daily."

"Where do you get the money from?"

"I have a job in the government where I can coax extra money from people."

Swamishri picked up on this point, "So you steal money. Your drug habit is one type of sin. Then you steal again from people to support your addictive habits; that's another sin."

After eight years of persistent effort, Swamishri was able to save Atul, the only son of a widowed mother, from the fatal grip of a silent killer.

Through personal meetings, letters and home visits, Swamishri's compassion has saved and pacified countless people. Whenever someone is in a difficult situation or condition, Swamishri is overcome with a feeling of pity: "How may I help?"

When Harshad Chavda, a youth who had been serving in the BAPS for many years, met with a car accident, Swamishri wrote him a 20-page letter to express his serious regret for not being able to serve him personally:

"The news (of your accident) brings me much pain. I am praying to Maharaj and Swami for your speedy recovery. I am praying for you in my morning puja as well. I also feel the pain you are suffering. I should be serving you in your time of need, because you have always selflessly served with great understanding and enthusiasm, and without concern for your health, hunger, thirst or time of day. I can never serve you enough to make it up! The fact that I cannot serve you now is causing me immense sorrow."

Prabhashankarbhai Pandya of Ahmedabad, an elderly devotee from Shastriji Maharaj's time, recalls a moving incident to illustrate Swamishri's compassion:

"Once, I arrived in Atladra for the Vasant Panchmi celebrations at around 2.00 a.m. Everyone was asleep and there was no place for me to sleep. I decided to rest in front of the steps leading up to the assembly hall, using my bag as a makeshift pillow. At around 5.30 a.m. I felt a hand on my shoulder. It was Pragat Bhagat – Swamishri's attendant. I saw a blanket wrapped around my body. 'Who covered me with this blanket?' I asked him. Pragat Bhagat replied, 'Pramukh Swami Maharaj had come in the middle of the night and covered you with his blanket.' "

On a sweltering hot summer afternoon in 1971, a procession had been organized through the streets of Nadiad. Swamishri was seated in a decorated chariot. The streets were baking under the blistering sun. Narayanprasad Swami did not have his sandals. Swamishri noticed and called him, "Here, take these sandals and wear them. It is not good to walk barefoot in the scorching sun. The sizzling pavement may damage your health."

Narayanprasad Swami accepted the sandals and wore them. After a few moments, he realized that these were probably Swamishri's sandals. So, he instantly removed them.

Swamishri noticed and said, "I didn't give you the sandals to hold them in your hands. Wear them!"

Swamishri notices the smallest details about his devotees.

Late on a cold winter night in 1977, Swamishri arrived in Ahmedabad with a few sadhus and youths. As everyone was getting ready to sleep, Narendraprasad Swami was looking for a blanket for a sick youth, Jagdish (presently, Narayancharan Swami – Swamishri's personal attendant sadhu), who had a fever and couldn't tolerate the bitter cold. It was already midnight and Narendraprasad Swami couldn't find an extra blanket anywhere. A few moments later, Swamishri walked into the room where the youths were sleeping, gave Jagdish a blanket and left. Only at dawn did everyone realize that Swamishri had given his own blanket and he himself had used only his thin upper garment for cover from the biting cold.

Swamishri willingly puts up with difficulties to lighten those of others.

In 2000, a young boy named Prashant, from the small village of Sagarkhedu Kharva, was seriously injured in an accident during the preparations for a festival in Surat. He was admitted to the ICU of Mahavir General Hospital for treatment. Swamishri heard of the incident and was deeply saddened on hearing of the child's plight.

Coincidentally, Swamishri arrived in Surat that day. The next morning, he decided to visit Prashant in hospital and left by car.

As they neared the hospital, they realized that the road leading to the hospital had been temporarily closed for repairs. Swamishri opened the car's door, stepped out and expressed his wish to walk the remaining quarter of a kilometre. Supported by his attendant sadhus, he began to negotiate through pipes and ditches as he made his way to the hospital. Swamishri was 80 years old, yet he was not deterred by the physical obstacles. When he reached the hospital and entered the ICU, he placed his hands on the boy's head and whispered, "Prashant, Prashant...Jai Swaminarayan..."

Prashant was unconscious, but Swamishri spoke to the boy as if he was listening to every word. He then placed Harikrishna Maharaj's garland around Prashant's neck and prayed for his wellbeing. Then, Swamishri comforted the boy's father. His compassion touched Prashant's family beyond imagination.

Swamishri left the hospital and returned to his car, walking over the uneven ground, and leaping over ditches and manholes. He was satisfied, since he had been able to soothe and care for an innocent young child and his family in their time of need.

Once, Janmangal Swami asked Swamishri, "What do you think of when you pray to Harikrishna Maharaj?"

"What else would we pray for? May everyone be blessed with peace and happiness. May no one have to suffer any miseries. May everyone offer devotion and may their circumstances improve."

Only a Satpurush who is beyond the attachments and needs of the body can truly and selflessly shower compassion on others. Only he can speak and live by the words.

"In the joy of others lies our own;
In the progress of others rests our own;
In the good of others abides our own."

That such a Brahmaswarup Sadhu engages in countless activities for the benefit of others is the result of his compassion, as described by Bhagwan Swaminarayan in the Vachanamrut: "For a devotee of God, even though *mayik* influences are overcome, intense compassion and affection for God and his devotees increases. But in no way are compassion and affection ever lost; they always remain" (Vachanmarut, Gadhada III 3).

The compassion of such a Sadhu is not shown only when he sees someone suffering. It is more than that. The ancient sages call it *akaran daya* – 'Compassion with no particular cause'.

Yogiji Maharaj called it *atyantik daya* or 'the compassion to free souls of the never-ending cycle of life and death'.

We are indeed fortunate to have such a sadhu in our midst.   ◆

Kshantihi

क्षान्तिः

Kshanti means to forgive.
It is an extraordinary quality of God and his Gunatit Sadhu.
Even if he is insulted, offended, robbed,
poisoned or killed a true sadhu always forgives.
He never seeks revenge or punishment
for those that have harmed him.
Such is forgiveness.

A person who can put the past behind him, forgive those who have wronged him and pray for their wellbeing has scaled the heights of forgiveness. Pramukh Swami Maharaj has attained those heights.

Since childhood, he has exemplified the virtue of forgiving. He has always tolerated others' mistakes and forgiven them. At times, his classmates would pull a prank and get punished by their teachers. Swamishri was often punished along with the group, though he had no role in the mischief. He would remain silent and accept the punishment. The teachers would realize that young Shantilal wasn't part of the group and apologize for punishing him, but he never harboured a grudge against them.

Brahmaswarup Shastriji Maharaj made Swamishri the President of the Sanstha in 1950, when he was only 28. His appointment caused envy among some veterans within the Sanstha. In 1954, one such individual tried to poison Swamishri. The poison had almost reached Swamishri's lips when the plot unfolded. Despite the heinous act Swamishri forgave the guilty person and cared for him in the Satsang till his death.

Swamishri made those who had witnessed the terrifying incident, promise that they would never mention it to anyone. He never mentioned the incident to anyone and looked after the perpetrator's every need. It wasn't until six years after the individual had passed away that Dharmajivan Swami revealed the story for the first time.

A famous historian, Professor Makrand Mehta, is touched by Swamishri's forgiving nature.

He narrated the incident to the sadhus at the 1989 Sant Shibir. Swamishri's eyes filled up with tears and he said, "Forget all that. There is no need to talk about it. Just talk about the service he had performed." Swamishri's profound compassion touched all.

In 1971 Swamishri became the spiritual successor of Yogiji Maharaj. He travelled from village to village, house to house, touching the hearts of people from all walks of life and teaching the messages of Bhagwan Swaminarayan. His selfless ways and humble manner inspired thousands. His succession and subsequent success as guru was met with strong resistance by some jealous individuals. To their surprise, their every act clouded by envy was met with love, mercy and forgiveness.

In 1977 a few conspirators plotted to have Swamishri arrested and falsely charged. They bribed a police inspector to have him arrested. Swamishri had just arrived in Gadhada and was doing darshan at Lakshmi Vadi, the farm of Dada Khachar sanctified by Bhagwan Swaminarayan. The inspector arrived there and announced that he had orders to arrest him. The devotees were taken aback and demanded to see the arrest warrant.

The inspector was caught off-guard and he revealed that he did not have it. Calmly, Swamishri asked him to come to the BAPS mandir. There, the devotees called the authorities and exposed the plot. The inspector panicked and thought, "What am I going to do?" He was trembling as he paced back and forth. Swamishri noticed that the inspector was near tears. He called him, placed his hand on his head and said, "Don't worry. It is almost lunchtime, so take lunch before you leave."

Swamishri asked the sadhus to seat the inspector before him during lunch. Swamishri lovingly served the inspector, as if he were an honoured guest! The inspector remembers Pramukh Swami Maharaj's mercy even to this day.

Ishwarcharan Swami, who was a witness to the incident, recalls a similar episode that occurred in 1966, "Yogiji Maharaj and Pramukh Swami Maharaj were seated in the evening satsang assembly in the grounds of Ahmedabad mandir. At that time a group of people arrived from Vidyanagar and demanded to meet Swamishri right away. Yogiji Maharaj and Pramukh Swami Maharaj met the group in the old assembly hall behind closed doors. There, the group angrily started insulting and shouting at Swamishri. They had been misinformed and, losing all sense of respect, were accusing Swamishri. A few devotees noticed the commotion and told us.

"Some youths quickly arrived. We pushed the door open and barged into the room. We were upset at the way the group was insulting Swamishri. But, Swamishri stood up and requested us to leave. We didn't listen. Swamishri forced us out of the room saying, 'All of you leave. There is no need for you to do anything. They are here to talk to me so let them finish. Now, leave.'

"The atmosphere was so charged that the meeting had to be called off. The group from Vidyanagar realized the tense situation and left the room. Swamishri safely escorted them to the main gate to ensure that nobody blocked their way.

"Swamishri has maintained his composure through many such incidents. He showed respect to people who didn't have the slightest respect for him. His ability to forgive and forget enabled him to mend the errant ways of others and reach a solution regardless of the complexity of the situation."

Not only does Swamishri forgive, he sees to it that those who are needlessly rude to him or have ill-will for him are not troubled in any way.

Swamishri was in Karjisan in 1994, when Natubhai Patel of Dangarva, who had arrived from America, started complaining.

"Swami, I want to invite you to my town, but there is a group of people that won't let me do so. They are jealous of your fame and are opposing your *padhramani* in my town. I have helped to build their mandir. I have financed most of their projects. But now I am not going to give them a single penny."

Swamishri smiled as he soothed Natubhai, "Do not think like that. You have done all that service to please God, and not for others. So whether or not they invite us, do not worry about it."

Swamishri's ability to forgive touches everyone.

"God is pleased when we forgive others…"

Former President of the Indian Historical Association and famous literary writer, Dr Makrandbhai Mehta, experienced Swamishri's forgiveness in a unique way.

During the Birth Bicentenary Celebrations of Bhagwan Swaminarayan in 1981, BAPS had organized a literary conference. After the event, Makrandbhai criticized the conference in the *Arthat* journal, defaming Bhagwan Swaminarayan's life and work. Many other Swaminarayan organizations were unhappy and opposed his article, and published responses to his accusations. The dispute fuelled a full-fledged battle between the two sides. Throughout this period, Swamishri had not reacted adversely towards Makrandbhai, but had remained silent and advised sadhus and devotees of the BAPS organization to stay calm. Not realizing the difference between BAPS and the other organizations, Makrandbhai developed a grudge against Swamishri as well.

A few months later, Makrandbhai had to visit the United Kingdom for an academic conference. He was worried about where he would stay and thought of his old friend Jaykrishna Patel.

Makrandbhai arrived at his friend's house and to his surprise realized that J.K. Patel was a devotee of Swamishri. He was apprehensive at the thought of having to stay in a Swaminarayan devotee's house for a month, but he had no choice.

During Makrandbhai's one-month stay, J.K. Patel never once mentioned the ongoing dispute. In fact, when Makrandbhai tried to apologize for it, J.K. Patel said, "There is no need to bring that up. It is in the past."

Makrandbhai was touched by his host's openheartedness and from him learnt about the saintliness and compassion of Pramukh Swami Maharaj.

In the next leg of his tour, Makrandbhai and his wife went to

48

Rome, Italy, for a conference. There, Makrandbhai suffered an unfortunate chain of events. His passport, along with all his cash, was stolen. He reported the incident to the police and the Indian Embassy but they could do little to help.

The historian was distraught. He didn't know what to do. He needed to find a way out of the situation. That night in his hotel room, out of desperation, he prayed to Swamishri, asking for forgiveness and help to resolve his difficult situation.

The next morning, to Makrandbhai's surprise, an Italian returned his passport. He was convinced that his prayers to Pramukh Swami Maharaj had been answered. So, on his return to India he went directly to meet Swamishri in Ahmedabad.

This was the first time he was meeting Swamishri after the furore over his article, yet Swamishri was calm and loving. There wasn't the slightest trace of anger or revenge on his face.

Makrandbhai was repentant of his past behaviour. He had never apologized or compromised with anyone in his life, yet Swamishri's ability to forgive and forget made him bow his head in reverence.

Swamishri welcomed him with a warm smile and asked him to make himself comfortable. Makrandbhai was fighting back his tears as he took a seat. He bowed down to touch Swamishri's feet and couldn't restrain himself any longer. He broke down as he expressed his remorse in a trembling voice.

"I have wronged you. Forgive me. I have never seen anyone as merciful as you. Please forgive me."

Swamishri gave him a glass of water and wiped his tears.

"Forget everything. It never happened."

Makrandbhai will never forget Swamishri's unconditional mercy.

Another incident explains how Swamishri is able to be so forgiving. Swamishri was in New York mandir having breakfast, surrounded by sadhus and devotees. Just a few days had passed since the magnificent 31-day Cultural Festival of India, inspired by Swamishri and organized by BAPS, had concluded. It helped to portray a true understanding of Indian culture to people living in the West.

Brahmavihari Swami walked into the room with a pamphlet in his hand. The pamphlet was full of slander directed at Swamishri and the Sanstha.

Pramukh Swami Maharaj asked, "What have you brought?"

"Nothing. It is not worth reading."

"Why do you say that?"

Swamishri insisted that Brahmavihari Swami read the article. Brahmavihari Swami read the outrageous title and Swamishri doubled up with laughter. The sadhus were surprised.

"We should give a stern rebuttal," someone suggested.

Swamishri immediately refused, "No, we should continue what we are doing. There is no need to argue. God is watching everything."

Again, someone reasoned, "Responding to their false accusations is not arguing. We are just clarifying their misconceptions. Gunatitanand Swami used to say, 'One should at least assert when needed!'"

"Asserting can be tiresome too. That has never been Shastriji Maharaj's 'policy'. If they insult us, curse us or even hit us, we should never retaliate. We should always forgive…"

"But there were only five sadhus in Shastriji Maharaj's time. They didn't have time to respond. Now, there are many of us…"

Interrupting in mid-sentence, Swamishri said, "If you have extra time, then pray to God and do bhajan. Don't retaliate."

Swamishri did not even ask how many pamphlets had been printed or where they had been distributed.

A prominent writer had for many months written false accounts about Pramukh Swami Maharaj and his work in a daily newspaper. Some sadhus couldn't take it anymore. They decided to respond to the articles. Swamishri found out and sternly told the sadhus, "There is no need for that. Did Shastriji Maharaj and Yogiji Maharaj ever respond to such things? I want you to promise me that you will never react to such articles."

The sadhus tried to explain their reason, "Even Bhagwan Krishna beheaded the evil demon Shishupal after one hundred offences."

Swamishri would not listen.

"Shri Krishna was God. He could act as he wished. We are God's servants."

In fact, when Swamishri met the writer on a stage at a public event, he invited him to sit next to him on the sofa. The audience was astonished by Swamishri's forgiving nature.

On 18 June 1988, Swamishri was in Toronto, Canada, at Chandrakantbhai's house in Markham. He was having his breakfast with the sadhus when one of them mentioned a letter that had arrived from the sadhus in Bhadra. It read: "We have been distributing *sukhdi* to the families ravaged by the drought. Many people are sarcastically saying that we are probably distributing only a small portion of what we have received."

Swamishri immediately replied, "People will always talk. We must perform our duty with God in mind. If you listen to such things, you

will not be able to do any work. Many of those people are speaking
out of ignorance. God and his holy Sadhu do not look at others'
faults. If God looked at our faults, we would never be liberated. Shriji
Maharaj always looked at the good in all. We should do the same."

Swamishri's greatest strength lies in his ability to forgive others
without ever reminding them of their mistakes. He remembers
the smallest service offered and forgets the biggest mistakes, as if they
had never occurred. This has inspired many of his disciples as well.

Swamishri was in Gadhada on 11 March 1995 when a devotee of
the Kshatriya community was speaking to him about avenging the
murder of his nephew, "I am going to kill that man. People in the
village are calling me a coward. I will show them that they are the
cowards."

Swamishri tried to calm the man by reasoning, "By killing the
man, you will be held accountable for his life. Your nephew will not
come back if you murder this man. Why would you want to increase
the bad blood? It's not like you are going to gain anything by killing
him. Stay calm and everything will settle down. People will try to
instigate you. But you have a family to provide for. None of the
instigators will come and support them. Therefore, think of your
nephew's death as an opportunity for peace and as God's wish. Do
not add to the bad feelings. Quietly pray to God."

Swamishri's sage advice relieved the tension.

In Rohishala, a village near Botad, a small dispute turned violent
and, in the heat of the moment, a youth murdered Amarshibhai, a
satsangi and respected resident of the village. The village was thrown
into turmoil. It looked as if a large amount of blood would be shed.

Swamishri called Amarshibhai's son, Jasmat, and said, "Stay calm.
Do not increase the animosity. Your father is in Akshardham and I am

Swamishri settles a feud that had devastated two groups for over 150 years by serving them water from each other's villages.

here for you. Do not worry. Withdraw the case from court. Forgive that ignorant youth and tell your mother to forgive him too."

Following Swamishri's wish, Jasmat's mother forgave her husband's murderer in front of a court full of people in Bhavnagar. Swamishri spent two days in Rohishala speaking to both sides and spreading the message of love and forgiveness. Swamishri thus saved a town from burning in the flames of revenge, murder and riots.

A villager who had witnessed the miracle said, "If Pramukh Swami Maharaj had not stopped both sides, God knows how many corpses would have filled the streets!"

In Gondal on 17 October 1997, Swamishri summoned two groups of Kshatriyas and Patels from Surat. The two clans had been fighting for three years, ever since a dispute had turned bloody. Swamishri sat with them after lunch until 4.00 p.m. and worked out a compromise between them. Everyone was getting ready to leave, when he asked them to sit down again, "There is one more thing that I want to talk about. To forgive is priceless. You have come to the Akshar Deri and this issue has been smoothly resolved. Forget that you ever had any animosity or prejudice against each other. Revenge fuels further revenge. Act so that you all work together and become happy. Now is not the time to show your valour. One has already died and others may follow unless you forgive and forget."

Swamishri asked for some sweets and fed both the clans lovingly, teaching them to love and lead by example.

Swamishri's merciful persona even helped to resolve a case that many, including, the Gujarat State government, the British authorities and the King of Bhavnagar Krishnakumarsinhji, had given up.

Kukad and Odarka are two villages in the Saurashtra region. A dispute over land turned into a gory and seemingly endless conflict involving a total of 45 surrounding villages. With each succeeding generation, the violence seemed to grow. The conflict threatened complete annihilation.

In the 80's, Swamishri sowed the seeds of peace after transforming the life of one of the most brutal members of the mob – Ramsang Bapu.

On 12 April 1990 Swamishri created history. He gathered the Kshatriyas from both villages under one roof for the first time in 150 years. He gave them water from each other's village to break the one-and-a-half century-old animosity. It was the first time the Kshatriyas had seen each other smiling, laughing and happy. The leaders were amazed at Swamishri's patience and ability to inspire forgiveness and said, "The work that the British and Indian Governments could not accomplish has been achieved by Pramukh Swami Maharaj."

One who shows mercy to all is able to lead others. Forgiving, even when one is capable of retaliating, is something that only a true Sadhu can do, a Sadhu in whom God resides.

Bhagwan Swaminarayan states in the Vachanamrut, "No one but the true Sadhu can forgive despite being able to punish."

Swamishri has accomplished that impossible feat, without even being aware of it.

Pramukh Swami Maharaj gives contemporary meaning to the Vedic concept of *ajatshatru* – one with no enemies.   ◆

Shortly after initiation, a photograph of Swamishri at 19 years of age, 194.

Tyagaha
त्यागः

Tyaga is renunciation:
letting go of those things that hinder one's quest for moksha.
This tradition of renouncing has persisted in
India for thousands of years.
The Upanishads explain the importance of tyaga:
"One who wants to attain God must let
go of all worldly attachments."
The ultimate form of tyaga is not just letting go, but also
selflessly sacrificing one's self for the benefit of mankind.
Pramukh Swami Maharaj has lived this true form of tyaga.
He left his home, his relatives, his ambitions and those dear
to him to selflessly give his all for humanity.
The tale of his tyaga begins when he was in his
teens and is exemplified by the ease with which
he had renounced on receiving the call of his guru,
Brahmaswarup Shastriji Maharaj.

"Life is like a box of chocolates. You never know what you are going to get." Mark Twain's thought-evoking words leaves us thinking: who likes surprises? Since, everyone wants their life planned. Often, so much time and energy is spent in planning that we forget that even our meticulous plans are subject to change. In his youth, Pramukh Swami Maharaj faced one such surprise, which entirely altered the course of his life. It was a test of his *tyaga* — he passed.

A short letter from guru Brahmaswarup Shastriji Maharaj is all it took for him to renounce his family and friends. He had aspirations of pursuing higher education to study English. But, at the word of his guru, his *tyaga* was spontaneous. Famous sages and kings have in the past renounced worldly life after months or years of contemplation: Gautam Buddha, Mahavir, King Bharat and Bhartruhari all

55

"Offering and surrendering everything to God is *tyaga*..."

considered their options and made a calculated decision based on their experiences. For young Shantilal the decision was instantaneous; and he shed the fetters of worldly life as easily as a snake sheds its skin.

On 11 November 1939, 18-year-old Shantilal was initiated into the *parshad*-fold at Babubhai Somnath Patel's house in Amli Vali Pol, Ahmedabad. It marked the beginning of a selfless life dedicated for the benefit of everyone. A few weeks later, on 10 January 1940, Shastriji Maharaj initiated him into the sadhu order, naming him Sadhu Narayanswarupdas. For almost seven decades now, Swamishri has lived by the sentiments with which he had renounced: to selflessly serve humanity. Swamishri has lived the principles of *tyaga* prescribed by Bhagwan Swaminarayan.

When Swamishri was 28 years old, the ageing Shastriji Maharaj wished to appoint him as the President (Pramukh) of BAPS in his place. However, Swamishri refused to accept the position or authority, since he only wanted to serve. But, after many weeks of convincing, he finally agreed. Delighted by his acceptance, Shastriji Maharaj arranged a special gathering at Amli Vali Pol in Ahmedabad on 21 May 1950 and declared, "I place Shastri Narayanswarupdas in my place. From now onwards, listen to him and follow his command as you would mine."

Being appointed the head of such a large organization at the young age of 28 imposed great responsibility on Swamishri, but he was undaunted by it. He saw it as a chance to serve. He pledged, "Today, in front of my guru and all of you present, I vow to loyally and faithfully serve the Sanstha, without concern for my body, and to repay the trust you have placed in me. I will work my hardest so that the Sanstha you have established and the Akshar-Purushottam *upasana* flourishes. I will pay attention to every detail and work with utmost determination and diligence to please all of the Satsang and earn your blessings and respect. I hope all of you will guide me."

Swamishri has lived by that promise all through his life. He has made sacrifices for people from all walks of life, giving up the personal element. In fact, volumes can be written just on his *tyaga* and sacrifices for the good of others.

Further, the BAPS Swaminarayan Sanstha has grown from its humble origins into a worldwide organization over the past 50 years. Yet, not even a square inch of land or a single penny is in Swamishri's name! Every single penny donated has been used to serve humanity in a variety of ways.

The Shrimad Bhagvad Gita defines *tyaga* in a unique way:
"One who renounces not the performance of good deeds, but renounces the desire for the fruits of those actions is a true *tyagi*" (BG 18.11).

This is truly hard to achieve.

Swamishri not only has sacrificed and acted for the betterment of those around him, but he has never expected anything in return, except God's and his gurus' blessings. He often speaks of it in his speeches: "We should serve with the intent of pleasing God. Never worry about the result; that is God's wish. For us the only expectation is that God is pleased; apart from that we should never wish for anything else in return."

In everything that he has accomplished Swamishri humbly

Swamishri gives credit for all his accomplishments to God and appreciates him with humble prayers and respect.

credits Bhagwan Swaminarayan for the success, be it Swaminarayan Akshardham in New Delhi, international cultural festivals, the outstanding relief work after natural disasters or the schools and hospitals he has inspired.

This represents his devotion and *tyaga*.

The following incidents demonstrate Swamishri's lifelong selfless service and sacrifice.

Shri Satyanarayan Kabra, a scholar of the Upanishads and the Shrimad Bhagvad Gita, came for Swamishri's darshan in Mumbai and confessed, "Even though I have studied the shastras, I feel lost and uneasy. I don't know what to do."

Swamishri's reply to Satyanarayan Kabra was based on the principles he had practiced in his own life, "We tend to carry the weight of our actions. However, as Bhagwan Shri Krishna advises Arjun in the Gita, we should perform actions, but without expectation of the fruits of those actions. If we offer everything to God, it does not cause attachment. Whatever happens in this world is due to the wish of God. All actions take place by his wish. We believe that 'I did all this', so we have to suffer the consequences of this. So, leave everything to God. Do not even wish for the fruits of those actions. The feeling that 'I do certain good deeds so I should get the benefits' nourishes one's ego. And that is why there is conflict. By desiring the fruits of one's actions, one suffers joy and sorrow and experiences unrest in the mind."

On 29 April 1995, after a long and taxing administrative meeting in Bardoli, Swamishri was getting ready to go to bed at 10.30 p.m. Swamishri's personal physician, Dr Kiran Doshi, asked him, "After the meeting do you feel stressed by the..."

Swamishri started laughing and interrupted him midway. Folding his hands over his head he said, "Jai Swaminarayan. Not at all. Why take the burden for it all? I always go to sleep believing that God is the all-doer. Whatever has happened and what will happen is due to the wish of God."

Ajay Varma, Superintendent of Police for Bihar State, came to Ahmedabad for Swamishri's darshan and said, "I have been very eager to meet the creator of Swaminarayan Akshardham in New Delhi."

Instantly, Swamishri attributed everything to God, "God is the creator of all. He is the one that inspires us all."

A sadhu once asked Swamishri, "People honour and respect you for all that you have accomplished. How does that make you feel?"

"The honour is for God. I am not capable of breaking even a dry leaf. It is because we follow God's wish and please him that we are respected. No one would even look at us otherwise. The only thing that we should focus on is serving and pleasing Bhagwan Swaminarayan. We should always serve humbly without expectations."

It may be easy to give up one's home and loved ones, it may be simple to renounce materialistic pleasures, but to let go of one's expectations and the credit that one feels one deserves is nearly impossible.

Who can do it? Only a person who is complete, content and wishes for nothing but God can achieve such a state of *tyaga*.

The Shrimad Bhagvad Gita says, "Wisdom is greater than knowledge, meditation is greater than wisdom and renunciation of the fruits of all actions is greater than this. The *tyag* of the desire of such fruits gives unlimited peace" (BG 12.12).

The Kaivalya Upanishad states, "Immortality cannot be achieved by wealth, power or good deeds. It can only be achieved by *tyag*."

Pramukh Swami Maharaj lives the great *tyag* that the Ishavasya Upanishad talks of in its first mantra. Immortality can only be achieved by letting go. Pramukh Swami Maharaj has attained that immortality by giving up everything.   ◆

Santoshaha
संतोष:

Arjavam
आर्जवम्

Arjavam is simplicity,
transparency and straightforwardness.
One who is very simple-hearted and does not have
a trace of deceit or trickery. He is not cunning or manipulative.
He is content with the divine joy of God.
Santosha is contentment or fulfilment in any situation.
Yogiji Maharaj used to say that one should adjust to circumstances by
"making do with whatever one gets, whenever and wherever." Swamishri
lives by this motto of guru Yogiji Maharaj. These qualities of arjavam
and santosha *are*
innate in Pramukh Swami Maharaj.

Since 1950, Swamishri has been the President of BAPS and the heart and soul of hundreds of thousands of young and old devotees around the world. He is a highly respected sadhu of India and has been honoured by hundreds of leaders for his services to humanity. Yet, Swamishri's life resonates with simplicity and contentment. In fact, these qualities are so natural that they are often taken for granted.

Due to his simple and straightforward nature, people from all walks of life find it easy to form a bond with him. They are able to present their problems and get practical solutions. Children, teenagers, adults, seniors, tribal folk, executives, community leaders and spiritual leaders all find peace and solace in his simplicity.

Swamishri has made over 17,000 city, town and village visits throughout the world, but his attendant sadhus report that not even once has he asked for a specific car, facility, bed, sofa or amenity for his use. When he was a young boy, his mother, Diwaliba, would have to make sure that he had his meals. He wouldn't ask for food, even when he was hungry, for fear that he might cause inconvenience to someone.

The absence of electricity and light couldn't deter Swamishri from working late into the night...

His ability to be simple, transparent and content has become more evident with the passage of time. Swamishri's ability to adjust is apparent through his spiritual tours in India and around the world. He never gets upset when there is lack of facilities. He smiles and says, "It is fine the way it is. Don't worry about it. A little hardship isn't going to kill us."

On 14 September 1975, Swamishri was on his way for the *murti-pratishtha* in the village of Kala Talav in Bhavnagar district. It started raining and the dirt road soon turned muddy. A few kilometres into their route, the Fargo van got stuck in the mud. The sadhus, devotees and even Swamishri tried to push it, but the van would not budge.

Someone suggested that by placing stones under the wheels the van could be pushed out.

It was still raining and Swamishri's clothes were wet. The sadhus suggested that Swamishri wait under a tree while they tried to get the car out. The sadhus and devotees began to gather stones to put under the wheels; Swamishri joined in as well. The sadhus tried to stop him, "There is no need for you to lift the stones, there are so many of us."

"There's nothing wrong with lifting a few stones. I used to lift stones in Shastriji Maharaj's time. I did physical work during Yogiji Maharaj's time too. It's nothing new." With this, Swamishri continued gathering stones. Then they tried again to push the van free. But it wouldn't move. Someone suggested getting another car from a nearby village, but Swamishri said, "There is no need to do that. Let's start walking and we will get to the next village in no time."

They walked until they reached Dudhadhar, where devotees helped get three bullock carts. They got in the carts and made it to Kala Talav in the pouring rain. Swamishri was unfazed by the situation, singing the Swaminarayan *dhun* all the way.

It is difficult to get even the bare necessities of life in some tribal villages of the Panchmahal District and in parts of southern Gujarat, but Swamishri is undaunted by the lack of comfort and has made many visits to such areas to inspire the devotees there.

Travelling with Swamishri in the Bhal region of Saurashtra was always a challenge. The region is known for its scorching heat, erratic electricity supply, hard water and dusty air. Swamishri would travel from village to village for months on end, satisfying devotees, not once complaining about the hardships.

In 1985, Swamishri was in Navsari getting ready to retire for the night when an attendant sadhu noticed a lot of dirt on the blanket. Swamishri asked him, "What are you doing? Is it dusty?"

"Yes, I'm cleaning it," the sadhu replied.

Swamishri commented, "Our body is made of dust as well." Swamishri's words reflected his understanding of this philosophical truth that night.

It was very cold in the night, but Swamishri fell asleep with just a light blanket for cover. In the morning, the attendant sadhu noted that in his sleep Swamishri had taken a mosquito net and wrapped it around himself for extra warmth. But he never complained about the arrangements, believing his body to be of dust.

It was summer vacation time at the end of the 1968-9 academic term and many students had gone home from the Akshar Purushottam Chhatralay in Vidyanagar. However, some students in one of the rooms were reading late into the night. At around 1.00 a.m. they heard a knock on the door. The door had not been locked, so Swamishri opened it and stood before the students.

Assuming that Jaykrishna Bhagat and the other *parshads* were asleep, Swamishri came to the room where the lights were on.

He looked exhausted from the travelling. One of the students offered to go and wake the *parshads* up. Swamishri stopped him, saying, "Let them sleep. We will just sleep here on the floor."

So, Swamishri, the president of the Sanstha, slept on the floor while the students went to sleep in their beds!

Swamishri's ability and spirit of accommodation has been the hallmark of his life, be it in matters of food, accommodation, rest, etc. A brief dialogue between Swamishri and the editor of the *Garavi Gujarat* magazine on 8 May 2004 in London brings this out.

"You travel around the world. Which city or place are you attracted to most?"

"I am attracted only to God," replied Swamishri.

Swamishri sitting on the steps outside his living quarters in Ahmedabad mandir and conversing with an elderly devotee, Shri Narayanbhai Mistry.

Acommon experience in small villages and large cities are the glitches in organizing Swamishri's schedule. This is especially evident during Swamishri's *padhramanis* or home visits for sanctification. At times Swamishri would end up doing 50 *padhramanis* instead of the five originally planned, thus upsetting the schedule. However, Swamishri would adjust himself to the unanticipated programmes. The devotees of that place would have to deal with it only for one day, but for Swamishri it was a regular occurrence. The following incidents may frustrate you as you read them, even today.

Swamishri was travelling in the Sabarkantha region on 14 January 1983 or the Uttarayan day. Swamishri arrived in Nadri village at around 1.00 p.m. In the scorching heat devotees had organized a procession, with horses, dancing children and... chaos. It was 3 o'clock by the time the procession ended. Swamishri sat down to have lunch and tried to rest for half an hour. Then it was time to address the devotees in the assembly. It was around 6.00 p.m., when Becharbhai asked Swamishri if he would undertake four or five *padhramanis*.

Swamishri readily agreed. From the four or five *padhramanis* that were scheduled, Swamishri ended up doing an incredible 102 *padhramanis*! It was 10.30 p.m. by the time Swamishri sat down for dinner.

This was a common occurrence.

Swamishri had just finished a few *padhramanis* in Piplag and arrived in Dabhan. Just as he was getting ready for a meal, a few

Eternal Virtues

devotees from Piplag arrived and requested Swamishri to come back, "There are a few more *padhramanis* that we have to finish. Can you come back to Piplag?"

Swamishri stood up and without saying a single word went back to Piplag. He sanctified houses until midnight. He did not return to Dabhan until 1.00 a.m.

Sometimes devotees would stand right outside their village waiting for Swamishri to pass by. Their intent being to take Swamishri to grace their village on his way to the next one. Their coercion and unorganized ways would test anyone's patience. Yet, Swamishri would remain calm and visit every devotee's house.

Swamishri had left Badalpur right after breakfast in the morning and was in a rush to get to Anand. However, by the time he got to Anand it was midnight. Swamishri had stopped to grace 13 villages on the way, not to mention a few dozen *padhramanis* in each village.

Devotees would often request the presence of Swamishri at various events in their lives – marriages, inaugurations, funerals, etc. At times, Swamishri would have to zigzag across the state and country to please the devotees. He would try really hard not to refuse a single devotee. Swamishri would give them what they wanted, when they wanted and how they wanted, always with a smile on his face.

Viveksagar Swami and other sadhus who have travelled with Swamishri for decades recall a few incidents.

Going from rooftop to rooftop in a neighbourhood of tenements in the Mahikantha region, Swamishri once walked from morning till night doing *padhramanis*. Such exertion would drain the energy of even a fit youth in no time, but Swamishri carried on day after day. Mahant Swami recalls a similar incident:

"We were travelling in Bamangam. The region is very hilly, with

Gracing a tiny tribal village in the Dang region, May 1999.

steep mounds to climb at every turn. It was around 3.00 p.m. and Swamishri looked exhausted. It looked as if his feet were in pain. In fact, I was on the verge of collapsing. Suddenly, I was overcome with pity for Swamishri. Why was he travelling like this at this age? He should rest. Just as I was about to say something, Swamishri smiled at me. I was getting annoyed. He was putting himself through so much, his body was giving way and here he was – smiling. He opened his mouth to say something. I thought he would admit that he was exhausted. Then he said, 'Yogiji Maharaj had travelled to all of these villages.' He wasn't even thinking about the hardships he was suffering."

The scorching summer sun in the Saurashtra and Sabarkantha regions is unbearable. To make things worse, the erratic electricity supply meant that the use of lights and fans was rarely possible.

On one such tour in the Sabarkantha region, Viveksagar Swami offered a suggestion, "It would be better if we travelled in these villages after the monsoon and stayed in Mumbai during the summer months. It's not as hot during the summer in Mumbai."

Swamishri disagreed, "It is better to travel in these villages during the summer. After the monsoon the villagers become busy with their farm duties and it would be an inconvenience for them."

In the following days, he visited over 87 villages in 27 days in the sweltering summer heat often reaching 45 degrees Celcius (113 degrees Fahrenheit).

Swamishri's ability to tolerate such inconveniences stems from his devotion to Bhagwan Swaminarayan.

On one occasion he was in Mumbai doing *padhramanis*. He arrived at Avinashbhai Popat's home in Mulund and the host apologized for the inconvenience Swamishri had to suffer on his way there.

Swamishri interrupted him in mid-sentence, "Where there is such love there is no trouble. One who wants to worship God should ignore the inconveniences. Make do with whatever one gets at the time. Never think about physical hardships. As long as one can worship God nothing else matters, even if one only has the shade of a tree."

Swamishri is a living example of this philosophy. It's not something that he merely talks about.

Swami Ramswarup Shastri, former chairperson of the Akhil Bharat Sadhu Samaj, says, "Pramukh Swami Maharaj is a simple, transparent and straightforward sadhu. This is the true definition of a sadhu. His actions are a practical lesson in simplicity and contentment."

For decades, Swamishri has travelled around the world. His passion to bond with every single devotee sets him apart from others. He has always insisted on meeting devotees individually. Sometimes it would take hours to meet all the devotees after an assembly, but Swamishri never lets go of such an opportunity. As Swamishri aged and his health started to decline, a few sadhus suggested alternatives.

On 9 December 1984, during Swamishri's 74th birthday celebrations in Mahesana, Narayanmuni Swami approached him. As usual, Swamishri expressed his wish to meet all the devotees individually after the celebration assembly. Narayanmuni Swami had other ideas, "We have organized things differently this time. Instead of each devotee meeting you individually, four separate lines of devotees will come to receive your darshan at the same time. They will be able to have your darshan at close quarters and you will be able to see them as well."

Swamishri tried to argue his point, but Narayanmuni Swami was very persistent. After a few minutes, Swamishri agreed, "It is best to listen to a sadhu. I will do as you say. God resides in all of you."

Swamishri adjusted to the wish of the organizing sadhus.

Yogiji Maharaj used to say '*Kat vadi javu*', meaning 'One should instantly adjust to the current situation'. Swamishri is able to do that even at the age of 89.

Despite being the president and spiritual guru of BAPS, Swamishri never forgets his primary role in the Sanstha as a *karyakar* or volunteer. His outstanding fame, power or influence has never diminished his ability to serve.

In May 1962, the *murti-pratishtha* of the BAPS Shri Swaminarayan Mandir in Shahibaug, Ahmedabad, had just been celebrated. Thousands of devotees had joined in the festivities. As night fell, all of them started heading towards their homes and villages after having dinner. Late into the night, a youth was trying to wheel a cart of waste up a slope to the dumpster at the back of the mandir grounds. He had been trying for a while, but the cart was just too heavy for him to push up the slope by himself. He tried looking for help, but not a single person was around.

Swamishri had just stepped out of a meeting discussing the festival. Swamishri noticed the youth struggling to get the cart up the slope. He ran to help the youth. He helped push the cart up the slope and to the dumpster. He helped empty the waste into the dumpster and stayed with the youth until he pulled the cart back to its starting point.

Today, that youth, now known as Narayanprasad Swami, remembers that incident and the ease with which Swamishri was able to join him in such a menial service. He recalls another incident revealing Swamishri's cooperative nature.

In Kolkata in 1968, a few of Narayanprasad Swami's works of spiritual art were to be displayed in an exhibition. The famous Bengali literary giant Tarashankar Bandopadhyay was also attending. According to the *niyams* laid down by Bhagwan Swaminarayan, sadhus have to travel in pairs. Narayanprasad Swami was looking for another sadhu to join him to go to the exhibition. He asked the few sadhus present, but all were busy in other duties. Swamishri walked by and noticed the gloom on Narayanprasad Swami's face. He immediately volunteered to accompany him. Narayanprasad Swami was perplexed. How could he take the Sanstha's president to go as his pair?

Swamishri put aside all his work and joined Narayanprasad Swami at the exhibition, leaving him touched by his simplicity and ability to adjust.

In 1972, Swamishri visited Kolkata for the *murti-pratishtha* of the BAPS Swaminarayan Mandir. He was passing by the kitchen the day before the inauguration and saw Devcharan Swami making *puris*, but no one was there to help him fry them. Immediately, Swamishri turned over an empty oil can, sat on it and started frying them. It was just a day before he was to consecrate the mandir, but Swamishri's simplicity made it possible for him to serve in any situation.

Once, Yogiji Maharaj and Swamishri were going to Rajkot from Limbdi. A few other sadhus were following them in another car. The sadhus decided to stop for darshan in Muli. Unfortunately, the driver of their car lost his way and they didn't get to Rajkot until about 12.30 p.m. The sadhus were worried that they were late in preparing lunch for Yogiji Maharaj.

However, to their surprise, Yogiji Maharaj was eating when they arrived and Pramukh Swami Maharaj was serving him. Yogiji Maharaj smiled and said, "Pramukh Swami cooked while I did *katha*. Taste it. It is amazing. It is so tasty, you will lick your fingers clean!"

Swamishri performed the duties of the attendant sadhus without the slightest hesitation.

Another aspect of his simplicity is his ability to do things without even a hint that he is the guru. His discourses are a prime example of this. Swamishri has never insisted on certain numbers of the crowd as a condition to speak. And the duration he is given does not matter. He speaks as he is requested. Sometimes he speaks for five minutes and sometimes for 50 minutes. On some days he speaks five to seven times during the day, but his speech is as simple as his life.

Swamishri was in Tradiya in the Saurashtra region. Amid the blistering heat of the sun and dusty hot winds he was taken out in a procession through the village. The procession terminated in the middle of the village and Swamishri was asked to bless the villagers.

Unknown to Swamishri the main assembly had been arranged in the evening. So, Jambha Bapu, a devotee travelling with Swamishri thought that it was unnecessary for him to speak now. He interrupted Swamishri's speech and hailing the *jay nad* announced the end of this impromptu assembly. Swamishri smiled and without the slightest trace of embarrassment stopped talking and went to a devotee's house for lunch. When asked about Jambha Bapu's rude behaviour, Swamishri said, "It's a good thing he ended the speech. I didn't know there was another assembly in the evening."

In spite of being the guru, Swamishri was able to adjust to and tolerate such embarrassing situations.

In 1994, Swamishri had just finished a satsang assembly in Nairobi, Kenya. It was around 11.00 p.m. by the time he got back to Chandubhai Patel's house to sleep. Before Swamishri arrived, a group of devotees had come for Swamishri's darshan and blessings. Harshadbhai Rana, a senior devotee, stood up and announced that Swamishri would say 'two words'.

Swamishri addresses the assembly in a humorous mix of Gujarati and Hindi, November 2004, Ahmedabad.

Swamishri followed his cue and literally said two words!

"Brahma-satyam, jagan-mithya…" meaning, "Brahman is the only eternal Truth and this world is perishable."

Another example of his simplicity is his simple language. His language is filled with experience and not superficial poetry, flowery language or an impressive vocabulary. Whether he is speaking at the opening of Swaminarayan Akshardham, New Delhi, in the presence of national leaders or addressing spiritual leaders during the Millennium World Peace Summit at the United Nations, Swamishri maintains a simple approach, never trying to stir the audience with a glitzy delivery.

His simplicity is what speaks volumes.

Internationally renowned photographer Raghu Rai had come to photograph Swamishri on his 70th birthday celebrations in Sarangpur. Thousands of people had gathered in the assembly to pay obeisance at Swamishri's feet. Many community leaders and sadhus spoke about Swamishri's greatness and dynamic personality, but Swamishri did not even look up once. It was as if he was alone on stage, untouched by all the praise or attention. He continued to read and reply to letters from his beloved devotees.

Raghu Rai was amazed, "Swamishri was reading and writing right up to the point where the microphone was put in front of him and the switch was turned on. He started speaking at a moment's notice.

No worries about what to stay. He seemed to be not even thinking about it."

Having experienced this simplicity, literary legend Harindra Dave writes, "I have met Pramukh Swami Maharaj several times. I have experienced profound peace in his simplicity. He has the right blend of a mother's love and a sadhu's care for humanity." Swamishri's unassuming ways allow him to laugh at his own slip-ups in public.

On 24 November 2004, during the Darshan Parishad, a conference of philosophers, who had come from different parts of India, was held in Ahmedabad. Several distinguished scholars were the stage guests of the evening assembly with Swamishri. Dr Ramjisingh and Dr Dubey addressed an assembly of several thousand devotees in Hindi. Thereafter, Swamishri started his discourse in Gujarati and then switched over to Hindi. Since he very rarely speaks Hindi, Swamishri started to mix both languages. The result was a humorous mix of Hindi and Gujarati. This caused the devotees in the assembly to start laughing. In fact, each sentence would set off a series of chuckles from the audience. Swamishri joined in the laughter and explained, "This is how I speak Hindi. It is not that good. So, don't laugh! Since the pundits spoke in Hindi, I decided to try it as well. In all honesty, Hindi is not my forte."

This brought about renewed laughter from the devotees, sadhus, scholars and Swamishri himself.

Once, in Ahmedabad, while delivering his blessings, Swamishri cited an inaccurate reference seven to eight times. That evening as Swamishri was sitting down for dinner, the sadhus were having a good laugh as they remembered Swamishri's blessings.

Swamishri innocently asked, "What are you talking about?"

"We were remembering," the sadhus said.

"Tell me, what you were remembering."

Aksharjivan Swami told Swamishri about the factual mistakes he had made in his blessings.

Swamishri started laughing, "Yes, I do get things mixed up. I am not as learned as Sakshar (referring to Aksharjivan Swami) so I forget sometimes."

Aksharjivan Swami hesitantly tried to explain himself, "No. I was just trying to…"

Swamishri said, "No. I admit that I was wrong. I am not learned so I mess up. Scholars may worry about their image or reputation if they make a mistake. For me, it does not matter. As long as we speak to please God, it is okay."

Swamishri readily admits his mistakes in front of his disciples.

His simplicity has a profound impact on many. The following stories of transformation echo the effect his quality of *arjavam* has on people of all backgrounds.

Vinodray Vala is from a small town named Badhada in the district of Bhavnagar. He had Swamishri's darshan for the first time while Swamishri was travelling on the road and he wrote:

"I have been a Christian for five years. On 1 March 1995 I had your divine darshan on Badhada road. On 3 March, I decided to come to Bhadra and listen to your blessings. Your speech is so simple yet divine. I received your blessings and the spark of truth lit within me. I smoke, drink alcohol and chew tobacco. I want to give up my addictions. Please help me."

A famous industrialist from southern Gujarat, Mr C.K. Pithawala, was at a friend's house in London. There, he saw a video of Swamishri's Suvarna Tula in 1985 at Alexandra Palace. Despite the great honour that had been bestowed upon him, Swamishri's speech did not reflect even the slightest trace of pride or ego. Swamishri's simple yet moving language touched him. Mr Pithawala was so impressed by Swamishri's simplicity that he became a *satsangi*.

Simplicity and a spirit of accommodation have become a part of Swamishri's life. He is always willing to adjust as long as his *niyams* are not compromised. Swamishri knows that adjustment is the key to world harmony.

Dr David Boddy is the Headmaster at the famous St. James Independent School for Senior Boys, which also teaches Sanskrit, in London. On 6 May 2004 he asked Swamishri an interesting question, "What is the answer to developing world peace? How can we teach the people of this world to live in harmony?"

"If everyone learns to compromise, world peace would become a reality."

Swamishri's simple answer touched Dr Boddy's heart.

Swamishri has always been able to compromise and adjust to any situation, and yet at the same remain satisfied and content.

In 1986 Swamishri visited Jamnagar and stayed in the apartment of Dr Harshadbhai Joshi, who was studying medicine at the time. There were leaks in many parts of his apartment. Water dripped from the ceiling and rain water would constantly flow from the bathroom ceiling.

While Swamishri was in Atladra in 2006, Dr. Joshi reminded Swamishri of his visit to his house in 1986, "I am sorry that I was not

Swamishri's straightforwardness and simplicity have touched thousands of hearts.

able to take proper care of you then. You must have had to put up with a great deal of inconvenience."

Swamishri put him at ease, "One should learn to deal with happiness and sorrow in life. That kind of experience trains one for difficult times in the future. One should learn to be happy and comfortable everywhere."

Swamishri often says, "If one learns to be content with what God has given us there will not be any sorrow. If we wish for things and then don't get them, we will be distraught and saddened. If one is content with whatever God gives us then peace is attained."

It is this profound spiritual understanding that enables Swamishri to be satisfied and transparent at all times.

In the Mahabharat, Veda Vyasji says, "Deceit is evil; transparency and simplicity are the way to God. This is true knowledge. What's the point of discussing the rest?"
♦

Samyam
साम्यम्

*Samyam is equality, fairness and impartiality.
It is a special quality of God and the God-realized Sadhu.
Maintaining one's composure and remaining happy in any
adverse or extreme situation is* samyam. *One who sees
God equally in the young and old, the rich and poor,
success and failure, joy and misery, the priceless and
worthless is described in the Shrimad Bhagvad Gita
as a Gunatit Brahmaswarup Sadhu.
Pramukh Swami Maharaj is such a Sadhu.*

Bhagwan Swaminarayan states in the Vachanamrut: "All of the attractive *vishays* are the same to me. Also, a king and a beggar are the same to me. Further, to rule all the realms and to beg for food carrying a broken begging bowl are the same to me. Even sitting with honour on an elephant and walking on foot are the same to me. Whether someone honours me with sandalwood paste, flowers, fine clothes, and ornaments, or throws dirt on me – all are the same to me. Whether someone praises me or insults me – both are the same to me. Gold, silver, diamonds and waste are all the same to me. Moreover, I look upon all devotees of God as being equal; i.e. I do not differentiate one as being superior and another as being inferior" (Vachanamrut, Gadhada II 13).

This is the highest form of equality. A true Gunatit Sadhu also has that level of equality.

The Shrimad Bhagvad Gita says:

"One that sees equality in happiness and sorrow, in stone and in gold, in beauty and repulsiveness, in insult and praise is a true Gunatit Sadhu" (BG 14.24).

In Miami in October 2000, President Bill Clinton met Swamishri for the first time. He was so touched by the meeting

Swamishri blesses a poor, tribal devotee

that during a visit to India the following year he altered his schedule and met Pramukh Swami Maharaj again in Gandhinagar on 5 April 2001. He was accompanied by 50 community leaders and prominent Indo-Americans.

President Clinton lost track of place and time as he continued to praise Swamishri's loving nature. The President took Swamishri's leave and had barely reached his car when Swamishri started searching for a group of villagers who had come from Kutch. The sadhus and devotees were preoccupied in discussing what President Clinton had said about their guru; but the guru was intent on meeting the villagers who had lost everything in the recent earthquake.

Swamishri treated Sidikbhai, Satishbhai and Jadavjibhai with the same deference and warmth that he had shown to President Clinton.

Holding their hands Swamishri said, "I hope you are doing well. It is a good thing that you have come here. You have faith in God and therefore he will help you get through this difficult time."

Swamishri asked them how they were going back. He told the sadhus to make arrangements for their return journey, "Make sure you book a sleeper coach. They will be tired travelling to Kutch in an unreserved compartment."

In the span of a few seconds Swamishri was able to meet one of the world's greatest leaders and also some of the poorest villagers, all with the same enthusiasm. He sees God equally in all.

Tens of thousands of devotees had gathered for Swamishri's birthday celebrations in Mahesana. After the assembly, Swamishri arrived at Mahendrabhai Sukhadiya's house. A poor villager was eagerly waiting to see Swamishri just as he arrived. Swamishri greeted the devotee from Mahiyel and began talking to him as soon as he entered Mahendrabhai's house. Doctor Swami was observing this remarkable event from a distance. Swamishri's birthday festivities had concluded a few minutes before. How could someone who had been praised and honoured by thousands forget all that and talk to a poor villager with the same enthusiasm!

Swaminarayan Akshardham in New Delhi was inaugurated on 6 November 2005. Thereafter, scores of community leaders and spiritual gurus came to congratulate Swamishri and offer their appreciations. On 19 November 2005, the President's private adviser and renowned scientist, Dr Y.S. Rajan, came for Swamishri's darshan. After meeting Dr Rajan, Swamishri greeted a villager who introduced himself as Hemraj, "Swamiji, I am from the same village and family as Sagram Vaghri in Bhagwan Swaminarayan's time."

Swamishri was overjoyed and asked him to bring his relatives to Akshardham. Finally he asked, "Do you drink, smoke or have any other addictions?"

Swamishri talked to him lovingly about his life and blessed him. Swamishri saw God in both the President's adviser and a tribal villager.

In 1994, Swamishri had just performed the *murti-pratishtha* of the BAPS *hari* mandir in New Delhi. One morning, he asked the sadhus if they had seen Dhanji Vaghri of Surendranagar, who lived in New Delhi. The sadhus were surprised by Swamishri's question, especially since none of them knew him. They told Swamishri that he had probably left after having darshan from a distance. However, Swamishri knew that Dhanji would meet him if he had come. So, Swamishri called Surendranagar, got his address in New Delhi and then sent Kishorsinh Rana to call him. On the one hand Swamishri was meeting some of Delhi's elite and at the same time he recalled his tribal devotee.

In 1997, Hira Bharvad, an elderly devotee who had served for many years in the livestock farm in Sarangpur, died. Swamishri called Tapodhan Bhagat, who took care of the livestock, and told him, "Hiro Bharvad was one of our own. Make sure the 12th and 13th day memorial rituals are observed. Also, go with his son when he immerses the ashes in the sacred rivers."

Swamishri made it a point to arrange the 13th day memorial rites

Swamishri gifts a pair of glasses to Hira Bharvad in Sarangpur.

and meal for his family and relatives. Ragho Bharvad spoke on behalf of Hira's relatives, "You have truly served Hira. Everyone in our family is amazed by the attention and detail you have paid to Hira's funeral rites."

To this Swamishri replied, "Hira was one of us."

Another example of Swamishri's equality and impartiality is his ability to think of and care for everyone, even those often forgotten by others. While most people are always busy organizing and planning for executives, community leaders, industrialists and politicians, Swamishri is often thinking a step ahead of them.

On 6 February 1997, Swamishri was in Atladra with an organizing group of sadhus and senior volunteers planning for a forthcoming celebration. The organizers explained their plan that would ensure the distribution of 70,000 *prasad* packets in just 15 minutes to the people that would be attending.

Swamishri listened to their plans patiently. Then he said, "People who are sitting in the assembly will get their *prasad* packets, but what about those who are waiting outside. The tractor, bus, car and other vehicle drivers will be waiting in the car park to take everyone back home. They should also get *prasad*. Make sure everyone gets a packet. No one should be left out."

This is a usual occurrence. Whenever politicians or community leaders come to meet Swamishri, everyone is looking after the main guest, while Swamishri also remembers the guest's driver and personal attendant or secretary. He will find a way to take care of them, whether it is by making arrangements for their lunch or dinner, talking to them or blessing them.

Swamishri always cares for those that escape other's attention. This is illustrated by the following incidents.

Swamishri has spoken at several gatherings of tribals and Harijans, "God belongs to all. He does not just belong to the wealthy, educated or powerful. God belongs to those that worship him."

Once, in Sarangpur, Swamishri was walking past a group of youths standing a few feet away. Swamishri called, "Come here. Why are you standing so far away?"

"Swamiji, we are *harijans*."

"We are also *hari na jan* (i.e., God's children). Come here. Do not hesitate."

The youths ran towards Swamishri and fell at his feet. They had never been addressed with so much love. They could see the respect and compassion on Swamishri's face as he spoke to them, "Friends, all of us have to become *hari na jan* someday. Do you have any addictions? Make sure you live a pure life and get a sound education. You have my blessings."

This impartial love and comfort from Swamishri brought a satisfying smile on the youths' faces; it built an aura of confidence and pride.

Swamishri was in Motibej, a tribal district. It was around 1.00 a.m. on a wintry night and the biting cold was making everybody shiver. Yet even to this day, his comforting words ring in their ears, "I see God in all of you!"

While in Dharampur-Dang district, Swamishri said something

"Your huts are as pure as the sacred places of pilgrimage." In a tribal devotee's hut in the Dang District.

similar to another group of tribal villagers: "*Adivasi* doesn't mean tribal or backward. It means one who is close to God. 'Adi' means God and 'vasi' means close to."

Dalubhai Madari lived in the small village of Dedvasan in southern Gujarat. After becoming a *satsangi*, he gave up all his former addictions. He became a vegetarian and gave up his violent ways. Now, he wished to invite Swamishri to his humble hut.

When Swamishri finally graced his hut, Dalubhai danced with joy. However, there was one small problem. He didn't have any space or arrangements to seat Swamishri. His house and cowshed were virtually one. How could he offer a seat to Swamishri?

Helped by the sadhus, he cleaned a small stoney portion of the shed and made room for Swamishri to sit. Swamishri helped Dalubhai perform Thakorji's puja.

When Swamishri found out that Dalubhai had given up all his former addictions, he got up from the stone he was sitting on, embraced Dalubhai and blessed him.

After learning that all the other tribesmen present had also given up their addictions, Swamishri hugged all of them.

"They may be poor, but even their darshan brings peace. They are pure. How could anyone call them backward? These huts are like places of pilgrimage."

It was difficult for the tribal folk to appreciate Swamishri's glory from a worldly perspective, but they were touched by his sense of equality and impartial love.

Swamishri was walking from his room in Sankari to the mandir. A few unkempt tribals were seated on either side of the road, totally uninterested in their surroundings. Swamishri stopped and greeted them, "Jai Swaminarayan."

The tribals paid no attention at first. After Swamishri repeated the greeting a few more times, they looked up at him. Having made eye contact with them, Swamishri continued, "All of you should come for darshan in the mandir daily. This mandir is not just for the wealthy and upper classes, but it is for all. Sit and pray for a while, you will experience peace. If everyone else comes to the mandir and you don't, we feel bad. So make sure you come. Also, if you have any addictions shed them. Addictions are a waste of money. The monsoon is approaching. If your house is not proper, it may collapse or leak. In the winter you will feel cold and in the scorching summer you will feel hot. By indulging in addictions you are inviting difficulties. You remain poor; cannot repair the house and your children are unable to study. But by saving money, by giving up smoking, drinking, etc., you can improve your house, educate your children and have decent clothes. All this will benefit you. We don't want your money. But, if you come and do darshan everyday, it is worth thousands of rupees for us."

Swamishri sees God in all. He not only treats everyone as equal but also asks others to do the same. Swamishri's practical applications and experience-based teachings help convince even the staunchly orthodox.

According to a tradition that had carried over into the Swaminarayan Sampraday, *parshads* from the lowest strata of society were not given the *bhagvati diksha* – initiation into saffron robes. In 1981, Swamishri discontinued it by initiating the *parshads* into the sadhu order. This is probably the first time something like this had happened in the Hindu community.

There are many such instances where Swamishri has offered his love equally to all who meet him. It could be a felicitatory function organized by the British and Canadian Parliaments or royalty, or an address to the UN or meeting *adivasis* and harijans in their humble huts. In each instance he has blessed and spoken with the same humility and enthusiasm. He truly sees God in everyone.

Swamishri often advises, "We are *atma*. We are not this body. We must eradicate our *dehbhav.*"

Many times the situation is so intense that it would have shaken the strongest of men, but Swamishri has maintained his composure.

In 1974, a grand welcoming assembly was held in honour of Swamishri at Alexandra Palace, London. A few days later, Swamishri was back in India travelling in the nondescript village of Rohishala in Saurashtra region. He was staying in a mud house. One morning, Subhash, a youth from London travelling with Swamishri, commented, "This is a far cry from Alexandra Palace!"

Without hesitation, Swamishri replied, "Subhash, a hundred Alexandra Palaces do not add up to this little mud house. Look at the affection of these poor devotees."

In 1982, just a few days after returning to India from London, Swamishri went straight to the villages in the Khandesh region of Maharashtra. The scorching summer heat was unbearable and the villages lacked even simple facilities, such as indoor toilets. Yet, Swamishri was equally at ease in these small villages as he was in London and toured them with the same enthusiasm.

Swamishri is held in high regard because of his spotless character and selfless service. His simple yet dynamic persona has touched millions around the world. Yet, for various reasons, some people have heaped insults on Swamishri. Even though he is capable of responding to such unfounded attacks, Swamishri swallows the poison, digests it and forgets it.

Eternal Virtues

Once, a group of individuals launched a media campaign against Swamishri. They published thousands of pamphlets and books and distributed them throughout India. At one stage they insulted Swamishri in a manner that went beyond all bounds of decency! Yet, Swamishri remained composed and didn't utter a single word and stuck to his daily routine. He met the devotees, blessed them and continued as if nothing had happened. Not a single expression on Swamishri's face changed. He remained as jovial and relaxed as before.

Swamishri could have easily given a response or a clarification, but Swamishri didn't say a word. He didn't even let the sadhus or devotees write or say a word.

Swamishri often says, "When you are praised, it feels great; you should feel the same when you are insulted. If you don't feel any ill-will for those that wrong you then you have attained a state of equanimity in honour and insult. We are *atma*. We are not this body. We must eradicate our *dehbhav*."

A leading scholar of the Bharatiya Vidya Bhavan, Shri Bhaishankar Purohit, who has witnessed Swamishri's equanimity for years, writes, "Swamishri has effortlessly accomplished things that the government and wealthy individuals could not with his calm and easygoing personality. He gives all credit to Bhagwan Swaminarayan. He can meet the leaders of this world and then meet an *adivasi* villager with the same affection. His voice and enthusiasm don't change for a second. He is a living example of what the Bhagvad Gita calls '*Samatvam yoga uchyate*', or a true sadhu that possesses equality towards all."

Bhagwan Shri Krishna states in the Bhagvad Gita:
"An ideal sadhu that worships God with his body, mind and soul is the only one that is able to love every living being equally. He is able to see God in them" (BG 12.3).

Tulsidasji states in the Ramacharit Manas:

"One who can maintain his composure in praise and insult is dearer to me than life. That sadhu is full of all divine qualities and is a storehouse of bliss." ◆

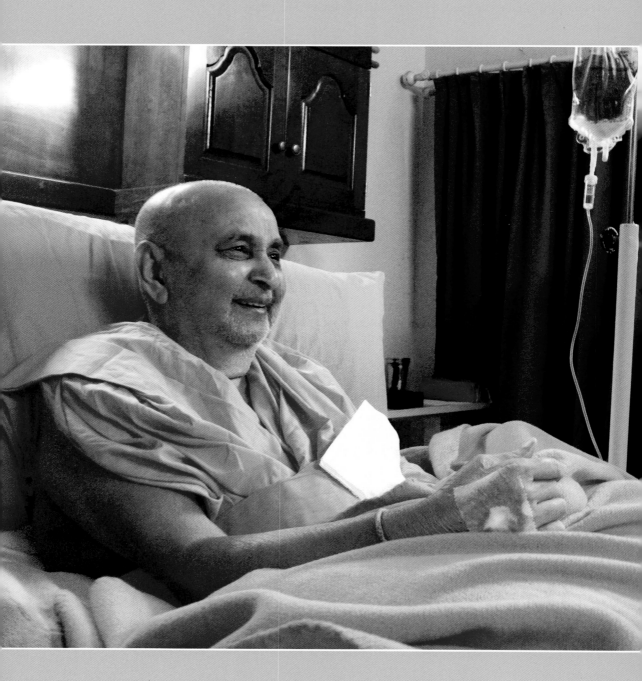

Titiksha
तितिक्षा

Titiksha is to tolerate with understanding.
Most people tolerate because they are forced to and
have no other option. Tolerating when you are in a position
to counter or respond is a great spiritual accomplishment.
Pramukh Swami Maharaj has tolerated all his life,
from serious physical ailments to a variety of bewildering
situations. Swamishri has perfected the ability to
tolerate physical, natural and spiritual problems with a smile.

Swamishri often describes the importance of tolerance: "This body is home to many diseases, just as this world is home to sorrow and unhappiness. Just as people are likely to come to stay at one's home, one is likely to get sick and to have to deal with difficulties. It is natural. Shri Rama, Shri Krishna, Shastriji Maharaj, Yogiji Maharaj and great devotees such as Mirabai and Narsinh Mehta have had to face and tolerate difficulties. If one lives with understanding and wisdom, obstacles do not appear like obstacles. One who has this understanding experiences happiness even in troubled times."

Swamishri speaks from personal experience. His ability to tolerate is amazing – be it heat and cold, hunger and thirst, illness or any other difficulty without a murmur. Swamishri has tolerated for us.

Swamishri has an in-built knack for silently tolerating without complaining since childhood. His life provides an ideal example of tolerance.

The largest chapter of tolerance from his life is his life-long *vicharan* to help mankind. Just as the sun doesn't take even a day's rest, Swamishri has continuously travelled around the world to assist those in need.

These travels take a toll on his body. They place physical and

Travelling in the remote villages of Gujarat, disregarding his age and health, Swamishri has blessed thousands of villages and tolerated untold inconveniences.

mental strain on Swamishri, but he has never complained. No regularity in his routine is possible because of the demand on his time. This plays havoc with his meal and rest times: one day he may get to have lunch at 1.00 p.m., while the next day lunch may be at 3.00 p.m. Schedules vary almost daily, and for the most part are dictated by others.

Swamishri also braves the climate to personally be with the devotees. He has offered his warmth to villagers during the freezing winter months in the Sabarkantha region, and cooled the hearts of villagers during the scorching summer heat in the Saurashtra region, saying, "Let the seasons do their duty. We have to do ours."

Attendant sadhus remember that upto the age of 65 they had to force Swamishri to wear a warm cap in the freezing winter cold. Often, during the hot summers, electric fans were a scarce commodity in the interior villages of Gujarat and Maharashtra. And, at times, when devotees would arrange for air-conditioning units, Swamishri would refuse the comfort, reasoning, "Why make it a habit? It is better to tolerate the heat than become dependent on rare facilities."

Many have witnessed Swamishri's ability to put up with hardships.

In June 1979, Swamishri was travelling in Mahuva district of Gujarat, visiting the homes, rather the huts, of *adivasi* villagers in remote villages like Kharpa and Fulvadi. On his way to Dedvasan, the dirt roads were littered with scrap metal, pipes, glass and jagged stones. It was near impossible for the driver to take the car any further. Just as they were thinking what to do, the clouds rumbled and the rain started pouring. Before the sadhus could say anything, Swamishri got out of the car and started walking towards Dedvasan. The sadhus protested, but Swamishri continued. A little while later,

Narayanprasad Swami requested him, "Let's go back. This is too much of a distance for you to walk."

Swamishri responded with conviction, "A little walking in the rain isn't going to hurt me. These devotees live here in such tough conditions, and all of you sadhus regularly travel here tolerating the heat, mosquitoes, tics and inconveniences of food, water and sleep. So, why shouldn't I do it?"

Swamishri silently continued to walk in the rain at an unmatchable pace.

In 1967, Swamishri left Gondal for Sarangpur via Gadhada in an open jeep. Torrential rains turned the roads into veritable streams. The driver took the Vallabhipur road and at around midnight they arrived in Khambhda. The driver was half asleep when Swamishri noticed that the jeep was on the edge of an irrigation channel. Swamishri told him to stop the vehicle; Swamishri got out and noticed that the muddy slope ended just a few feet ahead. Swamishri instructed the driver to turn the jeep around. To the driver's surprise the vehicle wouldn't budge as its fuel tank was empty. Without a trace of anger, Swamishri told the driver and a devotee to wait there while he and the others would walk to Sarangpur, about 10 kilometres away, and send fuel for the vehicle.

Taking his sandals in one hand and his *potlu* in the other, Swamishri energetically plodded through the muddy roads to Sarangpur, arriving there at around 3.00 a.m.

An ancient proverb goes, 'The toughest hardships are ones created by accident.' Swamishri tolerates and overcomes even those.

His ability to tolerate stands out especially when he is sick. Swamishri was travelling in southern Gujarat when he arrived in the village of Kapura on 28 September 1978. The previous

Swamishri has endured various difficulties while visiting the huts of tribal villagers, Chuli, April 1998.

few days had been rough. On the previous day, Swamishri had travelled through numerous villages while observing a waterless fast and had not had a chance to fully recover from this exertion. In any case, the schedule continued. Swamishri was at Sumanbhai Bhakta's house and an assembly was underway. As Viveksagar Swami was speaking to the audience, Swamishri sat peacefully turning his *mala*. The other sadhus started noticing a change of expression on Swamishri's face. His skin was changing colour and he looked really uneasy. Swamishri looked like he was going to collapse. As he spoke, Viveksagar Swami noticed this and in mid-speech put his hand on Swamishri's wrist to check his temperature. To his surprise, Swamishri's body was very hot.

Viveksagar Swami immediately ended the assembly and helped to get Swamishri to Jitubhai Shah's house. The sadhus helped Swamishri get to his room on the second floor. As soon as they brought him to the bed, he fell onto it, exhausted. A doctor was called, and in the meantime he was given some medicine, but his condition seemed to deteriorate by the minute. He was barely conscious when he started mumbling instructions. The sadhus tried to listen and make out his words. After a few minutes they realized what he was saying, "I hope Sumanbhai's father is not offended. I wanted to stay for the whole assembly. I didn't want to finish it early. We didn't get to go to Mahendrabhai's house. He has come all the way from Madhi."

Swamishri was so weak from the fever that he couldn't even turn in bed. At around 11.30 a.m. Swamishri mustered every ounce of strength in his body to sit up and said, "Have you prepared Thakorji's meal? Make sure you offer the *thal* on time." He lay down again after receiving a confirmation from the sadhus.

From the start until the end of this incident, Swamishri hadn't uttered a single word about himself or his discomfort.

In the following days, Dr Ramanbhai Patel of Bardoli treated Swamishri for jaundice.

Also, Swamishri was suffering pain from a gum abscess. Dr. Labhshankarbhai, an experienced dentist of Rajkot, came for Swamishri's darshan in Sankari. Upon hearing of Swamishri's toothache he decided to examine it. As Labhshankarbhai opened Swamishri's mouth and gently touched the gums, pus oozed out. Labhshankarbhai was amazed by Swamishri's threshold for pain, commenting, "Only Swamishri can tolerate so much."

Swamishri never complains about physical ailments. He endures them with a smile and without as much as a sigh. There are many more examples.

In 1984 Swamishri was in Nadiad for the mandir's groundbreaking ceremony. The mandir grounds hadn't been cleared properly and as Swamishri was walking a four-inch thorn pierced through Swamishri's slippers and lodged in his foot. He stopped in his tracks due to the sudden pain. A few sadhus ran up to Swamishri, but he pulled the thorn out of his foot before they could say anything. Blood gushed from his foot.

Swamishri turned around to the sadhus and instructed, "Do not tell anyone."

But how could such an event be kept a secret. Everyone came to know of the incident and a few sadhus decided to rebuke the organizers for not clearing the grounds properly. Swamishri called the sadhus and said, "There is no point in blaming anyone. You are bound to get hurt sometimes. You can get hurt outdoors, inside your room or even in your bed. You can't control such things."

Swamishri readily tolerated the physical pain, but made sure that the devotees or organizers were not hurt verbally.

A similar incident took place when a heavy duty staple entered Swamishri's foot while he was walking in Navsari mandir. Swamishri again tolerated the discomfort and continued his activities.

Sometimes an incident may seem really insignificant but the lesson learned from it is colossal.

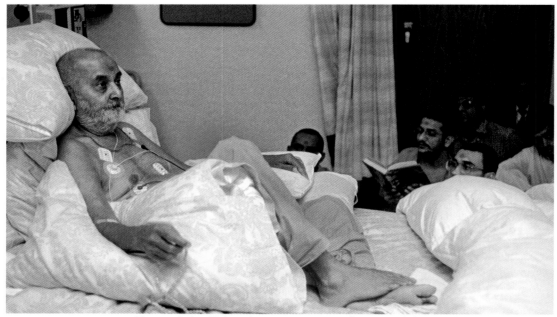
Moments before his heart bypass surgery, Swamishri attentively listens to katha, New York, 1998.

Swamishri has tolerated numerous illnesses without uttering a word. Ordinary complaints that are rather common with most people such as 'My head hurts' or 'My feet are killing me' are never heard from his mouth. In spite of frequent warnings from physicians, Swamishri has continued to serve the devotees, tolerating all that comes his way.

He has had operations to remove his gall bladder, cataracts and a benign tumour; he has suffered a heart attack and subsequently has had quintuple coronary bypass surgery; also, he has troublesome arthritis in several joints and is prone to an attack of frozen shoulder. In each instance, he proves to be an ideal patient, never complaining or asking for special arrangements.

In 1983, in Sundalpura, a town near Anand, Swamishri suffered a severe heart attack. His ability to tolerate touched all those present. His attention was not drawn to his own health; he was worrying about arrangements for others.

In 1996 during Swamishri's Satsang Tour to the US, physicians advised him to undergo coronary angiography. The procedure was done in Houston, Texas, by renowned cardiologist Dr Virendra Mathur. Touched by Swamishri's tolerance, Dr Mathur said, "He is an amazing patient. Swamishri didn't complain or let out a single moan throughout the procedure. He is very tolerant. This is the first time I have had a patient like this. "

On 7 July 1998, Dr Moses and Dr Schwarz performed an

angiography on Swamishri at the Lenox Hill Hospital in New York City. They walked out of the cath lab with a grim face and explained the complexity of the situation. Swamishri was still on the angiography table when one of Dr Schwarz's assistants was trying to communicate with Krishnavallabh Swami in English. Krishnavallabh Swami was having trouble understanding the doctor and couldn't respond since he didn't speak much English.

Swamishri was observing this comic interaction lying down on the table and started laughing out loud. The young doctor was amazed to see that Swamishri, still hooked up to the machines and moments away from emergency bypass surgery, was able to enjoy a lighter moment.

Explaining the results of the angiography the physicians suggested that Swamishri have immediate bypass surgery. Swamishri listened to them attentively and agreed, "Whatever God wishes."

Swamishri was turning the *mala* and then went soundly to sleep for two hours, as preparations were made for the operation. How can one sleep so soundly in such critical situations? Only Swamishri, who places everything in the hands of God, can.

In the weeks following the bypass surgery, Swamishri was recovering at Dr Mahendrabhai Patel's house in Westchester. Swamishri was suffering from aching pain in his shoulder and upper back. One day, when he was lying on the bed, Dr Kiranbhai Doshi and Yogicharan Swami noticed that Swamishri was in pain. Dr Kiranbhai broke the silence.

"Is that paining you?"

"Yes, it has been hurting for some time now." An immediate decision was made to start physiotherapy for this. So, a physiotherapist came to examine Swamishri's shoulder.

"Swamiji, my name is John. I am going to press on your shoulder. I will start off gently and then apply more pressure. Tell me to stop when you can't bear the pain. "

Swamishri nodded in approval. John started the therapy. Swami was silent. At one point, John's thumb was hurting him from the force of pressing down, but Swamishri remained silent.

John was startled by Swamishri's capacity to bear pain. He didn't remember ever having a patient like him before.

A couple of months after the bypass, Sam Pitroda, a renowned entrepreneur, came for Swamishri's darshan. In fact, Mr Pitroda had had bypass surgery a few years before as well and he reflected, "The first two months or so you will feel uneasy. You will feel heaviness in your chest, almost like having a brick hanging from your throat. Do you feel it?"

"Yes, I feel it. But it's getting better," Swamishri agreed.

The attendant sadhus were surprised by Swamishri's answer because he had never mentioned it to anyone before. He had tolerated it without saying a word!

After being diagnosed with arthritis in his heel, Swamishri started laughing and sang a famous bhajan, *"Junu to thayu re deval junu to thayu...",* meaning, "This body is old now, this body is old...".

Narayanmuni Swami interrupted, "You have gone through enough now. It is time for you to..."

It was Swamishri's turn to interrupt, "I haven't endured anything. Everyone is supposed to endure a little pain, but my body works fine. I have no other problems. I am not bedridden. I can sleep well. I can digest what I eat. What else can I ask for? How much more grace do I need from God?"

In Ahmedabad, cardiologist Dr Madhubhai Patel took Swamishri's ECG and commented, "Swamishri you need to rest. Your cardiogram looks a little different from what it had been last time. It looks like you have done a lot of travelling this past winter. "

Swamishri smiled and didn't say a word.

Later that afternoon at lunch time, Swamishri jokingly told Krishnavallabh Swami, who cooks Swamishri's meals, "My test results are not normal. The doctor told me that I eat too much. I am going to have to cut down!"

Imagine someone laughing at such serious test results. Swamishri tolerates everything with the understanding that his real form is not this physical body; he is the *atma*.

A few days later, Dr Bhuva had come for Swamishri's darshan to Sarangpur from Bhavnagar. He looked at the cardiogram reports and started to instruct Swamishri.

"It's called a lateral extension. Basically, the blood isn't circulating properly in your heart. It may permanently damage the heart. It's serious. You should stop vigorous travelling."

Swamishri answered with ease, "I have no problem sleeping, even though it's a different bed every night. I can digest what I eat. I don't visit that many houses now so there isn't much exertion. According to your theory, walking out of this room is exertion too! Plus, I am bound to face a few health issues as I am getting old."

Even after repeated warnings from physicians, Swamishri was adamant on continuing his *vicharan*. Most people who get such serious warnings would think twice before even climbing a flight of steps. Swamishri was undeterred.

Once, a few doctors from Mumbai had arrived in Sarangpur to

examine Swamishri's heart. Dr Kiran Doshi, Dr Panchal, Dr Samani and Dr Bhagubhai Patel examined Swamishri's cardiogram and were greatly concerned at what they found.

Dr Samani explained the situation, "The lateral extension is getting worse. Your heart muscles need a certain amount of blood and that is why we have arteries leading to the heart. If one of them is blocked, enough blood is not delivered and that could lead to serious problems. Therefore, take it easy and don't exert yourself too much."

Swamishri remained silent. Dr Samani was confused. Why was Swamishri ignoring him? "You are listening to me, right? Or would you rather just not talk about it?" Swamishri said nothing as he flashed an innocent smile across his face.

It was time to change the subject!

Swamishri was in Kolkata in 1993. He started having dizzy spells and was losing balance. Physicians suspected that there was inadequate blood circulation to the brain. They decided to rush Swamishri to Mumbai and told him to cancel his *vicharan* plans in Kolkata.

Swamishri refused, "I pray to God for everyone's wellbeing and bless the devotees; I am sure God will bless me. All of you pray daily too. Everything is going to be fine. A few more days here will not make a big difference. The devotees have worked very hard to plan the programme here, so let us complete the schedule here and then go to Mumbai. Leaving now would spoil their efforts. There is no need to rush. Nothing will happen."

Swamishri was willing to tolerate anything just so that he could please the devotees.

It is almost as if he enjoys tolerating and that is why doctors repeatedly have to beg to him to be frank, "Please tell us if something is not right or you are feeling uneasy. If you are feeling the slightest pain, tell us. Give us a chance to serve you."

How can they expect someone who has endured his whole life to stop doing what he does so naturally?

A devotee once asked Swamishri to take care of his own health; to which he responded, "God takes care of our health. How am I going to take care of it? He has given me this human body and will keep me healthy so I can serve all of you."

The secret behind Pramukh Swami Maharaj's ability to endure lies in his understanding that he is *atma* and not the body.

In 1994, Swamishri was travelling around Europe and arrived in

Swamishri in a joyous and divine mood.

Prague. One of the attendant sadhus was massaging his feet when he noticed a wound of some sort.

"How did you get hurt here? What happened?" he asked.

Swamishri gave no response.

The attendant forced the issue until Swamishri explained, "The body is bound to get hurt sometimes. It's not a big deal."

Swamishri brushed off the wound as if it didn't exist.

His physical tolerance is beyond imagination, his mental and emotional endurance surpasses even that. Swamishri listens to those that arrogantly and ignorantly insult him, without uttering a word in protest.

Harkishan Mehta, the editor of *Chitralekha,* a widely read Gujarati weekly magazine, interviewed Swamishri in Mumbai. He was curious to know about Swamishri's views on tolerance.

"How do you feel when someone insults you?"

"I am not bothered by it. If we are right, it doesn't matter what everyone else says. One day they may realize the truth," Swamishri replied.

"But don't you want to correct the misconceptions or answer the criticism?"

"No, not at all."

On 13 February 2007, Swamishri was talking to a few sadhus in Mumbai. The sadhus asked him, "You always tell us to endure, but

Eternal Virtues

for how long can one tolerate? Don't you think it is best to clarify and respond sometimes?"

Swamishri's response reflected the essence of his life, "Keep tolerating. There is no end to it. You have to respect and love even those that offend you. Look at Yogiji Maharaj's life. He endured till his very last breath. If you tolerate their mistakes and insults of others, one day they will realize their mistakes. You can change them without saying a word! He who remains silent achieves everything. Confronting the individual may cause more conflict. Be patient and humble. You will never be able to teach others a lesson. Tolerating will change them. Tolerate till the very end."

In 1987, the Mumbai bureau chief, Kanubhai Mehta, of the *Gujarat Samachar* newspaper came for Swamishri's darshan. He asked Swamishri a few questions.

"Do you ever have any regret for anything in life?"

"Regret? For what? I act according to God's wish, realize that he is responsible for everything and so I have no regrets," was the answer.

"What do you enjoy the most? Is there a specific incident or moment that you cherish?"

"I enjoy everything. Every incident in my life is joyful. God is the source of all joy."

Swamishri enjoys everything, including the hardships, difficulties and insults in order to please his devotees. Swamishri's tolerance is outstanding. ◆

Swamishri's aloofness from this world is reflected while chanting the holy name of God.

Uparatihi
उपरतिः
Viraktihi
विरक्ति

Virakti is lack of interest in worldly pleasures.
While most people seek happiness from worldly objects,
one who has achieved virakti does not care for
worldly enjoyment. Uparati means lack of interest
in material gains and worldly activities.
There is a subtle difference between tyag and virakti.
It is easier to physically let go of something than to harbour
disinterest towards it in the mind.
Bhagwan Swaminarayan defines virakti as disinterest in
the universe and all its material objects
(Vachanamrut, Gadhada I 44).
For all sadhus virakti is a required quality,
but it is seldom achieved completely.
Without virakti a sadhu has only reached the base
camp at Mount Everest.
During his 70 years as a sadhu and in the
18 years before initiation,
Swamishri's life show this disinterest and aloofness.

The *American Heritage English Dictionary* defines a river as being 'a body of water that flows'. Just as a river is defined by its motion or flow, Swamishri's *virakti* is defined by his continuous *vicharan*.

Swamishri is unaffected by any amount of wealth, material objects, comfort, fame and praise. There is no showcase or display of his *virakti*; it is a natural phenomenon.

In this chapter we will discuss one aspect of Swamishri's *virakti*, his disinterest towards the world and everything within it.

In a later chapter on 'Shilam, Shama, Dama, Tapa', we will discuss his control over and ability to regulate his mind and senses.

"Our only work is to turn the *mala* and worship God…"

Swamishri has been living within society, directly dealing with its problems to help people cope with the ups and downs of life. He is frequently honoured by local, national and international dignitaries, yet Swamishri has never sought or desired worldly fame or pleasures. He has never asked anything for his personal needs. Thousands of devotees place the world's comforts at his feet, yet he remains distant. It's amazing that nothing has ever been able to tempt him.

In 2004, Swamishri was on his way to an evening satsang assembly at the Raritan Centre in Edison, New Jersey. Jaimin Patel and Hitesh Patel were driving Swamishri to the venue in a new top-of-the-line luxury car. Knowing that Swamishri spends much of his time in a car travelling in the villages, they wanted to offer this comfortable car for Swamishri's use.

After taking the first few minutes to explain the features of this fine vehicle, they daringly posed a question, "This car would be perfect for you. Right?"

Swamishri understood their intention and replied, "I am fine with whatever we have in India. Old is gold!"

Swamishri tried to change the topic, but the youths persisted, "You build new mandirs all the time and each one is built differently with new architectural designs and patterns. So why not take this new car?"

"Mandirs are made for God. They benefit thousands of people

worldwide. This car will only give me comfort."

Hitesh tried to argue from a different angle, "When Shastriji Maharaj designated you as the Pramukh of our Sanstha, he told you to please and satisfy the devotees. We would feel satisfied if you accepted this car as a token of our devotion."

"We have always pleased and satisfied you…we sit with you, talk to you…"

Hitesh insisted, "Swami! We want you to take it. It's our deep wish…"

"Never wish for such things," Swamishri interrupted.

The youths were humbled by Swamishri's *virakti*. They were offering one of the world's finest vehicles to him, yet Swamishri was not interested. He was not tempted by it at all.

Swamishri has never asked for or accepted luxuries even in the name of convenience.

On 16 October 1994, Swamishri was sitting with a few youths and sadhus in Vidyanagar. One of the youths suggested buying a helicopter to help ease Swamishri's hectic and exhausting travelling routine.

Swamishri interrupted him and said, "One should desire liberation not worldly comforts."

Bhagvatcharan Swami added, "I agree with you, Swamishri. You don't need a helicopter, but I do think that you need a new car. I can barely fit in this car of yours."

Swamishri smiled and said, "Rather than changing the car, I think you need to lose a little weight! You should condition the mind and body so that it is comfortable anywhere. You should be able to sleep equally well on a dusty road or in a king-size bed."

Swamishri has lived that lesson throughout his life, travelling on

Swamishri inspires all to turn the *mala* and chant God's name to overcome worldly pains and pleasures.

dusty, potholed roads in open jeeps, farm tractors, bullock carts and even a Mercedes Benz to please devotees.

Once Swamishri said, "You can only be content if you develop the understanding that even when among the masses you are alone in a jungle, and if in a jungle that you are surrounded by the masses. It seems like simple and free advice, but it is the essence to living a happy life."

Swamishri's indifference to materialistic objects has inspired thousands of individuals to live this spiritual lifestyle.

Even when travelling to foreign countries, Swamishri seldom visits tourist attractions. At times when local devotees are insistent, Swamishri will very occasionally go along just to satisfy them. He is never influenced by or interested in these entertainment spots.

Swamishri never wishes recognition and power; rather he dislikes such things.

On 12 April 1995, when Swamishri was in Bharuch, a discussion on the Narmada Dam Project arose. Referring to the delays caused by political corruption throughout the project's history, a local community leader expressed his confidence in Swamishri, "If you were in office along with a team of your sadhus, you would complete the task in no time."

Taking Swamishri's silence as a sign of approval, the individual started discussing the plan in detail. Swamishri listened to him patiently and then expressed his thoughts, "For a sadhu devotion, *mala* and service are his main duties. It is not a sadhu's role to get involved in these things." Then Swamishri added, "The pleasures of the entire universe doesn't compare to the bliss experienced from worshipping God. For a sadhu worshipping God is his duty."

On 4 November 1997 Swamishri was travelling in the Eurostar train from London to Paris. He was quietly turning his *mala* when a devotee started discussing the government infrastructure. Harshadbhai Rana from Nairobi, who was travelling with Swamishri, said, "The government should place their power in Swamishri's hands. He would do a great job..."

In reply, Swamishri raised his right hand slightly showing his *mala*, and said, "My hands are busy turning the *mala*. I have no time for anything else."

Many a times, world leaders have expressed this same sentiment in public, but they haven't received as much as a nod of approval from Swamishri.

Pramukh Swami Maharaj's passion for peace and his outstanding work in restoring peace around the world have not gone unnoticed. Many politicians, including former Indian Ambassador to the UK, the late L.M. Singhvi, have suggested that Swamishri should be nominated for a Nobel Peace Prize. Many devotees agreed and in 1997 Brahmavihari Swami brought up the topic, "Dr K.C. Patel and many other senior devotees wish to nominate you for the Nobel Peace Prize. I have started doing some research."

Swamishri stopped him, "I have Bhagwan Swaminarayan and Gunatitanand Swami. That is the greatest 'Nobel Prize'. I don't need another prize. One's true greatness does not come from getting such a prize. We have Bhagwan Swaminarayan and gurus Shastriji Maharaj and Yogiji Maharaj. Is the Nobel Prize better than that?"

Priyadarshan Swami explained its benefits, "You work so hard to spread the teachings of Bhagwan Swaminarayan. If you get this award, thousands of people would be interested in our principles and benefit from them."

"If we offer our devotion to God and sincerely serve society, people will be interested and benefit from our teachings." Swamishri replied.

Swamishri added further, "The Nobel Prize may be something you can show the world. But understand that if you please Shriji Maharaj and (Gunatitanand) Swami, you have accomplished everything there is to do. That is true recognition. Worldly awards do not guarantee

Engrossed in meditation amid his hectic schedule.

true prestige and fame. So, stop thinking about trying to get the award. It is best to worship God."

No one was able to counter Swamishri's reply. Swamishri refused others to pursue the nomination for the award any further.

Wherever Swamishri goes, people around the world organize grand assemblies to welcome him. Yet, Swamishri never attaches importance to them. Though he adjusts to the organizer's plans, he never encourages people to hold such events and usually discourages it.

In July 1994, after a gap of many years Swamishri was scheduled to travel to the Kutch region of Gujarat. Devcharan Swami and Dharamsinhbhai Bhanushali told Swamishri of their plan to organize a procession with Swamishri riding a decorated elephant.

Swamishri immediately protested, "No, no, no… there is no need for all that." Instead, Swamishri made sure that the welcoming was a simple affair.

Once, Swamishri was scheduled to visit the Akshar Purushottam Chhatralay in Vidyanagar. The sadhus and students at the hostel had decorated the whole campus with flowers. It was truly a colourful and vibrant sight. Swamishri arrived and was joyously welcomed by the sadhus and students. After a few moments, Swamishri turned to the sadhus, "There is no need for such extensive decorations when we come. It's not like we are guests here. This is our home. You should only decorate like this if there is a special occasion."

In 1968, guru Yogiji Maharaj celebrated Pramukh Swami Maharaj's 48th birthday in Mumbai and instructed the devotees to celebrate it every year in a grand manner. At Yogiji Maharaj's insistence Swamishri reluctantly accepted the honour on that day, out of respect for his guru's wish.

Every year since then, Swamishri has attended the celebration assembly only because of his guru's command (*agna*). He permits the celebrations because of the devotees' devotion, but just moments after thousands of devotees have celebrated his birthday, Swamishri leaves the stage and forgets that it ever even happened!

As a gift to future generations, Swamishri keeps on building magnificent traditional mandirs and cultural centres. He has also created the magnificent Akshardham complexes in New Delhi and Gandhinagar. They inspire and promote spiritual, cultural and social activities in society. Yet, Swamishri is never physically attached to any one place. After inaugurating a new mandir and setting up the infrastructure needed to maintain it, Swamishri is on the move again, promoting world harmony, spirituality and cultural coexistence.

In 1996 the Duke of Edinburgh HRH Prince Philip was left speechless after visiting Akshardham in Gandhinagar. Swamishri was in Sunrendranagar at the time and therefore was unable to meet him.

Prince Philip asked the guide, "I understand that Swamiji is not here now, but he does live here, doesn't he?"

The Prince was surprised to learn that Swamishri did not live at Akshardham permanently and only sometimes visited there. He wondered how someone could create something so majestic and not live there.

On 10 November 1997, Pramukh Swami Maharaj honoured Prince Philip's invitation and graced Buckingham Palace. Prince Philip recalled his visit to Akshardham the previous year.

"Akshardham is marvellous! I am surprised that you have made such a beautiful place yet do not live there."

Swamishri listened attentively to the Prince and just smiled.

The Prince was puzzled by Swamishri's detachment from his own creation.

Swamishri's *virakti* towards his native village or relatives is reflected by the fact that he has never used his influence or the organization's resources for them.

Swamishri was talking with a few youths in an informal setting. They tried to coax him into talking about Chansad – his hometown.

Swamishri didn't let them finish.

"I don't have a hometown; I don't have a home or any relatives. I have God and that is enough! I worship God and teach others to do the same."

Swamishri is forever absorbed in God and disinterested in mundane things.

It doesn't stop there. Swamishri has such a carefree, indifferent attitude towards even his own self. He places the convenience of others before his needs. That is why even when he is suffering from fever he still pleases the devotes by gracing their homes. That is also why in 1980 he risked losing his eyesight due to cataracts so that the devotees would not have to reschedule the arrangements.

In 1998, two months after Swamishri's bypass operation, cardiologist Dr Dayanand Nayak performed a 3-D echocardiogram as part of a routine checkup. He strongly advised that Swamishri reduce the pace and extent of his strenuous travels. Yet, by the time Swamishri had returned to India, via London and Africa, Swamishri had vetoed all the restrictions put in place for his health.

Unfortunately, the body has its own limitations. Swamishri's rigorous schedule started taking a toll on his body. But that hasn't deterred Swamishri.

In 2007 while Swamishri was in Pune, physicians were concerned for his health and decided to get a full checkup done in Mumbai. After performing numerous medical tests, the physicians again instructed Swamishri to stop travelling. They strongly urged him to stay at one place.

However, less than three months later, drawn by the heartfelt devotion of the devotees, Swamishri embarked on an extensive six-month spiritual tour to Kenya, Uganda, Tanzania, the United States, Canada and the United Kingdom.

Eternal Virtues

Hitesh Patel had come to Bochasan for Swamishri's darshan from London. Upon arrival, he told Swamishri the first thing he had noticed, "Swami! You have lost a lot of weight. Your hands are all wrinkled. You don't look healthy."

Swamishri pulled him close so that others couldn't hear and told him, "That's what happens when you get old. God is calling!" Swamishri stopped for a few moments, smiled and added, "Hitesh! Don't worry about my body. I am getting old; I am bound to get sick. Talk about the *atma*. The *atma* is eternal. It never gets old. If you focus on your *atma*, you will always be at peace. That's the only way to eternal happiness."

Dr Bhaskarbhai Vyas had gone for Swamishri's darshan to Sarangpur from Ahmedabad. At the first instance, he commented on Swamishri's health, "Your body is shrivelling up! You have lost so much weight."

Swamishri spoke with indifference, "Of course it's going to shrivel up. In fact, one day it will disintegrate to dust as well! "

Dr Bhaskarbhai said, "There is so much left to do for Satsang."

Swamishri replied, "God will take care of all that. Once we are done with our work here on earth, we all go our own way!"

Swamishri's *virakti* can be summed up with one final incident. On 6 August 1994, Swamishri was visiting Prague in the Czech Republic, in response to Professor Fric's invitation. He was going to take the visiting devotees and sadhus sightseeing to a famous church. Swamishri who was staying back at his lodgings, called the sadhu responsible for his correspondence and offered, "You can go with them if you want. Just leave the letters here."

The sadhu replied, "I am not interested in going there, so I will stay back and catch up on the letters."

Instinctively, Swamishri revealed his inner feelings, "I am not interested in anything either, except for God."

This incident illustrates Swamishri's disinterest towards the world and it's material pleasures.

Swamishri desires nothing, except God.　　　　　　◆

Shrutam
श्रुतम्

Jnanam
ज्ञानम्

Shrutam is to understand and live the
profound messages of the shastras.
Jnana is to experience atma and Paramatma.
So, jnana is not just information.
Obtaining information from the shastras pertaining to
atma and Paramatma is called paroksh (non-manifest) jnana.
To fully experience and realize their bliss is aparoksh jnana.

The Shrimad Bhagvad Gita defines *jnana* or wisdom:
"Wisdom is to totally experience the true forms of *atma* and Paramatma" (BG 13.12).

Bhagwan Swaminarayan describes a *jnani* or wise person:
"A wise person is one who is *brahmarup* and fully understands the greatness of God" (Vachanamrut, Gadhada I 56).

Jnana is an elevated spiritual state. It is not something to merely talk about; it is something to live. Pramukh Swami Maharaj's life exemplifies *jnana* and that is why he can accomplish what seems humanly impossible.

Swamishri maintains his composure in the contrasting dualities of happiness and sorrow, success and failure, and honour and insult.

He remains humble and free of self-admiration despite worldwide fame.

Swamishri remains devout and thinks of Bhagwan Swaminarayan even while he travels around the world with a hectic daily routine.

Swamishri is the spiritual and administrative leader of a global organization and yet remains stress-free.

Talking or writing about *jnana* is relatively easy, living it is the real task. Swamishri has mastered that *jnana* and that is why he enjoys the divine bliss of God every moment of his life.

Swamishri blesses teenage members of a BAPS dance group after their performance.

"There is no happiness without jnana, even if you go to the moon...", London mandir.

Three youths from Sussex, England, had developed an interest in Hinduism and were visiting India to gain a firsthand experience. David, Daniel and Richard had met quite a few sadhus during their time in India but did not come in contact with Pramukh Swami Maharaj. One night, after their return to England, David had Swamishri's darshan in a dream. After discussing the information he recalled from the dream with his friends they all came to the BAPS Shri Swaminarayan Mandir in Neasden, London. On 5 May 1994, David and his friends came for Swamishri's darshan. David experienced peace, satisfaction and fulfilment upon seeing Swamishri.

David had a question, "Four days ago, you graced me with your darshan in my dream. You told me about *nirvikalp samadhi* or the divine experience of God. In fact, you gave me a practical demonstration where I experienced it as well. Do you constantly experience that bliss in everything that you do? "

Swamishri replied, "Yes. Because while I walk, talk and in everything else that I do I have God with me."

The ease and confidence with which Swamishri answered the question convinced David.

In 1993 Swamishri was in Kolkata, when he started having dizzy spells. He was immediately brought to Mumbai for a medical checkup to rule out the possibility of any serious illness which would require urgent treatment. The neurosurgeons recommended that an

EEG and a BERA scan be performed.

During the BERA test Swamishri was told to lie face-up on the examination table. An array of sensors and wires were attached to Swamishri's head and around his ears. After 15 minutes of trying the technician told the attendant sadhu, "I am not satisfied with the readings. Please request Swamishri to relax and calm his mind."

The attendant explained the instructions to Swamishri, but he found that Swamishri was completely calm and relaxed.

The second attempt yielded the same results. The technician again asked Swamishri to remain calm and free of thought.

Then he tried for a third time. Yet again, the readings were not satisfactory.

Swamishri then came back to the mandir after the incomplete test. As Swamishri was going to bed that night, the attendant sadhu explained that the physician had called and said they needed to do that test again.

Swamishri immediately refused.

The attendant sadhu explained the importance and urgency of the tests to diagnose the illness.

Swamishri again refused, "It doesn't matter how important it is. I am not taking that test again."

The attendant was astonished as to why Swamishri was being so firm. He tried to request one more time.

This time Swamishri raised his voice a little and said, "I was calm the whole time. I was imagining myself sitting in the Akshar Deri in Gondal, meditating on Bhagwan Swaminarayan. Is that not serene and calm enough?"

Swamishri can never be free from this thought, since Bhagwan Swaminarayan is forever ingrained in his mind.

S wamishri may not be at the forefront of philosophical debates that discuss the forms of *atma* and Paramatma, but he lives in tune with his *atma* and in constant rapport with Paramatma. Despite being swamped with various tasks and consistently travelling, each moment of Swamishri's life reflects his devotion to and oneness with God.

Once, while Swamishri was in Bochasan, Paramanandji and Adhyatmanandji, sannyasins of the Divyajivan Sangh, asked him a few questions about his constant rapport with God.

"We had the good fortune of your darshan last year in Kolkata during your birthday celebrations. Does that mean that you were 'born'?"

"All true happiness in this world is derived from God."

Swamishri answered with confidence, "From a worldly standpoint, yes. Spiritually, there is no birth or death."

The sannyasins were surprised.

"There is no death?"

"No, I am Atma, Akshar, eternal and indestructible."

"Akshar and Paramatma are two different entities?"

"Akshar serves Paramatma, yet they are inseparable. Paramatma lives within Atma."

Dr Raymond Williams, of Wabash College in Indiana, USA, had asked Swamishri a simple question, "Who are you?"

To which Swamishri gave a simple answer, "I am Aksharbrahman."

Responding to a letter written to him in English, Swamishri clearly illustrated his constant awareness of the *aparoksh jnana* that separates him from ordinary mortals. He wrote, in English, "I am Brahman."

The Taittiriya Upanishad declares, "Aksharbrahman as the living form of *jnana*." That is probably why Swamishri's wisdom practically resonates from his words.

A teenager once asked Swamishri how often he is able to experience the bliss of Akshardham. Swamishri responded in one word, "Always."

On 12 July 1994 a youth asked Swamishri, "Which is your best time of the day?"

"I enjoy every moment because Bhagwan Swaminarayan is always with me."

Once, after Swamishri had performed *arti* in the Akshar Deri in Gondal, two kids came to ask a question. Swamishri was in a rush, but he listened to the children attentively, "How do you experience God when you perform the *arti*?" they asked.

"I experience God as if he is standing right in front of me! Just like the two of you are standing in front of me."

The secret to Swamishri's bliss and constant serenity is his ability to experience God. He is able to apply the wisdom of *atma* and Paramatma practically.

Swamishri's oneness with God is constant – 24 hours a day, 7 days a week, 365 days a year. He stays amidst us and with us, yet he is on a divine plane. This is often portrayed in his conversation.

On 14 May 2004, Swamishri was getting ready to leave from London for New York. Nainesh Patel, a local youth, started talking to Swamishri while he was having dinner.

"London is like your home. You should never go from here."

Swamishri's understanding of the *atma* followed, "Friend! Wherever I go it is my home. Akshardham is eternal and everywhere. Whether I am in a palace or in a small villager's hut, I am always at home. Therefore, it doesn't matter if you are from London or anywhere else. Understand your *atma*. We are all from Akshardham."

Vishwavihari Swami phoned Swamishri, who was then in Nairobi.

"When are you coming back to Ahmedabad?"

Swamishri gave him a humorous, but philosophical answer, "I don't come or go. I am here in Nairobi and over there in Ahmedabad as well. I am everywhere."

Bhagwan Swaminarayan describes this *brahmarup* state in the Vachanamrut:

"Such a devotee may reside in a kingdom, thousands of people may be under his command and he may be wealthy. But he himself

"There is no happiness without jnana, even if you go to the moon...", London mandir.

does not feel, 'I have become very great.' Furthermore, if the kingdom is destroyed and he begs for food from house to house with an earthen begging bowl, he does not feel, 'Now I have become poor.' This is because he remains absolutely carefree in his own bliss, and he knows the greatness of his own self and that of God" (Vachanamrut, Loya 10).

In 1992, soon after Swaminarayan Akshardham in Gandhinagar had been inaugurated during the Yogiji Maharaj Birth Centenary Celebrations, Pramukh Swami Maharaj left Gandhinagar for Nadiad. In Nadiad, Swamishri was sitting with a few devotees and sadhus when one of the devotees said, "Do you feel lonely here? There were tens of thousands of people in Gandhinagar and there are only five people here."

Swamishri replied, "I have God with me, so I am never lonely. I continuously enjoy his company. If you don't have God, you would feel lonely even if you are with all the people in the world."

Once, Janmangal Swami noticed how busy Swamishri was, "You are always busy doing work."

Swamishri replied, "I am never busy doing work. I am always worshipping Bhagwan Swaminarayan."

Being able to remember God even in the midst of constant activity is one of Swamishri's great abilities. Swamishri calls it the 'atma-Paramatma technique'.

A prominent Hindu spiritual guru and lifestyle reformer, Sri Sri Ravi Shankar, came to visit Swaminarayan Akshardham in New Delhi and to meet Swamishri. As he was leaving, Swamishri gave him a framed picture of him standing in front of the Akshardham monument taken just a short time before.

Sri Sri Ravi Shankar was amazed by the speed with which it had been edited, printed and framed.

Swamishri smiled and said, "This is the magic of technology, but the greatest technology is of *atma* and Paramatma. There is nothing greater than that!"

Swamishri not only lives with this technology, he teaches it to all those around him. He wants those around him to experience that same bliss of God.

Yogivandan Swami was preparing to return to Chicago and requested Swamishri, "Please give me a *niyam* to follow until you come to America in 2007."

"The greatest *niyam* is believing yourself to be *atma*. All *niyams* are included in that. Maintain that understanding even when you are facing difficulty. That should be our goal and the ultimate *niyam*."

In Nadiad, during a special meeting for the planning of Amrut Mahotsav in 1995, Bhagvatcharan Swami asked Swamishri for specific instructions, "They have put me in the fundraising department this time. What am I supposed to do?"

Swamishri replied, "Believe yourself and others to be *atma*. That is all you have to do in life."

Swamishri was in a youth assembly in San Jose, California. He explained this *jnana* to the young aspirants, "All of you have to become *brahmarup*. That's what the Bal Mandal and Kishore Mandal are for — to attain this spiritual state. Then all of you will experience this spiritual bliss. Once you master this *jnana* you will never be unhappy. You will be able to experience bliss regardless of the circumstances around you and in all of the activities that you do."

On 4 December 1994, Swamishri spoke to the Chief Secretary of Gujarat, Shri Balakrishnan about seeking this *jnana*, "Believe yourself to be *atma*. This is at the foundation of our principles. If you believe yourself to be *atma*, you will become free of worldly desires, attachments and hatreds, and will experience peace. Bhagwan Swaminarayan has given us this *jnana*. Only by believing your true self to be *atma* can you be focused during devotion. Otherwise there will be difficulties."

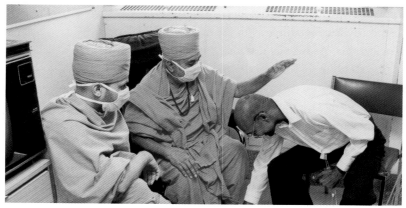

Swamishri blesses Bhagwanjibhai Mandavia, July 1988.

Swamishri was seated in a Board of Trustees meeting in London on 23 October 1997. Dr I.P. Patel said, "Swamishri! Jitubhai often has to listen to people insult him when he is trying to get work done for the mandir. He tolerates it because it is for the mandir."

Swamishri was pleased and said, "Our *jnana* is useful in these situations. Someone might call you a fool. Stop and think for a second. You know that you are not a fool. One who understands the *atma* is not bothered by insults or curses. Shastriji Maharaj also faced a great deal of abuse. People would write and say terrible things about him. But he was not at all affected by it. Those people are not around today, but Shastriji Maharaj's legacy has lived on. If we master this *jnana*, we will be able to live peacefully."

On 28 September 1996, Swamishri was in Los Angeles when an acclaimed writer and teaching expert named Brian came to meet him because he was experiencing depression. He had thoughts of committing suicide and attempted it a few times; such had been the state of his mind.

He asked Swamishri, "Who are we? What is the meaning of life?"

Swamishri lovingly explained the purpose of our existence, "We are not on this earth by accident. Life has a special meaning. We are *atma*. This body will perish one day, but the *atma* lives on. We should use our body to liberate our *atma*. Our goal in life is to liberate our *atma* by living peaceful, loving and moral lives. Our actions shouldn't hurt anyone or bring pain to any other living being. We should live an addiction-free and pious life."

Swamishri's words helped soothe Brian and give direction to his life.

In Auckland, New Zealand, on 10 October 1996, Thakorbhai asked Swamishri a few questions on how to attain spiritual progress. Swamishri's response, "We are *atma*. Paramatma lives within the *atma* and that is why you find happiness in the cars you drive, houses you live in, food you eat and clothes you wear. Once your *atma* leaves the body, there will be no pleasure. In fact, people will rush to get rid of the body.

"Therefore, all the happiness that you see in this world is derived from God. God is in everyone and everything around us. That is why we are attracted to them. God is in you. That is why you are enjoying everything as we speak."

Swamishri has helped many of his devotees attain that state of spirituality. These devotees have been able to live that practical wisdom or *aparoksh jnana*. These devotees have been living life and been able to cope with all the difficulties since they focus on their true self – the *atma*.

Bhagvanjibhai of Canada is one such example. He was a prominent community leader and successful entrepreneur. He had deep political ties and led the Indo-Canadian Federation. His caring and dynamic personality was appreciated by those around him. In 1985, doctors diagnosed him with blood cancer. Bhagvanjibhai was undeterred and continued his daily routine.

His condition continued to deteriorate, yet he refused to tell anyone. In 1988, he had a bone marrow transplant. Within the confines of his room in the hospital, Bhagvanjibhai was content and satisfied. The fatal illness had not affected his spirit; he continued to smile and live as if nothing was wrong.

Doctors told him of his worsening condition and that he had only a short time to live. The doctors were surprised to see a man that was unaffected by the news of his own fatal condition. Whenever he called his friends and relatives from the hospital, they were confused as to whether he was calling from his office or his death bed. His outlook remained very satisfied, energetic and comfortable.

With Swamishri's grace, Bhagvanjibhai was able to live the wisdom of the *atma* that he advocated, as the following letters demonstrate.

Just a few days before he passed away, Bhagvanjibhai wrote a letter to his brother:

"Physical illness is a part of everyone's life. Even great souls and sadhus such as Ramakrishna Paramhansa have suffered grave ailments. Therefore, never fear death! Pramukh Swami Maharaj is a Gunatit Sadhu. Don't ever think about leaving him. Serve him loyally and have firm faith."

He wrote a letter to a spiritual leader, which also illustrated his strength and stability.

"I have a fatal illness, yet I am content and happy because I have had the chance to serve an ideal sadhu like Pramukh Swami Maharaj."

Just a few days later, Bhagvanjibhai passed away at 43, his face gleaming with serenity and satisfaction.

On 23 October 1994, Chhaganbhai came for Swamishri's darshan in Gondal. Those surrounding Swamishri thought Chhaganbhai to be a small-time farmer from a village in Kathiawad. They soon realized that he was anything but common.

Just a few days previously, Swamishri had gone to Lilakha in Junagadh district for the *murti-pratishtha* of the new BAPS *hari* mandir there. At that time Swamishri had sanctified Chhaganbhai's house and taken lunch there. There, Jnanprasad Swami had told Chhaganbhai that Swamishri wanted him to help wind up after the celebration in his town and then come to serve at the Akshar Vadi in Junagadh.

Chhaganbhai then narrated the events after Swamishri's departure, "We helped clean up the festival grounds after you had left. It was early evening by the time I got home. My wife was sleeping in the room where you had your lunch a few hours before. She said, 'This room has been blessed by Swamishri. If I sleep here, I will definitely go to Akshardham.' I reminded her that we had to get our pictures taken so that we would be able to get our voter identifications. She wasn't interested, 'I don't want to vote in the elections. I vote for Akshardham! I don't want to come to get my picture taken.' I told her that I would leave for Junagadh the following morning as you had assigned me to serve at Akshar Vadi.

"She was in a different mood and said, 'Swamishri may have assigned you to serve at Akshar Vadi, but he has assigned me to serve in Akshardham!' I didn't quite understand her repeated references to Akshardham.

"We went to the mandir and everyone insisted that I perform the first *arti*. After *arti*, we came home and she went to milk the buffalo. Just as she was entering the house, she collapsed. She breathed her last. I thought in my mind, 'She is lucky. You took her to Akshardham!'"

Chhaganbhai spoke clearly and without the slightest sorrow in his voice. He was convinced that his wife had attained Akshardham.

Chhaganbhai made the arrangements for his wife's funeral and then immediately left for Junagadh, as he had been instructed by Swamishri.

When Swamishri learnt of the situation he called Chhaganbhai to

Gondal. He told Chhaganbhai to go back home and to complete his wife's remaining funeral rites.

"Chhaganbhai! You have done like Parvatbhai! You must go back home and stay there until all the rites are finished. Do not rush to Junagadh. You have to carry out your worldly duties as a husband. Both you and your wife have achieved a great understanding of Satsang."

Chhaganbhai folded his hands and agreed to follow Swamishri's wish. He was not in the slightest upset or dejected by his beloved wife's demise, since he knew that she was in Akshardham.

Sant Swami was an aged and senior sadhu from Shastriji Maharaj's time. He was suffering from a severe heart ailment in his final days, yet he remained surprisingly calm. Swamishri came to visit him in Sarangpur, when he expressed his conviction, "If Bhagwan Swaminarayan wants to take me to Akshardham, I am ready. If he wants me to stay, I am ready. I have served Shastriji Maharaj, Yogiji Maharaj and you. I am content. I have no desires, fears or regrets."

Swamishri's wisdom has helped countless devotees cope with circumstances that would otherwise cause trauma, depression and mental instability. Yogendrabhai Parmar is one of these people. Losing his 16-year-old son, Shriji, Yogendrabhai digested the news with ease. He calmed and consoled those around him. He distributed sanctified sugar crystals, an ancient tradition expressing joy, since he believed that his son was now in Akshardham.

Virchandbhai Modi and Maganbhai of Navsari are others with such high spiritual understanding. Thousands more have learned to live successfully in this world, without losing sight of the ultimate wisdom – knowledge of the *atma*.

There is another aspect to Swamishri's eternal *jnana*: *shrutam*. *Shrutam* means to experience the profound message of the ancient shastras.

Swamishri often jokes, "I was born a farmer..." Yet, Swamishri is able to reveal the profound meanings behind many scriptural verses as if he has experienced them firsthand. His ability to enlighten even the scholarly has continued to amaze Viveksagar Swami, Shrutiprakash Swami, Bhadresh Swami, Shvetvaikunth Swami and other learned sadhus.

In Sarangpur, on 24 April 1987 Swamishri and a group of scholarly sadhus had gathered to discuss spirituality and philosophical issues. In the morning discourse on the previous day, Swamishri had explained parts of the Bhaktachintamani. The sadhus wanted further clarification on a particular verse: *"Chho to ek ane diso chho doy..."*, meaning, "You are alone, yet it appears as if there are two of you."

Swamishri explained, "The sages had gathered in Badrikashram. They were awaiting the arrival of Nar and Narayan. The sages first saw Nar alone. The sages felt as if they had seen God because they had the darshan of his ideal devotee. Nar was an ideal devotee of Bhagwan Narayan. We often hear people say, 'He is a man of God'. Similarly, you can see God through his ideal devotee. That doesn't mean that God is dependent on his devotee. God can choose to give darshan as he pleases, whether it is through his devotee or alone.

"In the Shikshapatri Bhagwan Swaminarayan has said that when God is seen to be alone, understand that his ideal devotee is enveloped in God's form due to their divine love and oneness. Similarly, when the devotee is seen alone, God is always within him. That doesn't mean that God is the devotee or the devotee is God. It is a matter of understanding."

Swamishri's explanation wasn't mere rhetoric; it was from experience.

In 1984, a group of scholarly sadhus conducted a series of philosophical discussions to further explore and understand the Vedic philosophy revealed by Bhagwan Swaminarayan. From these discussions some questions remained. So, a letter was written to Swamishri detailing these tricky questions in order to understand the subject matter proficiently. Some of the questions were quite difficult to write about let alone read and understand.

Shvetvaikunth Swami wrote to Swamishri asking him about the different types of *muktas,* or liberated souls. The letter read: "There is only one Aksharbrahman and he is eternal. Anyone who understands his greatness and realizes him rises above *maya* and becomes a *mukta*. Therefore, it is not possible to have differences amongst liberated souls. Yet, in Vachanamrut, Sarangpur 17, Bhagwan Swaminarayan states that there are many differences amongst liberated souls. Sant Swami used to say that Bhagwan Swaminarayan said that these are differences amongst liberated souls on earth, not in Akshardham. The differences exist because of the different spiritual states of the *muktas* in Satsang today. Some are just beginners, some are at an intermediate level, while others are advanced. He gave the analogy of a doctor: a medical student still working through his rotations is addressed as a doctor and so is a reputed neurosurgeon. But there is obviously a difference between the two. Similarly, a new *satsangi* can be called a *mukta* and so is someone who has perfected this spiritual wisdom in his life. But again, there is a difference. What is your understanding of this?"

In his reply, dated 29 December 1984, Swamishri wrote, "The difference between the *muktas* is not in their spiritual state but rather in their *upasana*. The differences in the *muktas* are dependent on their devotion. The differences lies not in their spiritual state but their conviction of *sarvopari* or supreme God."

Swamishri's simple, yet profound answer satisfied Shvetvaikunth Swami.

On 7 October 1997, Swamishri was having lunch in Sarangpur. The sadhus were discussing the *Purushottam Mahatmya* by Nityanand Swami. The particular discussion revolved around an unfamiliar description of Akshardham and Bhagwan Swaminarayan.

It equated the voice of God to being as dynamic and powerful as the sound produced from a cymbal the size of the earth rattled by a drumstick the size of the tallest peak in the world.

A sadhu that was seated nearby joked that Akshardham must be very noisy and boisterous. Swamishri immediately corrected him, "There is a difference between loud and noisy. It is definitely loud, but it is pleasant, melodious and divine."

Swamishri's answer illustrated his personal experience of Akshardham.

Swamishri has never pretended or acted being wise. He has lived and helped others live by that *aparoksh jnana* or experienced knowledge of *atma* and Paramatma.

The Shrimad Bhagvat affirms his greatness, "A sadhu with such *jnana* (who has experienced the *atma* and Paramatma) is the only true guru and he is the form of God." ◆

Shilam शीलम्
Shamaha शम:
Damaha Tapaha दम: तप:

Shilam is a morally sound character.
Shama is to control one's mind and free it from worldly desires.
Dama is to curb one's senses from excessive and immoral
indulgence in the five sense objects.
Tapa is to control one's senses from indulging in
the sense objects and to focus them towards
one's atma to experience the divine bliss of God.
God in human form is above the influence of the
mind and senses. The virtues of shama, dama, tapa and
shilam are innate to God. This is equally true for the
Gunatit Sadhu who beholds God.
Pramukh Swami Maharaj's life is proof of this.

The perfect virtues of *shilam, shama, dama, tapa* are evident in Pramukh Swami Maharaj's life.

How does he control his senses?

How is he so austere?

How does he maintain his spotless character?

All these questions find an answer in his presence. Observe his life and the answers become obvious. His daily routine and lifestyle are proof of his mastery in these qualities.

Pramukh Swami Maharaj has conquered his senses. His stringent control over his senses and mind is evident to those around him.

Bhagwan Swaminarayan has said, "One who conquers his sense of taste has conquered all."

Swamishri's control over his sense of taste is probably one of the first things noticed by those who observe him.

In 1959-1960, Swamishri had joined Brahmaswarup Yogiji Maharaj for the first time in his *vicharan* abroad. Arunbhai (presently,

Ishwarcharan Swami) was travelling with Yogiji Maharaj before being initiated as a sadhu. He was one of the first to observe Swamishri's control over taste, "I had joined Yogiji Maharaj on his trip to Africa in 1959. I used to cook for the sadhus. Most of the sadhus preferred mild food. Yogiji Maharaj, Sant Swami and Balmukund Swami all used to prefer bland food that was very light in spices and salt. That left Pramukh Swami Maharaj. Swamishri used to prefer spicy food and in fact, he used to enjoy it. For nine months, Swamishri ate the food that I made. Not only was the food bland, but I was a beginner in the art of cooking. Yet Swamishri never commented on the food or even suggested ways of improving my mediocre cuisine skills. Swamishri would eat whatever I had prepared and served to Harikrishna Maharaj, praising it to further motivate me. That was the first time I came to realize that he was no ordinary person. He had controlled his sense of taste."

Former Chief Minister of Gujarat, Shri Babubhai Jashbhai Patel, was born into a Swaminarayan *satsangi* family and had over time studied Bhagwan Swaminarayan's Shikshapatri, a moral code of conduct. He was amazed by the lifestyle prescribed for sadhus and, in particular, their eating habits. He met Swamishri on various occasions and noted his observations in a letter:

"I have noticed that Swamishri has conquered all desire for taste. He never asks for anything or shows interest in fancy dishes, sweets or snacks. He mixes everything and is content with whatever he is given. Having conquered his sense of taste, he is a sadhu who has conquered all his senses."

This observation is a daily experience for Swamishri's attendant sadhus. Krishnavallabh Swami has served meals to Swamishri for over two decades, yet he can't recall a single instance where Swamishri has asked to cook a particular dish for himself. He smiles and eats

Eternal Virtues

whatever is served to him with the thought that the food has been served to and sanctified by Harikrishna Maharaj. He never comments on or complains about the meals.

Even when, occasionally, the attendant sadhus make a mistake in preparing his food, Swamishri eats what he is served without a fuss. Swamishri never gets agitated or frustrated and always stops the sadhu in the middle of his apology, saying, "If Harikrishna Maharaj is offered the same food, then why should I have a problem in eating it? Whatever is served in his *thal* is *prasad*."

Children and youths often ask Swamishri whether there is a particular dish, fruit or vegetable that he prefers or likes. In each instance his answer remains the same, "I like everything that has been offered to Harikrishna Maharaj."

In 1990, Swamishri was in Cardiff, England, and was attending an assembly in the local community centre. The attendant sadhus left from the hall early to prepare Harikrishna Maharaj's *thal* and cook for the rest of the sadhus. When they arrived at the devotee's house, they realized that there was still a lot to be done.

They hurriedly prepared the meal and offered *thal* to Harikrishna Maharaj. After a while, Swamishri arrived and sat down to have his dinner. There were still a few *padhramani*s left before Swamishri could call it a day. The sadhus hastily served Swamishri and prepared for the remaining house visits. Swamishri was attentively listening to a devotee's report and speedily eating his meal. At the end Swamishri ate *khichdi* and *kadhi*. The attendant sadhu served some more *kadhi* to Swamishri; he drank it without the slightest hint of displeasure and completed his meal.

In the meantime, a sadhu came running from the kitchen, and called out, "Don't give Swamishri any *kadhi*. It tastes weird and has a foul odour!"

The attendant sadhu rushed to see what was wrong with the *kadhi*. After looking around he realized that instead of using yogurt, he had used sour milk to make the *kadhi*.

He tasted the *kadhi* and barely got it past their lips when he was forced to spit it out! He realized that the spoiled *kadhi* would probably irritate Swamishri's sensitive stomach. He ran to where Swamishri was seated and started to apologize, "Swamishri! I am sorry. I should have been more careful…"

Swamishri stopped him in mid-sentence and smiled, "It really isn't a big deal. Harikrishna Maharaj was offered the same *kadhi* in *thal* and I have no problem with eating his *prasad*."

Over the years, during his travels from village to village, such occurrences have been common. Swamishri has pleased devotees by accepting whatever they bring to him with devotion: bitter orange juice in Mumbai, fresh green *chana* still covered with dirt, bitter cucumbers and excessively salty dishes have all been eaten by Swamishri without a murmur.

Once, a devotee brought some flour that he had ground with his new hand-mill. He was so excited to provide flour for Swamishri that he forgot that the new hand-mill had to be used a few times to make it free of any lose particles before grinding the flour for making Swamishri's meal. Yet, the flour was used to make *rotlis*. Swamishri finished his meal and when the sadhus sat down to eat the *rotlis* made from the flour they realized that there were very small grains of stone in it.

Yet, Swamishri had eaten the *rotlis* without the slightest change of expression on his face.

For many years now, Swamishri has been eating the same simple food everyday. He never eats anything different even on special or festive occasions. If someone brings something with a lot of love for him and tries to force him to have some, he is usually never successful. If he is, Swamishri has a pinch of the delicacy – just to satisfy the devotee.

Once while Swamishri was in Sarangpur, Yagnesh Swami brought some sugarcane juice. As soon as he entered the room, Swamishri stopped him, "I told you not to bring any yesterday and yet you have again brought some today. I don't want any. Please take it back."

The sadhus tried to persuade Swamishri, "Just have a little since he has brought some. He won't bring any tomorrow."

Swamishri smiled but remained firm, "No. If I have some today, he is sure to bring some more tomorrow."

Swamishri often says, "Don't accept everything that you are given. Learn to accept only what you need." This saying has been the foundation of his lifestyle.

In the afternoon, after the sadhus offer fruits and fruit juices to Harikrishna Maharaj, they used to bring some to Swamishri. He accepted a few kernels of popcorn or a few slices of fruit and told them to take the rest back. Swamishri stopped this routine since long back.

In fact, since 2007, Swamishri has stopped having lunch and subsists on a frugal breakfast and dinner.

In the Shrimad Bhagvad Gita, Bhagwan Shri Krishna explains the three different types of *tapa* or austerities.

The first type is physical, which includes respecting the learned and wise, purity of the body and mind, simplicity, celibacy and non-violence.

The second aspect is verbal. One should never say things to hurt or offend others. One should always be honest, caring and helpful.

The third aspect is that of the mind and involves freeing one's mind of all desires.

Bhagwan Swaminarayan also states in Vachanamrut, Kariyani 10 that *tapa* is the way to earn God's bliss.

Swamishri lives all three aspects of *tapa* in his life, setting an ideal example for others to follow.

He always neglects his physical needs and is an advocate of fasting. Until the age of 57, Swamishri used to do *dharna-parna* during *chaturmas*. He would always observe a waterless fast on Ekadashi days. Even while fasting Swamishri never relaxed his schedule. Once, even though he was fasting and had a 102 degree fever, he visited over 122 homes! Now, which category of *tapa* does that fall under?

The Hindu sacred texts state that if you are ill, you are allowed to eat fruits and other *farali* foods. Yet Swamishri, even after suffering a heart attack at the age of 63, refused to eat or drink anything on the five major fasting days specified by guru Shastriji Maharaj. At times when the attendant sadhus were persistent in their efforts to make him eat or drink something with his medicine, they saw a side of him usually unseen by others. He would tell them in a stern voice, "I am not going to die if I don't eat for one day!"

To stop him from observing a waterless fast is a great challenge in itself. In fact, he has been like this since he was six years old.

Chhotabhai of Bhadran had gathered about 50 children for a feast at his house. Young Shantilal was the first to be invited. All the children started gathering and were getting ready to eat, whereas Shantilal moved away from the dining area. Chhotabhai asked him why he did not eat. Shantilal explained, "Today is Ekadashi and I am fasting."

Chhotabhai and the other kids tried to persuade six-year-old Shantilal to eat, but he didn't budge! He even started crying when they tried to force him to eat. Chhotabhai had to bow to his faith and conviction.

Till the age of 87, he was adamant. Despite advice from his physicians and attendant sadhus about taking care of himself and maintaining regular eating habits, Swamishri always looked for a chance to do some *tapa*.

According to Vedic tradition, sadhus and devotees are required to observe certain dietary and other restrictions for the period before and during an eclipse. The rules can be relaxed for those above the age of 80. Yet, Swamishri is never willing to compromise.

In 2006, Swamishri was in New Delhi when the sadhus started preparing for a lunar eclipse. The moon was entering the penumbra right after lunch and so the sadhus were not going to have dinner in the evening. The elderly are exempt from the dietary restrictions and are allowed to eat until the eclipse begins, yet Swamishri refused to have his dinner. Ishwarcharan Swami and Viveksagar Swami tried to reason with Swamishri, "According to the sacred texts, there is nothing wrong with having dinner. You are allowed to eat."

"I will be okay. I just ate in the afternoon and I don't feel hungry. There is no need to eat." Despite this, the sadhus offered *thal* to Harikrishna Maharaj at around 6.30 p.m. and then Krishnavallabh Swami brought it into Swamishri's room. Swamishri was reading a few letters. He said, "There is no need for all this. I am not going to eat anything."

Krishnavallabh Swami, who has been one of Swamishri's personal attendants for over 20 years, has witnessed many such incidents. This time he tried to insist upon Swamishri, "We have offered the *thal* to Harikrishna Maharaj. It is *prasad*."

"If Harikrishna Maharaj has eaten then the spiritual benefit of preparing the meal has been attained."

"The benefit would be twice as much if you eat as well," Krishnavallabh Swami added.

"Serving Harikrishna Maharaj includes everything."

"By the time you sit down for breakfast tomorrow morning it will be really late. Why don't you have just a little..."

"I am not going to starve if I skip one meal."

Krishnavallabh Swami's efforts yielded no results. Everyone gave way to Swamishri's conviction. For Swamishri this isn't just *tapa*, but it is following the *agna* of God and guru. Swamishri is willing to endure any amount of hardship so that he can follow their *agna*.

Swamishri's persistence for *tapa* has inspired thousands of sadhus and devotees to follow in his footsteps.

His ability to control his mind is unmatched. Swamishri's control over his mind is reflected in his *nishkam dharma*.

In more than 70 years as a sadhu, Swamishri's celibacy is spotless. He lives his life according to the eight-fold celibacy or *brahmacharya vrat* prescribed by Bhagwan Swaminarayan.

In a general satsang assembly in Dubai, Acharya Pushparaj recognized this unsurpassable achievement, "Regardless of which God and principle Pramukh Swami Maharaj believes in, I am attracted to the way he lives his life. I am amazed by his spotless character and self-control. Even the *devas* bow their heads at the door of a man that follows eight-fold celibacy for even one day. Pramukh Swami Maharaj has observed *brahmacharya* throughout his whole life. I am not exaggerating when I say that he is the greatest celibate of our times!"

This is evidence of his spotless character and controlled mind. It is also a continuation of Bhagwan Swaminarayan's legacy. More than 150 years ago Bhagwan Swaminarayan had said, "I swear by the lives of these *paramhansas* that from the day I was born to this very day, I have never harboured an improper thought regarding women or wealth, either in the waking state or in the dream state." (Vachanamrut, Gadhada II 33).

Swamishri is at a spiritual state where his mind and senses experience the constant bliss of God. He desires nothing.

The Shrimad Bhagvad Gita says:

"The great ascetic soul that continuously experiences God's bliss, never stumbles from that peak of spirituality" (BG 6.21).

That is control. That is *nirvikalp samadhi* – constant rapport with God. ◆

Aishvaryam
ऐश्वर्यम्

Balam Bhagaha
बलम्   भग:

*Aishvaryam is the power to sustain all living beings. Balam is the
strength to control the mind and life force of all. Bhaga is the perfect
blend of aishvaryam, balam, jnana, strength and courage.
The Bruhadaranyak Upanishad sings the glory of God:
"Eternal, omniscient and omnipresent God
controls and sustains all by residing within."
The Gunatit Sadhu is blessed with these qualities of
aishvaryam, balam and bhaga through his
constant rapport with God.
It is God's power that works through him.*

Bhagwan Swaminarayan describes the strength and
capabilities of a true sadhu in Vachanamrut, Gadhada I 27:
"Consequently, by the grace of God, that devotee attains countless
types of powers and liberates countless beings. The powers of such
a person are such that since it is God who sees through his eyes, he
empowers the eyes of all of the beings in the world; and since it is
God who walks through his legs, he is also capable of endowing the
strength to walk to all the beings in this world. Thus, since it is God
who resides in all of the *indriyas* of such a sadhu, that sadhu is able
to empower the *indriyas* of all beings in the world. Therefore, such a
sadhu is the sustainer of the world."

In Vachanamrut, Gadhada II 22, Bhagwan Swaminarayan goes
on to say: "In a kingdom, the queen's authority is equal to that of
the king."

Thus, Bhagwan Swaminarayan describes that the Gunatit Sadhu
is blessed with God-like powers.

God is usually very discerning in showing and using his powers
when he is present on earth. The Gunatit Sadhu acts in the same
manner. Despite his efforts to shy away from the limelight, God's
powers radiate from him.

Thousands of individuals have experienced this divine power at various stages in their lives. There are enough incidents to fill many volumes.

The first experience of that divine strength is evident through his ability to amaze and pacify the minds and thoughts of all those around him.

Bhagwan Swaminarayan's divine persona had touched many great minds, including, the learned Gangadhar Shastri, the powerful Maharaja Gaekwad and the renowned poet Dalpatram.

Swamishri's presence evokes similar experience. Even those meeting him for the first time, and that to for only a brief moment, are overcome with bliss and joy – almost as if experiencing God. That experience stays with them as a part of their life. It is indescribable and eternal.

This is felt by people from all walks of life, belonging to different religious, ethnic, intellectual, social and spiritual backgrounds. They are captivated by his darshan, loving eyes, caring touch or simply from being in his presence!

The following are just a few of those touching experiences.

The founder of the BITS Pilani University in Rajasthan, India, Dr A.D. Bohra came to meet Swamishri in Jodhpur on 13 March 1994. Narrating his experience, Dr Bohra said, "We are very fortunate to have such a great soul here today in this relatively small assembly. Such a sadhu is very rare to find. His darshan makes me feel at ease and pacifies my mind. I had first met Pramukh Swami Maharaj 15 years ago in Nairobi. I felt a spiritual current that calmed my senses as I touched his feet. He put his hand on my head. I was left speechless. It was a unique experience. He looks the same today. He is as loving, energetic and peaceful as he was then."

The late Dr L.M. Singhvi, former High Commissioner to the UK, had felt something similar when he first met Swamishri in London on 9 November 1997. Dr Singhvi recalled, "Swamishri's touch has left me spellbound. It is not his speech or articulate manner that impresses me. I was simply bound by his divine touch. I have met many sadhus, but nothing compares to this experience."

Speaking to an assembly in the BAPS Mandir in London, he continued, "Since receiving the blessings of Swamishri, I feel that I have developed a relationship with someone divine. The relationship is not with a human or an organization; it is with God! God is present with us in his human form. God has been mentioned in our sacred texts, but the form of God is present today through Swamishri's love and care. It is not this marvellous mandir or the hundreds of educated sadhus, or the thousands of devotees that worship him that really impresses me, but it is the feeling that I can experience God through him."

Dr Faisal Zeera, a renowned physician and President of the International Hospital in Bahrain, is a devout Muslim and has also been attracted by Swamishri's divine persona, says, "Pramukh Swami Maharaj holds a very important place in our lives, in our thoughts and in our spirituality. He is my guru and serves as a guiding light in everything that I do. The first time I met him, I felt as if he was surrounded by angels and liberated souls!

"We live in an era, where 'seeing is believing'. We only believe in things we have seen, heard or experienced. The first time I met Swamishri, I experienced something that is really hard to describe. It was a realm totally foreign to me. I had never experienced anything like this before. I felt as if I was in the presence of the ultimate divinity. The experience was constant. It is impossible to describe it. It is an experience of the soul not one of the mind. This wasn't a one-time experience. I have experienced divinity every time I have met Pramukh Swami Maharaj. This is only possible because of the divine entity that resides in him. God works through him.

"It is true that all religions are different paths that lead to God, but I believe that the path leading to God that is most appropriate and suitable is the one prescribed by Pramukh Swami Maharaj."

On 22 September 2007, a prominent surgeon in Atlanta, Georgia, Dr Asif Taufik came for Swamishri's darshan during the Muslim holy month of Ramadan. The next morning he returned for Swamishri's darshan and described his experience, "I felt a divine wave surge through my body when Swamishri placed his hand on my head. I couldn't even sleep at night because of that divine joy. Swamishri's divine face was in front of my eyes throughout the night."

R.K. Laxman, the creator of 'Uncommon Man', is the renowned cartoonist of *The Times of India*. He has been featured on the cover of *Reader's Digest* and is hailed as India's, if not Asia's, greatest political cartoonist. He is a close friend of former Indian President, Dr APJ Abdul Kalam. After the opening of Akshardham in New Delhi, the President repeatedly suggested that he visit the newly opened complex. R.K. Laxman visited Swaminarayan Akshardham for two days and at the end came to meet Swamishri. He was mesmerized by Swamishri's darshan, commenting, "The president flew me in from Mumbai. He asked me to stay with him at the Rashtrapati Bhavan. He urged me to visit this complex. If I hadn't accepted his invitation, I would have missed out on the chance of a lifetime. I don't have words to describe it. I will never forget this experience."

There was silence in the room as Laxman stopped abruptly. He was lost for words. His lips were moving as if trying to say something, but his eyes were still, focused on Swamishri. Tears fell from the corner of his eyes, reflecting the deep emotional impact Swamishri's presence had made on him in that brief meeting. Everyone was amazed to see the nation's boldest critic in tears! After a few minutes he managed to repeat three words, "Nothing to say. Nothing to say."

Leaving the room after having Swamishri's darshan, he said, "It feels like I was swept in a whirlwind of peace and stability."

The experience changed R.K. Laxman, and his wife was the first to notice, "I have never seen my husband so amazed, so touched. It is a miracle."

Jeanette is a native of Holland and was introduced to BAPS through a long-time family friend and devotee, Han Kop. She was touched by the social services carried out by BAPS and Swamishri's life and work. She became a devotee and started actively participating in satsang activities. Her husband was taken aback by her sudden involvement and was worried about her sudden change in lifestyle. In 1984, when Swamishri was visiting Antwerp, Belgium, Jeanette persuaded her husband to have Swamishri's darshan. He went to meet Swamishri and sat down next to him, quite uncomfortable with the whole idea. A few minutes later as he walked out from Swamishri's room, he was convinced, "It was improper to form an opinion before meeting him. I never let anyone touch me, but the way he put his hand on my head left me speechless. I liked it. It was different. Very peaceful! Very Peaceful!"

Mosari Imam lives in Cairo, Egypt. He has a liking for India and

the Hindu way of life. After visiting Swaminarayan Akshardham, New Delhi, he decided to meet Swamishri. He made the trip to Gujarat and arrived in Sarangpur on 20 March 2007. He sat for darshan in Swamishri's morning puja and was touched by Swamishri's devotion towards Harikrishna Maharaj. He came to meet Swamishri afterwards and was gripped in a spell of joy, "You are an amazing person. I am going to tell my friends in Egypt about you."

On 7 October 1997, Shri Kothari came to Sarangpur for Swamishri's darshan from Nanded. He had come out of curiosity. He had made up his mind to leave if he felt the slightest discomfort or uneasiness. To his surprise, he felt himself at home. He spent five nights in Sarangpur enjoying Swamishri's divine bliss and mentioned to a volunteer that he had never slept so peacefully before.

Peter Henkel, a resident of Trinidad in the West Indies, first had Swamishri's darshan in Atlanta in 1988. He was so impressed by Swamishri's persona that he changed his name to Parikshit and became a practising Hindu. Nineteen years later, in 2007, he clearly remembered his first experience of Swamishri's darshan in New York, "I was sitting in Swamishri's puja in the morning. After completing the puja he looked at me; I still remember that divine glance. That image is forever inscribed in my heart."

On seeing Swamishri countless experience peace and joy.

Swamishri was in Chino Hills, a suburb of Los Angeles, California, in September 2007. Hale, an African-American youth living in the neighbourhood, came for darshan. He was so attracted to Swamishri that he started coming for Swamishri's darshan everyday. On 9 September 2007, Hale met Swamishri and expressed his feelings, "Every time I come into this campus or I am in your presence, I feel at peace and experience that state of bliss that you are always in."

In a satsang assembly organized in Forest Hill, New York, on 5 June 1988, Congressman James H. Robert had come to welcome Swamishri. After meeting him, he addressed the gathering, "I was in England last month attending an international summit on politics and religion. I had the fortune of meeting various religious and community leaders, including the Archbishop of Canterbury, Mother Teresa and the Cardinal of Austria. I thought it was a unique experience, but the divinity that I experience today in Pramukh Swami Maharaj's presence is something totally different."

On 7 June 2007, Swamishri was flying from Mombasa to Chicago. A steward was observing Swamishri during the flight. As the plane approached Chicago, he came for Swamishri's darshan, "I have met many religious leaders, but only a few of them I felt were spiritually inclined. In your presence, I feel divine peace. The way you interact with people and talk to them shows that you have no hidden agenda or ulterior motives. You are straightforward and transparent. It is that transparency that attracts me."

The President of the Gujarati Samaj in Dubai, entrepreneur Bharatbhai Shah, was not accustomed to recognizing anyone's authority. He was introduced to Swamishri for the first time in 1997 in Dubai. On 30 November 1997, he addressed a satsang assembly in Surendranagar, "I never believed in God. Swamishri's darshan made me realize that there has to be a source of ultimate divinity. Now, I believe in God. The love and affection in his eyes made me tearful and I felt great comfort in his presence. I decided to give up my addictions and lead a morally pure life. Six months later I tried a small wad of chewing tobacco, but spat it out immediately! I knew I was forever changed. I want to dedicate the rest of my life to serving this community. I want to help his cause."

Cardiothoracic surgeon Dr V. Subramanium describes a similar experience. On 20 December 2000, he shared that experience in an interview on Zee TV. The interviewer asked him, "You have performed over 20,000 heart operations. Have you ever had any special experiences?"

He thought for a second and said, "Nothing out of the ordinary. Yes, actually there was one such experience. I was operating on Pramukh Swami Maharaj, the spiritual leader of BAPS, at Lenox Hill Hospital in New York City. Usually, I feel a sense of pity and sorrow for the patient, but when I took Pramukh Swami Maharaj's heart in my hand, I felt a sense of divinity around. It felt as if some divine being had entered the operating theatre. I had never experienced this during any of the other operations."

In 1988, while Swamishri was in Nairobi, Councillor Sayam also had a similar experience. He explained it in the satsang assembly, "I felt a cool breeze sweep over my heart. This is the first time I am meeting him, but I am confident that God is working through him. Today, I vow to Swamiji that I will become a vegetarian and never again eat meat or eggs."

Thousands of people are attracted to Swamishri at first sight and experience an indescribable state of bliss. With each meeting that attraction deepens into a bond of unconditional love.

Swamishri's pure character not only attracts people, but also inspires life-transformations.

There are thousands of youths around the world that are successful in their careers and personal lives yet are deeply attached to him. They are reluctant to leave his presence. In fact, whenever they part from Swamishri they do so with tear-filled eyes. His attraction is above age, educational and social backgrounds, and communication barriers like language and culture.

This was experienced during his stay at the Lenox Hill Hospital after his bypass surgery in 1998.

From 7 to 13 July, Swamishri was recovering at the Lenox Hill Hospital in New York City. In those seven days, he had captivated and attracted the entire staff in the ICU. Everyone from Dr Subramanium to the nursing attendant Robert had experienced a sense of personal connection with Swamishri. In fact, even the female nurses who only had Swamishri's darshan on the closed-circuit monitoring system were impressed by his divine persona.

After one week, as Swamishri was leaving the hospital, the staff of the cardiothoracic department lined his exit route to bid him farewell.

There are scores of incidents like the ones mentioned above, each one affirming the idea that this attraction is not human. It is a divine attraction, God's power working through him.

Jashbhai was the leader of Sokhda-Matar village in the Kheda region. He was very vocal about his dislike for sadhus and *bawas*.

Eternal Virtues

He had sworn to never let them into his town. In the meantime, the local devotees had arranged for Yogiji Maharaj to visit the town. Purushottamdas begged Jashbhai to let Yogiji Maharaj visit. Jashbhai agreed because of Purushottamdas' pure character and lifestyle.

There was, however, one problem. None of the devotees' homes could accommodate all the sadhus and devotees. The only house big enough was Jashbhai's. Purushottamdas hesitantly approached Jash-bhai and requested the use of his house. Jashbhai clenched his teeth and agreed on one condition, "I am not coming for your guru's darshan. Don't ask me or force me to come. I am going to stay elsewhere while your guru visits."

Purushottamdas agreed, made the necessary arrangements and awaited Yogiji Maharaj's arrival.

Due to certain circumstances, Yogiji Maharaj was not able to come and had sent Pramukh Swami Maharaj in his place. After staying at Jashbhai's house for a few days, Swamishri asked the question that Purushottamdas had feared, "Who is the owner of this house? I want to meet him. Why won't he come?"

Purshottamdas explained the situation and thought it would be best not to invite him. Swamishri smiled and insisted, "The least we should do is thank him for letting us stay in his house. Call him. Tell him I want to meet him."

Purushottamdas spoke to Jashbhai and as expected, the latter wasn't interested. But Purushottamdas persisted and finally Jashbhai agreed to come.

The moment he saw Swamishri his inner feelings changed completely. He fell at Swamishri's feet and apologized, "Swamiji, I was unfortunate that I didn't come to serve you the past few days. Will you stay at my house for a few more days? I want a chance to serve you."

Everyone was surprised by the sudden change, but Jashbhai knew that he had experienced divinity. He couldn't explain it to others, but there was certainly something different about Swamishri. He became a devotee and served Swamishri for the rest of his life.

On 28 August 2007, the board members of Asian-American Hotel Owner's Association (AAHOA) came for Swamishri's darshan in Atlanta. A priest from a Christian church had also joined them for Swamishri's darshan. On meeting Swamishri, he tried to explain his experience, "I feel as if God is present in you. I feel like God resides in this marvellous mandir you have built. I feel like all of your devotees are like God's children. Everything is so divine here."

Chief of the Western Air Command of the Indian Air Force,

Air Marshal A.K. Singh, had come for Swamishri's darshan on 4 September 2006 in New Delhi. He was a decorated fighter pilot and an experienced veteran who had won numerous awards. After meeting Swamishri, he described his feelings to other sadhus, "He has to be God. I feel divine purity in his presence. When he put his hand on my head, I felt as if I had been blessed with everything I ever wanted."

This has to be God's *aishvarya* in Swamishri!

Swamishri's aura of divinity is so powerful that it often 'lingers' for a long time, even with an individual who has left his presence.

Dr Navinbhai C. Mehta is one of the biggest names in ENT and Reconstructive Surgery in New York. He has treated famous entertainers, actors, actresses, models, and political and spiritual leaders. But his experience with Swamishri stood apart.

Dr Mehta was driving Swamishri from New York to New Jersey on 21 September 1998. This was the first time he had had the privilege of driving Swamishri and he was excited. A police escort was guiding him through the heavy New York City traffic. Swamishri was speaking to him about spirituality in life and in the middle of their conversation Swamishri stopped. He looked at Navinbhai and said, "This particular road doesn't take us to where we want to go. Why is the police escort taking us this way? We should have taken the last exit."

Dr Mehta was dumbfounded. He had been driving these roads for the past 20 years and he still did not know the roads as well as Swamishri did.

The next day, two sadhus came to his clinic in New York City for a checkup. Even though 24 hours had passed, he described the incident as if it had just occurred, "The joy of those three hours is indescribable. I have met Pope John Paul II and many other religious leaders, but Swamishri is different. The only word I can think of is divine. God is present in him. No, he is definitely God!"

Many prominent community leaders and dignitaries have experienced a similar state of excitement and joy. They find it hard to compare this experience with anything else in their lives. The only words they seem to pull from their word banks are 'inexpressible' and 'unparalleled'.

There is another facet to Swamishri's *aishvarya* – seeking out and protecting devotees. Many choose to call such incidents miracles. Thousands of devotees have noted instances, where the impossible was made possible by Swamishri's grace.

Swamishri says in response, "All I do is pray for the devotees. Bhagwan Swaminarayan listens to our prayers and helps the devotees. But miracles do not lead to *moksha*. They are a hindrance to *moksha*. They raise body-consciousness, so one should not expect them and should just faithfully worship God."

Yet, such true experiences cannot be refuted.

Dr A. Srinivas Raghavan, a scholar of the Ramanuja school of philosophy and respected for his work throughout India, experienced such a miracle. During the Birth Bicentenary Celebrations of Aksharbrahman Gunatitanand Swami in 1985, he had come to Ahmedabad for three days from Chennai to chair the 'Bhakta-Bhagwan Relationship' conference hosted by BAPS. He writes about a personal experience that changed his life forever, "After the conference, I was flying back to Chennai. I was thinking about the three days that I had stayed in the festival. It was a splendid environment. The plane landed and I was one of the first to get off the plane. As I was putting my foot on the first step, I felt a sudden weakness in my body. I thought that something was happening to me. I couldn't even muster the strength to ask for help. I thought I would collapse. I was even having trouble breathing. All of a sudden, I felt divine intervention. I felt as if some divine strength was helping me up to my feet and helping me breathe. I saw Pramukh Swami Maharaj right before my eyes on the steps of Chennai airport. The divine experience filled me with great spiritual joy. I gained my composure and realized that I was still on the steps; only now, I was fit to continue my journey."

Han Kop is a retired Dutch teacher who lived in Holland for many years. His experiences alone can fill an entire section of this book!

As a youth, Han Kop set off with his brother in 1971 to see the world. When he saw a *murti* of Yogiji Maharaj at the BAPS Mandir in Mombasa, he wished to meet him in person. He learnt that Yogiji Maharaj was no longer alive. So, Han Kop and his brother changed their plans so that he could meet Yogiji Maharaj's spiritual successor, Pramukh Swami Maharaj. They travelled to India and arrived in Gujarat. The rest of the story is better told in his own words:

"We finally reached Gondal after travelling by road and struggling to cope with the scorching summer heat. I had a terrible headache, was starving beyond belief and could barely function. When we reached the mandir, Swamishri was having lunch. After lunch, Swamishri came to meet the devotees. This was the first time I had seen Swamishri. There was something different about him. The transparency and innocence I had seen in Yogiji Maharaj's picture in Mombasa was clearly evident in Swamishri. What surprised me the most was that I felt I had just had Yogiji Maharaj's darshan. My regrets for not being able to have Yogiji Maharaj's darshan while he was alive vanished. I was not hungry, nor did my head ache anymore. It felt as if his darshan and presence had satisfied me for eternity. After a few days, we took leave and flew to Karachi. We had a room at a nice hotel on the seashore and were planning on staying there for about 10 days. It turned to be a life changing experience.

"On a beautiful summer day, my brother and I decided to take a walk on the seashore. We noticed that there were a lot of children playing in the shallow sea water. Some of them were playing with inflated tubes, dancing and jumping to the beat of the pounding waves, giggling and smiling as we passed them. I noticed that one child had lost grip of his tube and it was floating away in to deeper waters. The child started to cry. I told him not to cry. I would get the tube for him. I was an experienced swimmer and had often swum in the ocean. I jumped into the deeper waters to try get back the child's joy. The tube was about 300 feet into the ocean, where the waves were pounding hard and the winds were gusty. I kept swimming towards the tube and it kept floating further and further away. I gave one last thrust with all my effort and finally made it to the tube. I was a bit tired from the exertion and decided to sit on the tube and relax on my way back to the shore.

"I floated on the tube for about five minutes and then I was greeted with another unpleasant surprise. My eyes seemed to widen as I couldn't believe the scene in front of me. There was a killer shark a few feet away from me. I had heard frightening stories from my uncle about sharks. I knew that the only way I would survive was if I could scare the shark away, because there was no way I was going to out swim the shark! I started splashing my hands and legs in the water with all my might with the hope that I would scare it away. To my surprise, the shark seemed to come closer to me with each stroke I made in the water. My life started flashing before my eyes. I knew it would all soon be over. In the middle of that mental state of chaos, Pramukh Swami Maharaj came before my eyes. Those loving transparent eyes and that radiating smile were all I could see. I closed my eyes and started chanting the Swaminarayan mantra. I prayed to Pramukh Swami Maharaj to come save me and there he was, I saw him standing right in front of me. I felt an inner voice telling me to let go of the tube and quickly swim to the shore. For the next five minutes, I couldn't see the water or the sky, the tube or the shark, the waves or the shore; all I saw was Pramukh Swami Maharaj's *murti* in front of me. To this day, I relive that moment and realize that there was no way I could have survived, if it wasn't for Swamishri."

Former Member of Parliament and former Solicitor General of Canada, Bob Kaplan, has also had two such experiences which he fondly remembers. He often publicly speaks of these incidents in front of thousands of people. He last spoke of them at the opening of the BAPS Shri Swaminarayan Mandir in Toronto, Canada in 2007.

In 1984, Bob Kaplan had requested Swamishri's blessings so that the candidate for his party, Pierre Trudeau, would win the country's general election and become Prime Minister. Swamishri wasn't in Canada at the time, but he wrote a letter in response to his request and gave his blessings.

Unfortunately, the letter didn't reach Canada until after the elections. After receiving the letter, local devotees, Bhagwanjibhai Mandaviya and Narsinhbhai Patel, hand-delivered it to Bob Kaplan. He read the letter, in which Swamishri had written that Trudeau would again become Prime Minister, and was a bit taken aback. He didn't know what to make of it. He thanked the gentlemen for bringing the letter and went to meet Pierre Trudeau. He gave the letter to Trudeau and waited for him to read it. Trudeau read the letter and gave a wry smile. He put the letter on the side and thought nothing of it. There was no point. He had already lost the elections.

A few months later, a political crisis gripped the nation and the government fell. Subsequently, Trudeau became Prime Minister. Bob Kaplan was convinced that the unimaginable only happened because of Swamishri's blessings.

He described a similar incident about his skin cancer. Swamishri's blessings had completely cured him of it.

These are just some of the many incidents that illustrate Swamishri's *aishvarya*. But Swamishri does not consider them as important. Instead, he always emphasizes God's grace, God's wish and prayers.

World renowned magician K. Lal views Swamishri's *aishvarya* from a different perspective, "Mahavir and Buddha were able to attract people with their ideology. If there has been a great soul since their time that has been able to attract people, it is Pramukh Swami Maharaj. I say this from the bottom of my heart. What is it about him or his eyes that inspire thousands of people to follow him and worship him? It is magic. Divine magic!"

Swamishri's spotless character and charismatic persona have transformed thousands of wayward lives...Valio is one of them.

Swamishri's personality not only attracts people, but transforms their lives. This is Swamishri's true *aishvarya*.

He works a different type of miracle. He doesn't change copper into gold or walk on water, but his ability to mould the character and lives of individuals is his specialty. A collection of such incidents would again fill volumes, but given below are a few examples:

Valio was a notorious character who terrorized the tribal villages of the Sabarkantha region. His name and actions reminded many of the ancient Valio, who was later transformed into Sage Valmiki, the famous author of the Ramayan.

Under the scorching afternoon sun, the drunken Valio would walk into Poshina town and eye a store with his bloodshot eyes. That would seal the fate of that store and its owner. Valio and his men would pillage that store at night and celebrate. He would even steal their livestock and prepare a feast for his men.

On one occasion, the police came to a large pillaged livestock farm and only found 50 kg of raw meat. They were wondering as to what happened to the remaining hundreds of kilos of meat.

Valio was a gone case; he was beyond redemption. That was until he met Swamishri. Pramukh Swami Maharaj's satsang activities have transformed Valio into Valabhai. Valabhai walks with that same confidence and pride, but now with a *tilak-chandlo* on his forehead.

Valabhai was indeed grateful, "There was no satsang in my town (Paliyabiyana). My men and I used to live like animals. No one had the guts to say a single word to me and my goons. But now, there is peace everywhere. The sadhus come to my village and I go to the satsang assemblies. Not only have I become a devotee, but all 60 of my men and their families have started leading devout lives. We promised Pramukh Swami Maharaj that we would never steal again. We earn our money by honest means."

Eternal Virtues

Valabhai has a small tape deck in his hut and you can hear the Swaminarayan *dhun* and *arti* playing on the hills of Paliyabiyana even today.

What type of transformation does Swamishri's *aishvarya* bring about in people of the lowest moral order? Barkubhai of Apti in Dadara-Nagarhaveli region is well qualified to answer that question.

Barkubhai would rob villages in broad daylight with a machete. The only way he would answer questions was with his machete. However, after coming into contact with Pramukh Swami Maharaj he changed his lifestyle. He stopped stealing, started serving the community and began devoting himself to Satsang. He now earns an honest living driving a rickshaw.

Once, after dropping off a passenger, he realized that the passenger had left his cellular phone in the rickshaw. Barkubhai immediately set out to find the owner and returned the phone. The owner appreciated his honesty. Little did he know that a few months ago, Barkubhai would have ripped the phone out of his hand, let alone look for him to return it.

A similar incident occurred when a father who was shopping for his daughter's wedding forgot to take a bag full of cash from the rickshaw. Barkubhai spent a good portion of the day looking for him and returned the cash to him. The owner was overjoyed and decided to reward him for his honesty. But Barkubhai refused, "I don't deserve a reward. I did what I was supposed to do."

The owner enticed him with some drinks, "You tell me where you want to go and I will pay for your alcohol for the night."

Barkubhai replied without a moment's hesitation, "I am afraid that is not possible. I quit drinking a long time back."

"Now is the time for you to drink and have fun. Why did you quit? You are not going to get your hands on alcohol when you're old."

"I have met a pure guru like Pramukh Swami Maharaj. I don't need to drink and 'have fun'. My only goal in life is to become *brahmarup* and go to Akshardham."

The owner was startled by this poor rugged man's conviction.

Sunsar. Just the name of the rowdy village in the Patan district of northern Gujarat used to give the creeps to police. There isn't a child in all of northern Gujarat that hasn't heard of the thugs from Sunsar. The people of Sunsar were known for two things: theft and alcohol.

Swamishri's aishvarya at work – transforming the village of Sunsar.

If there happened to be a robbery in any village of the Mahesana district, police would first raid Sunsar. Unfortunately, the Police did not have the courage to raid Sunsar without asking the town chieftain.

Even the prominent Gujarati social worker Shri Ravishankar Maharaj lived for seven years in a small home in the village with the hope of bringing about some sort of reform. There came a time when the people of the village even stole the sandals that he was wearing.

However, in 2006, the chieftain and the thugs of the town came for Swamishri's darshan at Mahesana mandir. They promised to give up all their vices and stop stealing.

Amongst them was 35-year-old Badkamdaar Monghaji Laluji Darbar. He was born into this violent culture. Even his schooling was centred on violence and theft. He would drink eight to ten mugs of beer and then fight with anyone he could get his hands on. His gang comprised of 30 other thugs of a similar violent and immoral nature.

Yet, Swamishri's serene presence and soothing words changed their lives.

To repent for their actions, they vowed to buy land in their hometown and build a mandir so that their children would learn a different set of values. Swamishri has been able to instil spirituality in the lives of those the world had given up on. He has developed ideal communities, one person at a time.

Subhashbhai Patel of Dar-es-Salaam, Tanzania, had also experienced a similar transformation. Subhashbhai relished alcohol, violence and vices to the extent that even the local police would fear his presence. In fact, it's hard to put a number on how many people and law enforcement officers he must have assaulted.

In 1995, Swamishri visited Dar-es-Salaam. Maheshbhai had known Subhashbhai for a long time and had decided it would be in his best interest to have Swamishri's darshan. Giving in to Maheshbhai's persistence, Subhashbhai came for Swamishri's darshan. Swamishri recognized him, "I know you. You had come for Yogiji Maharaj's darshan with your father in 1959."

Subhashbhai was surprised. How did this sadhu remember such a trivial detail from over 36 years ago! He felt a divine glow in Swamishri's presence. Swamishri looked into his eyes and told him to change. Subhashbhai felt as if a divine power was guiding him in the right direction.

Today, Subhashbhai performs puja, *arti*, listens to discourses and attends satsang assemblies regularly. His transformation even startled his good friend and ex-classmate, the Tanzanian President Kikiwete.

Subhashbhai is just one of many.

There is a small village called Odarka in the Saurashtra region. Odarka was the home of the infamous Ramsang Bapu (Ramsinhji Takhatsinhji Gohil), a notorious fighter and thief. His occupation was to steal from people and terrorize villages! He was so good at it that Bhupat, a nationally feared gangster himself, offered a partnership. Bhupat had told Ramsang Bapu that with you on my side, I can even rattle the national government. He offered half his profits to Ramsang Bapu, but the latter was not interested in such high profile action. Describing his original nature, he would say, "If you had seen me before, you would have thought I was Ravan and Kansa's brother! I was destined to die a very painful and humiliating death, but Pramukh Swami Maharaj changed my life."

Swamishri visited his house in Odarka and talked to him about the repercussions of violence, theft and hurting others. Ramsang Bapu followed Swamishri's wish and started to live a morally pure life, giving up his vices and violent ways. Pramukh Swami Maharaj had transformed him into a devotee.

His transformation helped the people of the region sleep better at night. For the rest of his days, Ramsang Bapu lived a pious life based on the codes of Satsang.

On 13 October 1997, Swamishri promised Ramsang Bapu that Bhagwan Swaminarayan would take him to Akshardham very soon.

In just 13 days, Ramsang Bapu breathed his last while telling his son Janaksinh, "Bhagwan Swaminarayan and Pramukh Swami Maharaj have come to take me. I am going..."

Changing misfits in society is common, but what is not obvious is the type of transformation Swamishri brings about. His divine *aishvaraya* enables people to rid themselves of anger, lust, greed and arrogance. This is by no means a small feat to accomplish. Though most people would not like to talk about such personal 'inner' change before others, the following are representative of people's experiences.

Virchand Modi of Kheralu has changed a lot. His current joyful and devout nature bears no signs of his previous hot temper. He admits, "I don't know how it happened, but it did. Swamishri's grace helped me overcome my anger."

A youth from Dallas, Texas, came to meet Swamishri on 18 July 1996 and professed, "I came for your darshan last time you were in Dallas and you had lovingly put your hand on my head. Since that day I have never lost my temper. You rid me of my anger, I started believing in God and now I live a morally pure life and eat a vegetarian diet."

The elderly Purushottam Bhagat who serves in Bochasan mandir, Joseph Maturia, the former Kenyan Minister for Lands and Settlement, and many others testify that Swamishri has cleansed them from within and inspired them to progress on the spiritual path.

Joseph Maturia had Swamishri's darshan in 1985 and, in an assembly of thousands, promised to stop drinking alcohol. Not only did this come as a surprise to those present there, but also to the people of his country. He didn't stop there. He returned to Kenya and convinced scores of his friends to stop drinking alcohol.

He came for Swamishri's darshan on 12 May 2007 at Nairobi mandir, and confessed, "Swamishri helped me stop drinking 22 years ago. I have never had the urge to drink after that. It has really changed my life."

There is more to Swamishri's *aishvarya*. Hundreds of thousands of children, youths and adults the world over lead upright lives inspired by Swamishri's *aishvarya*. Hundreds of young, talented and educated youths are giving up their ambitions and devoting their lives physically and mentally to help society by becoming sadhus due to his *aishvarya*.

His *aishvarya* can be seen in the smiles of inner satisfaction gleaming on the faces of those that have purified their body, minds and souls.

Miracles tend to overwhelm the common people. The popular conception is that the greater and more frequent the miracles, the greater the guru. But, according to the Hindu shastras miracles are not evidence of ultimate spirituality and divinity.

One of Muktanand Swami's bhajans emphasizes this point:

"Parcho icchhe tene pāmar jānvo...", or "Know one who expects miracles to be spiritually inferior..."

A sadhu's greatness is measured by his sterling qualities and not by the miracle he performs. The greatest *aishvarya* of a God-realized Sadhu is spiritual in nature: God resides in him eternally. A more detailed explanation:

God works through him; walks through him; sees through him; hears through him; speaks through him; breathes through him and resides in him.

The Supreme Being that is responsible for creating, sustaining and regulating this universe is present in him. A certain level of spiritual insight is required to grasp this profound truth.

One way to understand this is to recognize his servitude towards God. Despite possessing God's *aishvarya*, Swamishri never forgets that he is God's servant.

Dr Sureshbhai Patel, a longtime friend of Swamishri's heart surgeon, Dr Subramanium, had been observing Swamishri's work for several years. On 19 May 2004, he came for Swamishri's darshan, "Just as God is able to govern the universe with his unlimited powers, you have governed innumerable souls on the path to spirituality. They have joined in your cause to help humanity. Therefore, I believe you are God."

Swamishri started shaking his head in disapproval, "No, no. I am God's humble servant. God works through a sadhu." This wasn't just a memorized reply. He believes this from the bottom of his heart and lives in that way. The fact that God has graced him with his *aishvarya* and yet, Swamishri has never let it go to his head is a special strength in itself.

'Me', 'I' and 'Mine' are words that are common in most successful people's vocabulary. Swamishri has never used them or bothered to learn their use.

Is that not *aishvaryam?* ◆

Svatantryam
स्वातंत्र्यम्
Shauryam Tejaha
शौर्यम् तेज:

Shauryam *is courage.*
Teja *is the ability to be free from influence.*
Svatantryam *is to be free of expectations.*
These virtues of God contrast his qualities of patience,
truthfulness, compassion and tolerance.
But the truth is that these are also God's divine qualities.
The Gunatit Sadhu is blessed with these
Godly attributes as well.

There is a side of Pramukh Swami Maharaj that most of us are familiar with — a compassionate, tolerant, honest, fair, unattached, forgiving and loving sadhu. There is another side that we will get to know more in this chapter; his courageous, illustrious, invincible and independent side. Yet, his valour doesn't hurt or offend others. His invincible personality does not defeat others. His independence does not constrain or limit others.

Swamishri's *brahmatej* or divine aura does not overshadow others, instead, it makes them shine brighter.

His courage is evident in his observance of *niyams,* and the traditions and principles given by Bhagwan Swaminarayan. He does not compromise on these principles and doesn't let others compromise on them either. Those who associate with him cannot remain cowardly in their thoughts or actions; and those who are cowardly are unable to remain in his presence. Yes, Swamishri is forgiving, but he does not uphold cowardice. This is a unique combination of virtues.

Sadhus and devotees alike have experienced Swamishri's warm and loving personality over the years. Yet, there have been times when the divine radiating flare from Swamishri's eyes has been unbearable.

Over the years Swamishri has always openly supported these principles. At times, when he has felt the need to raise his voice,

"Whether people like it or not, the important thing is to obey God's command."

he has done so without insulting or offending those advocating relaxation. He is very careful with the choice of words and is firm yet polite, direct and fearless in voicing his thoughts. He is not influenced by anyone's manipulation, and following Bhagwan Swaminarayan's *niyams* and principles come first.

In Vachanamrut, Loya 2, Bhagwan Swaminarayan defines courage: "One who is courageous and brave never falters from following God's *agna*, even in the hardest of circumstances."

Swamishri is scrupulous in following the *niyams* prescribed by Bhagwan Swaminarayan for sadhus. The stories below illustrate this.

In 1981, as part of Bhagwan Swaminarayan's Birth Bicentenary Celebrations in Ahmedabad, the Bharat Sadhu Samaj held a gathering to commemorate its Silver Jubilee. The celebrations were to take place in Swamishri's presence. Pujya Harinarayananandji, Secretary of the Samaj, suggested honouring a female national leader on the stage. Swamishri said, "You can do that, but according to the *niyams* of celibacy prescribed by Bhagwan Swaminarayan, I will not be able to attend the event. Please forgive me."

Social reformer and editorial columnist, Ishwarbhai Petlikar, came for Swamishri's darshan in 1981. He told him, "If you want to allow your organization to grow, you should relax the celibacy *niyams* for your sadhus."

Swamishri was direct and to the point in his answer, "I do not believe in growing by transgressing the *niyams* laid down by Bhagwan Swaminarayan. There is no need for that type of growth. Bhagwan Swaminarayan looks after the growth of the organization, but we have to stick to our *niyams*. Many community leaders and politicians have suggested the same thing. They say this organization will not last long because of the stringent *niyams*. So be it. We will sit in a corner and worship God, but we will not sacrifice our *niyams*."

Today, Ishwarbhai is not alive to see the organization's growth — all without sacrificing those *niyams*.

Former Finance Minister of India, Shri H.M. Patel, had suggested a similar idea. Swamishri replied, "There is no way we will compromise the *niyams* prescribed to us by Bhagwan Swaminarayan."

The well-known journalist Kanti Bhatt had once asked Swamishri, "Have you ever thought that you should change your celibacy *niyams* to cater for the modern way of thinking?"

He got the answer, "Things are fine the way they are. There is nothing to change. People might call us orthodox, but it is our duty to follow the *niyams* given to us by Bhagwan Swaminarayan. It's not like we are insulting or hurting anyone by following them. So, whether people like it or not we have to follow Bhagwan Swaminarayan's *agna*."

Swamishri has observed these *niyams* even while meeting world leaders and international dignitaries. Even when meeting the likes of President Bill Clinton, Tanzanian President Julius Nyerere, the Sheikhs of the Arab Nations, UN Secretary General Kofi Annan and others he has never relaxed the *niyams*. Through his courage and valour he has ensured that these *niyams* are observed even while addressing the United Nations and during his own emergency bypass surgery. It seems impossible for a common man to be so bold; then again, Swamishri is not so common after all.

While following these *niyams*, Swamishri isn't orthodox, inconsiderate or insensitive in the process. He has shown tremendous courage in supporting changes to empower women. He has proved that it is possible to follow the *niyams* of celibacy and yet work tirelessly to meet their needs.

The BAPS Swaminarayan Sanstha has worked around the clock to meet women's educational, medical, spiritual, cultural, social and domestic needs. In fact, the BAPS women's activities have impressed many in several ways.

Dr Hanna Kim, a Ph.D. from New York University, has studied the BAPS Women's Wing for the past 15 years. She comments, "I have observed the devotion, creativity and inspiration the organization has provided to these women. It is all possible because of Pramukh Swami Maharaj's blessings. I have witnessed their organizational skills, execution skills and motivational skills. Not only do their families benefit from them, but this helps society as a whole. Women are fortunate to have a platform like this where they can develop and present their talents. Pramukh Swami Maharaj's guidance provides them with direction for a brighter and more promising future. It is truly an amazing gift that empowers and guides women."

Swamishri has also stressed education and academic excellence for women in tribal villages, "Educating a woman helps to educate the whole family. It has been 50 years since India's independence and the illiteracy rates are still high in this country. If women are educated, it will help us create a brighter future for our children and community. Women may think that they can make more money if they start working now, but in the long-run, it is important to have an education. Education gives independence and vision. There is also a greater chance of being cheated or duped if you are not educated. I strongly request everyone to get an education. We must educate the women and children in our community. It is a necessity for the future. Bhagwan Swaminarayan had started initiatives to educate and empower women even in his times."

Under Swamishri's guidance and inspiration, The Sanstha has been able to set up numerous academic institutions and programmes for women all over the world. His courage to maintain his *niyams* and yet empower women has astonished many.

Swamishri's *brahmatej* emanates when people attack God and his avatars.

A popular singer came to Ahmedabad to sing in a satsang assembly. In a partly comical and partly sarcastic approach he commented on Bhagwan Rama and Sitaji in a demeaning manner and praised the evil King Ravan. He intended to humour the audience. But, when Swamishri subsequently blessed the assembly, he said, "Bhagwan Rama was God and Sitaji was his ideal devotee. Their lives were perfect. Sitaji stayed loyal to Bhagwan Rama despite numerous temptations. Ravan was evil and immoral. There was nothing good in his character or life and he is not an appropriate role model for anyone!"

Swamishri responds with a similar sharpness when people try to discredit the sacred texts, sadhus and mandirs. There are many people that question the need for mandirs and their use. They argue that mandirs are just piles of stones and have no meaning.

Swamishri explains to remove their misconceptions, "Many people argue that mandirs are a waste of time and money. Do we need them? The answer is yes. We do need them. Our community needs schools, because we have to fight illiteracy. We need hospitals,

"Everyone has a right to live. It is not humane to live by killing others."

physicians, police officers, politicians, educators and armed forces, because they all serve a purpose. Similarly, mandirs serve a purpose. They pacify the mind and soul. They provide peace. Students would have a tough time learning if we didn't have schools. Similarly, where is one to worship God if we don't have mandirs? Mandirs are needed as a haven for spirituality. India has survived centuries of aggression because of the mandirs.

"Mandirs teach morality and values. One can go for God's darshan in mandirs. Mandirs instil spirituality, ethical behaviour and compassion. We have to have faith. Mandirs, religion and our sacred texts are all necessary. We have to learn to live a pious and harmonious life. That will help us become better as individuals, families and communities. If we look after our culture and religion, they will look after us."

Swamishri is also very vocal against the anti-social practices that trouble and divide our homes and society. He speaks openly against the iniquity of dowry, "People spend ridiculous amounts of money to maintain their name and status. Many people still collect dowry. They think it is absolutely necessary. They don't realize that marriage is not a business deal. Marriage is about respect and love. People end up having to sell their homes and belongings so that they can get their daughters married. It is a shame. That is why we organize *samuh lagnas* where many couples can use the same facility

"God is the source of all strength."

to get married and not have to spend ludicrous amounts of money. Taking dowry does not lead to a happy marriage. Why take money that doesn't belong to you? It does not bring peace."

The rising clash of cultures and widening communication gap between the parents and children have given birth to old-age homes. Swamishri's heart aches when he hears of such stories, "We should teach our children to care for our parents and elders, so that they take care of them as they grow old and not send them off to old-age homes."

In one particular instance, Swamishri told a youth who was considering sending his parents to an old-age home, "Take care of your aging parents. They clothed you, fed you and cared for you while you were growing up. They were patient with you and gave you what you wanted. Now, it is your turn to return the favour. Be patient with them and take care of them."

Swamishri valiantly opposes immoral activities, even those that take place under the authorization of religion or spirituality. He was very forthright on one such occasion.

In 1984, Catholic Bishop John L. Markovsky met Swamishri in Houston. He was explaining the various community activities supported and funded by his diocese. He mentioned that holding bingo sessions helped to financially support many of the schools and hospitals the diocese ran.

Swamishri asked, "Has the Bible sanctioned gambling?"

"No, it hasn't been mentioned in the Bible," said the Bishop.

"Then how can you promote gambling in the name of God? If religious institutions sanction gambling, children and youths will think it is okay to gamble and try to make money the easy way. Gambling can lead to stealing and debts."

The Bishop was left searching for an answer. He did come up with one in a few seconds, "We are all humans. Humans need some sort of entertainment."

Swamishri replied, "There are a lot of other ways to entertain people. Let them do whatever they want to outside your church, but it is wrong for a religious organization to sanction such immoral activities. Religion is supposed to prevent people from engaging in adultery, robbery, gambling and substance abuse."

Bishop Markovsky agreed, "You have set the bar very high, but we will try to follow your ideals."

Swamishri is against gambling, bribery and lottery games since they promote immoral ways. Swamishri says that people should work honestly to earn their rewards. You cannot expect to always get a free ride. To people seeking to gain through such means, Swamishri says, "Trying to profit without working is wrong. Playing the lottery and gambling promote laziness. Students go on strike and try to bribe their professors so they do not have to work hard to pass. That is wrong as well. Teachers fight for their rights, but they do not want to teach. Businessmen try to make money by selling impure and faulty products, but they do not want to work hard. How is that going to help the country? If everyone worked honestly and diligently for eight hours a day, India would have one of the strongest and most efficient work forces in the world."

When people discuss the rise in substance abuse, animal slaughter and drug trafficking, Swamishri is unable to remain quiet. His valour is evident, "There is a rise in the number of slaughterhouses and fishing centres all over the world. People like to spread propaganda to make money. They say that eggs are very nutritious and some people even claim that eggs are part of a vegetarian diet! Do eggs grow on trees? They have catchy marketing slogans to get people to start eating them. Slaughterhouses have changed the state of our nation. How can one be happy by taking innocent lives? Every living being has the right to live. You cannot become happy by taking the life of others."

Swamishri has clearly told community leaders, politicians and

Through his innate brilliance and efforts Swamishri transforms the lives of people and society.

even industry leaders about his views. He was very bold in pushing for the Narmada Dam Project too. He has bravely inspired people to petition for it and has spoken about it to thousands. He has courageously campaigned for those suffering in Gujarat.

Swamishri has strongly reasoned against conversions as well, "Is it fair to bribe and coerce people into changing their beliefs? You are taking advantage of their ignorance."

In 1980, in a dialogue with the Archbishop of Canterbury, Swamishri reasoned, "A true Christian should flawlessly follow the Ten Commandments. How many Christians in the world follow the Ten Commandments?"

"Very few, Swamiji," replied the Archbishop.

"Then wouldn't it make more sense to focus on making those Christians 'true' or 'perfect' Christians? What's the point of focusing on conversions? If every person follows his or her religion properly, world harmony would become a reality."

Swamishri is a strong believer of preserving Indian and Hindu culture. He has built hundreds of mandirs and cultural complexes around the world to preserve Hinduism and present its true greatness to the contemporary world. Yet, there isn't the slightest hint of force, insult or degrading of others. That in itself is another example of his courage, to strongly believe in one's principles and ideology while equally respecting those of others.

At the age of 85, Swamishri inaugurated Swaminarayan Akshardham in New Delhi and at 87 he consecrated traditional mandirs outside India. Taking on such mammoth tasks even at this advanced age is another symbol of his courage.

The former Director General of the National Human Rights Commission and former Director of the CBI, Shri D.R. Karthikeyan, was impressed by Swamishri's courage, "He has to be the bravest soul on earth. Swaminarayan Akshardham is probably the greatest wonder of the modern world. Every Indian should be proud of it. This is one of Pramukh Swami Maharaj's miracles.

"I don't think any king, government, or international organization can build Akshardham. God is working through him. All of the world's leaders should come to look at this and gain inspiration. This sadhu has given up everything so that he can give back to humanity. You need courage to build something so majestic. I think he is the most courageous man I have ever met. He is an ideal for the rest of the world."

There are countless examples of his courage, valour and brilliance. The Shrimad Bhagvat defines *shauryam* as conquering ones desires and inner instincts (20.19.27). In Vachanamrut, Loya 2 Bhagwan Swaminarayan states that one who is truly courageous makes his senses tremble in the knowledge that they will not be allowed to indulge in material pleasures.

Swamishri's courage is evident through his obvious control over his desires, as already discussed in a previous chapter.

Swamishri's brilliance doesn't overshadow others but it motivates them to reach the heights of spirituality that he has scaled.

Pramukh Swami Maharaj lives a life independent of attachment and influence.

As one famous journalist said, "Courage is the ladder on which all other virtues mount."

Swamishri's courage is the foundation of all his other virtues. ◆

Smrutihi
स्मृतिः

*Smruti does not mean only memory or the act of remembering.
It is God's most precious blessing upon mankind. God remembers
his devotees and the services they have rendered to the smallest detail.
This shows God's unconditional love for his devotees.
The Gunatit Sadhu, who constantly remembers God,
also showers his love upon the devotees in a similar fashion
by remembering them and the services they have rendered.
Pramukh Swami Maharaj remembers,
appreciates and rewards all devotees.*

Swamishri's personal contact with people is phenomenal. He meets hundreds of people everyday, listens to their problems and guides them in the right direction. For decades, he has lent his ears to his devotees; not merely for the sake of appeasing them, but because he really cares about their well-being.

Travelling to almost every corner of the world, Swamishri has not merely given his physical presence but has sanctified the homes and touched the hearts of millions. He has provided them with selfless love and has become a part of their families.

This selfless love has helped him remember the details of thousands of individuals, their families, their difficulties, their homes and their forefathers.

His sharp memory and unflinching loyalty continue to amaze those around him. He remembers everyone.

These memories are undiminished even after half a century and are spread across the globe.

The following are just a few of the countless experiences that show his love, affection and appreciation towards the devotees.

Swamishri has nurtured a closely knit satsang family. On 23 February 2006, while Swamishri was having lunch

Countless devotees have experienced Swamishri's selfless love at first hand. For Swamishri they are all like family members.

in Vidyanagar, the sadhus were introducing a few of the hostel students.

Mitesh stood up and was introduced as a native of Jesangpura. Swamishri immediately asked if he was from Narsinhbhai's village. Mitesh nodded his head in agreement. So, the sadhus asked him to mention the names of his father and grandfather.

Swamishri immediately stopped them in mid-sentence, "I know his entire lineage."

Swamishri asked him his name again and then rattled off the names of his family, "Your name is Mitesh. Your father is Ramesh. Ramesh's father's name was Narsinh and Narsinh's father's name was Narayanbhai. Right?"

Swamishri started talking about the *seva* they had rendered in Shastriji Maharaj's time, "Narsinh had an older brother named Girdhar. They have been *satsangis* from the beginning. They had served Shastriji Maharaj. Where is Gunjan?"

Mitesh was surprised that Swamishri remembered his neighbour and replied, "He still lives next to us."

Swamishri also recalled that Narsinhbhai was Devcharan Swami's maternal uncle.

Oddly enough, the day before Sadhujivan Swami had complained to Swamishri, "I am having difficulty remembering things."

Swamishri had also confessed, "I also have trouble remembering things."

That obviously wasn't the case when it came to remembering his devotees.

On 26 December 1998 Swamishri was in Sarangpur. Paramswarup Swami introduced a devotee to him, "This is Becharbhai. He is from Rohishala."

Swamishri looked at him and thinking that he had met him before, he asked, "Where did you live before you moved to Rohishala?"

Paramswarup Swami said, "He has always lived in Rohishala."

Becharbhai moved forward and had passed Swamishri, when he was called back. Swamishri was still in doubt, "Where were you living before you moved to Rohishala."

"I used to live in Chakampar. I had lived there for 15 years."

There was a sparkle in Swamishri's eyes and he grabbed Becharbhai's hand, saying, "Now, I remember. We had come to your house twice in Chakampar for *padhramani*. How is everything? I hope you are doing well. When did you move to Rohishala?"

Swamishri thereafter engaged in a lengthy and loving conversation with Becharbhai. As Becharbhai was leaving Swamishri's room, Paramswarup Swami asked, "How long ago did Swamishri visit your home? How does he remember?"

"About 45 years ago!"

Becharbhai couldn't answer the second question and was left speechless.

Most people are simply amazed when Swamishri remembers such minor details about thousands of his devotees. They can't seem to figure out how he does it.

On 13 September 1993, Swamishri was returning to his room on the 5th floor at Dadar mandir in Mumbai after his walking session. Viveksagar Swami was waiting by the elevator with a devotee. Swamishri recognized him from a distance.

"Ahh Narendra! When did you get here?"

Swamishri hadn't seen Narendrabhai for over 50 years!

"We had held a *parayan* in Karachi decades ago. You were barely a toddler. You are Jivrajani's son. Swami used to travel in your father's car."

On 28 December 1994, Kanubhai Amin from Mumbai had come to Ahmedabad for Swamishri's darshan. He had brought a relative who was visiting from America. Swamishri interrupted as he was starting to introduce his relative, "I know him quite well. Your father is Ramesh, his father was Bhailalbhai, his father was Chaturbhai and his father was Shyamalbhai. Chaturbhai had five sons – Somabhai, Hirabhai, Hathibhai, Chunibhai and Chhotabhai. Hirabhai had three sons. Somabhai had two and you have two other brothers…"

On his overseas *vicharan* tour in 2004, Swamishri was in London and a few youths were introducing themselves.

One said, "My name is Haresh and I am from Shrijipura."

Swamishri remembers the lineages and history of so many families.

Swamishri asked him his father's name. He replied, "Ramji Chhagan."

Swamishri had visited every single home in Shrijipura many times. He knew all the devotees and their families. He started telling the sadhus, "They were originally from Ugamedi. Shastriji Maharaj had brought them to Shrijipura to take care of the Sanstha's property. His father's name is Ramji, whose brother's name is Dayal. They were the two sons of Chhaganbhai. Chhagan had three other brothers – Trikam, Narayan and Talshi. Haresh's brother is a sadhu in Sarangpur. They are related to Manilal from Surat."

Haresh stood still with the microphone in his hand. He was at a loss for words. Swamishri knew more about his family then he did!

On 25 May 2004 a youth came to meet Swamishri in Edison, New Jersey. When Swamishri asked him where he was from the youth said he was from Dungri-Timba.

"What's your dad's name?"

"Hirabhai."

Swamishri instantly revealed his lineage, "Hirabhai Govindbhai, Govindbhai Mathurbhai and you are originally from Sarsa…right?"

The youth meekly nodded in approval. He was stunned by Swamishri's ability to recollect his ancestry.

Swamishri was returning to his room after darshan at the Yagnapurush Smruti Mandir in Sarangpur. Sadhus and devotees had gathered for Swamishri's darshan. At the front of the crowd were two children. Swamishri pointed at one of them and said, "This is Devraj and that one is Arvind. They are Ravjibhai's sons. They are from Tajpur. Ravjibhai's dad's name was Dharamshi. Dharamshi, Kanji and Lakhman were brothers. Their father, Becharbhai, had become a sadhu at a very old age. He was very wise, used to memorize kirtans and verses in Sanskrit, too."

On 11 November 1994, a devotee from Petlad came for Swamishri's darshan in Bochasan. Swamishri asked him if he was related to Ramanbhai.

"He is my father."

That's all it took to get Swamishri started, "Shastriji Maharaj has stayed at your place many times. In fact, I used to study at the Sanskrit institute your family runs."

Swamishri went on to mention Ramanbhai's brother's name, too.

Swamishri was in San Jose, California on 6 September 2007. One of the activity coordinators began to introduce one of the youths, Ghanshyam. Swamishri recognized him and asked, "You are Ramanbhai Choksi's son, right?"

"Yes."

"You used to come to the youth assemblies in Ahmedabad. You used to play the *tabla*, too. You have an older brother…"

"Manibhai."

"Yes, that's it. Manibhai Choksi."

Ghanshyam was moved by Swamishri's recollection of such minute details. But Swamishri knew that the details were anything but minute for Ghanshyam. They were the gateway to his heart.

On 29 June 2007, Swamishri was in Chicago meeting a devotee from Detroit. He asked him about his native place in India. He said, "Paliyad."

"You are from Paliyad? One of our devotees lives there. His name is Govindbhai Shivabhai."

"That's my father!"

"Govindbhai has a lot of energy. He can rattle windows with his *jay nad*. Why don't you do the same? Call out the *jay nad*."

Realizing that Swamishri remembered this distinctive detail about his father, the devotee hailed the *jay nad* with great enthusiasm. Swamishri laughed and blessed him with a pat on his back.

A sadhu was introducing a devotee to Swamishri.

"He is from Bhavnagar."

"What's your dad's name?"

"Shyamjibhai"

"Shyamjibhai T.T.?"

"Yes!"

"Shyamjibhai T.T. lived in Bhavnagar. He had performed a lot of *seva*. He was Khodabhai's nephew, originally from Tajpur," Swamishri recalled.

On 7 August 2007, devotees from East Windsor, New Jersey, were introducing themselves to Swamishri in Edison. A youth decided to be upfront with Swamishri, "Every time we talk, Chandresh tells us that you know him. Do you really know him personally?" Swamishri said, "Yes, he was a satsang volunteer who lived in Gana, not too far away from Anand."

Viveksagar Swami asked Chandresh to mention his father's or grandfather's name, but Swamishri beat him to it, "Fulabhai Muljibhai, right?"

"Right! That's my great grandfather's name."

On 14 August 2007, Swamishri was meeting devotees in Atlanta, when one of them introduced himself, "I am Purushottam Lallu's son."

Swamishri instantly remembered him, "I knew him very well. He used to live in Bhadran. His wife was also a faithful and devout *satsangi*. When we were studying in Bhadran, she would regularly send groceries with Purushottam Lallu on the day after Ekadashi so that we could prepare food for *parna*."

The devotee was surprised that Swamishri remembered and appreciated his parents' *seva* even after so many years.

In Houston on 3 July 2007, Swamishri was being introduced to a local *karyakar*, "This is Vasudevbhai. You know him pretty well."

"Not just him. I know his father, his grandfather, his brother. I know all of them and everything about them," Swamishri said.

It was a moment that Vasudevbhai would savour for the rest of his life.

Swamishri not only recalls people, places and names. He remembers the history and meaningful events in the devotees' lives to the smallest detail. At times, his accuracy and detail make those present feel as if the event just took place yesterday, or rather, it is taking place now, in front of their eyes.

On 28 April 2004, Bhanubhai Patel of London came for Swamishri's darshan with an elderly relative. The relative told Swamishri, "You undertake a lot of hard work."

"Everything is due to the grace of Bhagwan Swaminarayan," Swamishri said, and then turning to Priyadarshan Swami, he explained, "This is Bhanubhai's father-in-law. His name is Somabhai. We had gone to Kampala in 1959 to bless Bhanubhai on the day of his wedding."

The 87-year-old Somabhai was nearly in tears. Swamishri had remembered him after all these years!

On 8 August 2007, devotees of Edison, New Jersey, were describing their satsang discussion sessions to Swamishri. They introduced Natubhai, who supervised the sessions.

Swamishri immediately recognized him, "You used to live in Ahmedabad...right?"

"Yes, in Ambavadi."

"We have been to your house in Ambavadi."

In 1994, Swamishri was in Bhuj when he pointed to an elderly devotee walking towards him and said, "That's Govindbhai. He is 85 and still moves around independently. In Shastriji Maharaj's time when the first Swaminarayan mandir in Nairobi was built he was a trustee. He had helped to build it, working with Harmanbhai and Maganbhai. He has always supported us."

Swamishri probably hadn't seen him for decades. Govindbhai was surprised that Swamishri recognized him. He had not expected him to.

His memory is above all expectations. Mohan, a small time farmer from Sarangpur, can attest to that. In Sarangpur, on 3 March 1995, Swamishri recognized an elderly devotee and said, "Mohan! How are you?"

Mohan had loyally served Shastriji Maharaj and that was enough

For Swamishri the entire Satsang is one big family.

for Swamishri to grace him with his affection. Swamishri held Mohan's hand and led him into his room. He was taking care of him as if he was a VIP guest.

Swamishri sat him down and started introducing him to all the sadhus, "Mohan is an old devotee. His father's name was Moti. He was the administrator for the Shermia of Dholka. The land on which we had celebrated Fuldol was his."

Mohan was lost in reminiscing the good old days. He started to recollect and remember the days when he had worked along side 'Narayan Swami'. His failing memory and toothless mouth made it hard for others to make out what he was trying to say, but Swamishri listened attentively and paid close attention to every single word.

Swamishri repeated his stories to the others and added his own memories, "He has been in the mandir since Shankar Bhagat was *kothari*. He had worked with me when we were building the gate and the powerhouse… Shastriji Maharaj had kept him with us while building the mandir in Atladra. He was a very diligent worker. He was an expert in stone cutting."

Mohan added his own memories from 1945, "Narayan Swami (Pramukh Swami Maharaj) used to shovel and dig by himself. He would always join the workers and help them. He would carry a headload of 15 bricks at a time. Even when we were working on the gate here in Sarangpur, he would drive the oxen by himself."

Everyone had grown fond of Mohan during the short exchange of sweet memories between him and Swamishri. His son, standing on the side observing all of this, could not hold back his tears.

On 30 December 1994, an elderly devotee from Nagasar had come to Ahmedabad for Swamishri's darshan.

"Welcome Popatbhai! I haven't seen you in a very long time. I hope all is well."

Eternal Virtues

Popatbhai was startled, "This is the first time I have met you in years. How did you recognize me? I still remember when Shastriji Maharaj was in Kathlal and I had come for his darshan. Shastriji Maharaj got up from his bed and hugged me. You were sleeping on a small blanket in a corner of the room. I still clearly remember those divine moments."

On 20 March 1997, Swamishri was in Bochasan when a few devotees from Limbasi came for darshan. Viveksagar Swami saw one of the devotees and said, "Swami! This is Mafatbhai."

Swamishri was quick to correct him, "That's not Mafatbhai. Mafatbhai is the one behind him. That's Manibhai!"

Dr Ghelani had come to meet Swamishri from Palitana. He talked about his father-in-law, Bakubhai. Swamishri asked him what Baku-bhai's father's name was. Dr Ghelani hesitated. He thought long and hard but couldn't recall the name.

Swamishri smiled at him and teasingly asked, "Shankarbhai?"

"Yes! That's it."

Dr Ghelani was touched by Swamishri's *smruti*.

Once, in Sarangpur, Swamishri had just finished dinner and scores of devotees were waiting to meet him. Swamishri noticed Ramjibhai from Mojidad.

"Ramji! It's a pleasure to see you after such a long time! Who are all these people with you? Introduce your relatives to me."

With this, Swamishri turned to the sadhus standing next to him and said, "Ramji's father Kanji Gokul was a dedicated devotee of Mojidad. They used to donate regularly. They were very particular about that." Swamishri started talking to Ramji's relatives, as if they were his own.

Swamishri was walking to the Yagnapurush Smruti Mandir in Sarangpur, when he noticed an elderly man sitting on the side.

"Darbar! How is everything? What are you doing now?"

"I have a small shop."

Swamishri blessed him and told the sadhus with him, "This is Tapubha's brother. He had served a lot when I was here between 1946 and 1948."

Swamishri saw a cowherd walking in the mandir grounds and called him.

"How are you Ratno? I hope all is well."

"I am well due to your blessings."

The sadhus were surprised to see Swamishri speaking to him.

Even amid the flow of new devotees, when Swamishri meets old devotees he affectionately greets them.

Everyone started wondering who Ratno was.

"This is Ratno! Our old neighbour in Sarangpur. He used to own the farm next to our tamarind farm."

Swamishri noticed an old man standing at a distance from his seat in Sarangpur. Swamishri called out to him, "Vitthal! I hope all is well. What are you doing? Do you come to the mandir regularly?"

Vitthal was surprised that Swamishri recognized him after so many years. Swamishri introduced him to the rest of the sadhus, "Vitthal is a potter by profession. The three of them – him, his brother and Hari used to do a lot of *seva*. When I was Kothari here 40 years ago, they used to help me distribute the Annakut *prasad*."

On 30 August 2007, Swamishri had just finished lunch and was heading towards his room in Dallas. His eyes fell on the corner of the large dining room, where an elderly gentleman was intently staring at him. Swamishri asked all the sadhus and devotees to make way for him; he wanted to meet the devotee. He made his way to the corner of the room and blessed him and lovingly talked to him.

Swamishri started telling the sadhus as he was walking back to his room, "That was Rasikbhai from Bhadran. His father, Somabhai, had looked after us when we were studying there. His house is near Kashidasbhai's house."

Pramukh Swami Maharaj remembers one and all. He is especially keen on meeting devotees that have served his gurus, Shastriji Maharaj and Yogiji Maharaj. He takes interest in their well-being and talks about their *seva* to the younger sadhus and devotees.

On 12 September 2003, devotees from Nenpur had come to Sarangpur for Swamishri's darshan.

Swamishri was very glad to see them, "How is everything in

Eternal Virtues

Nenpur? Do you go to the mandir regularly? Make sure you do satsang. Shastriji Maharaj was pleased with the devotees of Nenpur. Atmarambhai, Somabhai and others were very dedicated. The devotees were very loyal and faithful. Do you know Somabhai's story?"

Swamishri didn't wait for an answer. He started narrating the story, "Somabhai and his three sons, Dahyabhai, Narayanbhai and Manibhai, wanted to build a mandir in the village. They were farmers and had planted vegetables in over two acres of land. It kept them very busy. They would grow the vegetables and then go to sell them. Somabhai realized that they would never finish the mandir unless they stopped farming. He called his sons and told them to uproot the crops. The mandir comes first. The entire family joined in the *seva*. They were very faithful and courageous. They were loyal to Bhagwan Swaminarayan, Shastriji Maharaj and Yogiji Maharaj. Today, Shantibhai is still in Satsang. Somabhai's son was Dahyabhai. Dahyabhai's son is Shantibhai."

Pointing to Shantibhai's son Swamishri said, "You are the fourth generation of the family in Satsang. I have seen all of you."

How many people can he remember? It seems as if the list is inexhaustible.

Swamishri was in Mumbai in October 2006 and the sadhus were showing him some very old video footage from the time of Shastriji Maharaj and Yogiji Maharaj. As expected, Swamishri could put names to the faces in a flash, "That's Jashbhai from Vaso, grandfather of Dinubhai Amin. That's Jashbhai Bhailalbhai and Bhailalbhai Purshottambhai. Purshottambhai had had darshan of Bhagatji Maharaj. Jashbhai was a great devotee. If Shastriji Maharaj was coming to Mumbai, Jashbhai would walk from house to house telling the neighbours about his guru's arrival. If the plans changed, Jashbhai would again go from door to door telling them his guru was now not going to come. He was very dedicated..."

Swamishri not only remembers and appreciates those in his presence, but even remembers those faces which have left the world for decades. They are eternally inscribed in Swamishri's memory.

Yagnapurush Upanishad, a publication based on photographs taken during Shastriji Maharaj's time was being prepared. The photographs were shown to Swamishri. He looked at each picture and described the scenario; he identified the people in the pictures, described their families and their contributions to Satsang. He even recalled their distinctive habits and characteristics. The sadhus realized that

Swamishri remembered everyone and everything.

But there are times when Swamishri is not able to put a name to a face, or remember the village of the devotee. On such occasions he frankly admits, "I recognize him, but don't remember his name."

Swamishri would search through his extensive mental database and eventually come up with a match. Meanwhile, the conversation would carry on, until Swamishri interrupted, saying, "His name is Purshottamdas and he is from Nar..."

A similar experience is noted when the extensive biographies of the gurus and other publications are being read in front of him. He remembers and at times corrects the villages, names and incidents noted in the books.

The devotees of Khandesh in the state of Maharashtra had served Shastriji Maharaj with great enthusiasm. Swamishri knew all about their services in those early days of the Sanstha.

On the occasion of his 80th birthday celebrations in Sankari in 2001, Swamishri was to sanctify *murtis* for some new mandirs in Khandesh. However, Swamishri was ill. He had a fever and had been battling a severe bout of cough and diarrhoea. Upon seeing the devotees from Khandesh, he was overcome with enthusiasm. He started calling and talking to all of the devotees. He remembered their forefathers and the other devotees that were unable to make it to Sankari. He had recalled so many of them that even the devotees started losing track of them. Swamishri remembered his *vicharan* on the dusty paths of those remote villages. In fact, whenever Swamishri travelled to Khandesh, he visited the homes of all the devotees.

For decades, Swamishri used to take his meals seated amid sadhus and devotees. So, he was familiar with their likes and dislikes. He knows their dietary restrictions and requirements.

He is often heard whispering instructions to the sadhus: 'Bhaikaka prefers *galka na bhajiya*, make sure you prepare some...', 'Ghanshyam Bapa! Have some *mathiya*...', 'Shrihari Swami, would you like some *papad*?', 'Has Kothari Swami finished eating? Make sure you give him some *dal* towards the end of his meal...', 'Go give this *ghughro* to Viveksagar Swami', 'I don't see any yogurt in Haka Bapu's dish. Give him some from mine...', 'CM they have made *jalebis* for you today. Try some!', 'Mahant Swami usually eats mild and saltless food. Make sure you take some out for him...', 'Sant Swami would love this papaya. Is anyone going to Sarangpur? Send some for him.'

Swamishri has served and cared for thousands. His unconditional love has left a lasting impression in the hearts of many individuals.

Caring for and accommodating other peoples' needs have always been his forte. His specialty though, is remembering the specific needs of each individual.

After having darshan at Akshar Deri in Gondal, Swamishri was walking to the assembly hall for his morning puja when he called Dharmacharan Swami, "Dr Mangaldas and the others are probably leaving today. Make sure you give them *prasad* and send some for Verma Saheb as well."

Once, after puja, Swamishri called Jnanprasad Swami and told him to make arrangements for Ramanbhai, "Ramanbhai is leaving today by bus. See to it that you send someone to drop him off at the bus stop. Jagdish is going back with him so make sure you send *prasad* for Tulsibhai, Lallubhai, Bhailalbhai and Dahyabhai. Do not give *prasad* for Kanti. He is here, so make sure you give his *prasad* to him directly."

In 2005, thousands of people had come for the inauguration of the Swaminarayan Akshardham in New Delhi. Hundreds of people would come to meet Swamishri everyday and he would oversee the arrangements for all of them. He would give special directions for them and remind the sadhus of their needs. He would also remember and call those who hadn't come to see him.

Tyagvallabh Swami writes of one incident that he witnessed, "I was in Dharmaj with Swamishri. We went to A.P. Patel's house. He was an elderly devotee and was bedridden due to illness. Swamishri blessed him and sat in the car to return to the mandir. Four sadhus were seated in the Fiat car in front, waiting for the sadhu that was supporting Swamishri to join them. Then C.M. Patel of London went to sit in that car, which would leave the sadhu on his own. So, I told another devotee to explain this to C.M. Patel and ask him to walk to the mandir, which was nearby. Swamishri immediately disagreed. He told the devotee to tell two sadhus to come out of the car and walk so that C.M. Patel would not have to walk to the mandir. The cars took off and on our way to the mandir, Swamishri explained that as C.M. Patel has arthritis he would not have been able to foot the distance."

He remembers the specific needs of his devotees: "Make sure you put a chair for Ishwarcharan Swami in the meeting. He has a back problem. Don't let him sit on the floor." "Have you made arrangements for Balmukund Swami? Make sure his room is on the ground floor. He cannot climb the stairs." "Don't force Tyagvallabh Swami to eat sweets. His sugar level is really high." "Make sure you feed Sarvamangal properly…he is not well…"

Another important aspect of Swamishri's *smruti* is his desire to meet each and every one of his devotees. Travelling around the world, meeting tens of thousands of devotees, Swamishri remembers exactly which ones haven't come to see him.

In 2007, when Swamishri was in Edison, New Jersey, thousands of people were attending the evening assemblies. One evening after dinner, Swamishri was meeting hundreds of devotees and noticed a grey-haired gentleman fold his hands and walk past Swamishri. Swamishri stopped him and called him out, "Kanti! Don't walk away like that. Come here. Where have you been?"

Kantibhai replied, "I come everyday, but I do darshan from a distance. I don't like to bother you."

Swamishri was quick to comment, "You have always kept your distance. But now you should come." Then Swamishri turned to the sadhus standing nearby and said, "Kanti is a gentleman. He is very faithful. He had come to be a sadhu with the first batch of 51 youths in Yogiji Maharaj's time. He is related to Doctor Swami and he always helped Tyagvallabh Swami in the kitchen." Swamishri lovingly smiled at him and blessed him.

A few days later, a youth came for darshan. Swamishri himself introduced him, "This is Narayanbhai's son. He is from Sunav." He then turned to Jitendrabhai and said, "I haven't seen you at all this time. Where do you live?"

"I live in Parsippany, New Jersey," replied Jitendrabhai.

"Make sure you come to mandir regularly. Your father was the president of the Satsang in Dar-es-Salaam. You belong to us."

Swamishri put his hand around his neck and noticed that there was no *kanthi*.

"Where is your *kanthi*? You don't have one? Here, wear this *kanthi* and inspire others to wear it."

In Sarangpur, on 30 March 2006, Swamishri had met about 150 devotees when he recognized a familiar face in the crowd, "That's Bhagvat Joshi from Anand."

Bhagvat Joshi had travelled a great deal with Yogiji Maharaj between 1956 and 1958. Swamishri hadn't seen him for many years and affectionately asked him, "Where have you been? Just recently, I was in Bochasan for many days. Why didn't you come to meet me there?" Swamishri repeated the question several times. Then, Bhagvat hesitantly answered, "It's so difficult to meet you nowadays. No one lets me in."

"Why wouldn't they let you in? If you wanted to come, they would. I haven't seen you in a long time." There was a sense of belonging in Swamishri's voice, "Before you used to come so often. Now, whenever I come make sure you come and see me."

Viveksagar Swami added, "Just look for me. I will bring you in to meet Swamishri."

Swamishri reasoned, "Why do you need to bring him? He can come by himself. He can manage that much at least." Swamishri's paternal love left Bhagvat in tears.

Swamishri was leaving Nadiad on 5 December 1994. He realized that he hadn't seen Natubhai, a physically disabled devotee. Swamishri requested, "Someone phone him and tell him that we are coming to meet him on the way." Then Swamishri told the driver to take the car to his house. He went inside and blessed him.

After an assembly or darshan in the mandir, there have been many times when Swamishri has told Dharmacharan Swami or other sadhus to call devotees he had spotted on the way. He would say, "Call Dinubhai, we have to send some letters back to Ahmedabad. Make sure he comes to see me before he leaves."

No one would seem to recall seeing Dinubhai, but Swamishri would know where to find him. "He is sitting on the bench under the tree..." Swamishri would tell them.

Swamishri observes his devotees and their whereabouts, paying attention to every single detail.

On 20 October 1994, Swamishri was having darshan in the Akshar Deri in Gondal. The sadhus and *parshads* were inside, seated around the Akshar Deri. Govindsinh Chudasama was seated behind one of the pillars, virtually out of sight. While doing *pradakshina*, Swamishri glanced at him from the corner of his eye. Swamishri finished doing darshan and as he was leaving, he picked up a rose from the Akshar Deri, went to where Govindbhai was sitting, bent down and placed the rose in his lap. Govindbhai was left trying to figure out when Swamishri had seen him.

The most amazing thing is how Swamishri practically remembers all of this. He doesn't take notes in a journal or a diary. He doesn't have an office to work from. He flawlessly remembers everything and everyone – every time.

His constant *vicharan* is a reminder of his *smruti*. He visits the homes and villages of thousands of people, with one thought in mind: 'They have served the Sanstha.' He has never bothered to think of the physical strain or exertion that it has caused on his body.

Once, during the Guru Purnima festival in Bochasan, Swamishri was writing a few letters on stage. While the assembly was in progress, Gordhanbhai Jhaverbhai Patel of Narsanda came to the edge of the stage for Swamishri's darshan. He wanted Swamishri to look at him and so started talking to him.

Swamishri couldn't hear him properly, so he walked over to the edge of the stage and bent down to listen to him. He realized that Gordhanbhai was inviting him to grace his house. Swamishri explained to him that he was short on time, but would definitely come another time.

A local sadhu had heard this dialogue and turned to speak to Swamishri after Gordhanbhai left, "Don't bother going to his house. It's not worth it."

Swamishri asked him why he said that. The sadhu explained, "The last time we went to his town, you had a temperature and he had told us that there were only two *padhramani*s. It turned out that he had scheduled fifty."

Swamishri kept silent for a moment and then responded, "Do you know how much he has done for Shastriji Maharaj? No one would let us into Narsanda and he had bravely opposed everyone to let Shastriji Maharaj stay in the village mandir. He used to send food from his house. It's a different story that we can't make it, but you should never say that it's not worth it!" The sadhu apologized and the incident was forgotten.

Then, a few days later, Swamishri had gone to Vartal for darshan. He stopped his car and turned it towards Narsanda. Gordhanbhai was sitting on the swing in his yard when he saw Swamishri's car. He started crying with tears of joy. He couldn't believe his eyes. Swamishri had come to Narsanda.

Gordhanbhai welcomed Swamishri into his home and took him upstairs, where he had just added a second floor. Swamishri showered sanctified flowers there, and then prepared to leave. Gordhanbhai was at a loss for words. But Swamishri spontaneously said, "You have done so much for Shastriji Maharaj."

Swamishri has shown up unexpectedly at many homes – Dahyabhai Patel, the poor farmers of Bhadra, former Prime Minister Gulzarilal Nanda and Ishwarbhai of Jitodiya are just a few of them. The reason? They have served his guru and the Sanstha.

Swamishri always remembers to give credit to the responsible individuals. Many times when reading about festivals or events in the Sanstha's Gujarati monthly, *Swaminarayan Prakash*, Swamishri remembers names that have been inadvertently left out: "How can you forget to mention Shivlal Parmar when writing about Ahmedabad mandir..."; "You forgot to credit the Petlad Textile Mill for its help during the cattle camps we organized in Bochasan..."; "Why did you forget to mention R.K. Patel from London when you were discussing the construction of Swaminarayan Akshardham, Gandhinagar..."; "Shambhusinh is a senior and dedicated devotee in Rajkot..."

In many instances, he has insisted that the appropriate names be included in the next issue.

From the dirt roads of Gujarat to the five-lane expressways in America, Swamishri remembers many routes. When sadhus are singing verses from the Bhaktachintamani, Satsangijivan or other shastras, Swamishri is the first one to hint the next line when someone blanks out. He even remembers the morning discourses and where the reading of a particular text stopped in the previous session. There are countless incidents that demonstrate his *smruti*.

Though his memory is sharp in all respects, there is one particular area that he never forgets. Swamishri has a knack for remembering peoples' strengths, talents, skills and positive characteristics. They are inscribed in his heart forever!

This one incident illustrates that ability to its fullest extent.

Swamishri was staying at Dr Mahendrabhai Patel's house in Westchester, New York, recovering from his bypass surgery. Not too far away in Purchase was the beautiful Pepsi-Co Park. It was an ideal place for Swamishri's daily walk. Extremely quiet, yet buzzing with nature's animation. It soon became a daily routine; Swamishri would go to walk in the park everyday. On 30 August 1998, what started as an everyday event, turned out to be a not so ordinary evening.

Swamishri finished his walk and sat in his wheelchair in a serene green corner. The evening continued as usual, the sadhus performed *arti* and then Swamishri explained Vachanamrut, Gadhada I 27. He was ending the discourse when he started talking about Yogiji Maharaj's life. He said, "All these qualities are present in Yogiji Maharaj's life."

He praised Ishwarcharan Swami for writing the six-part biography of Yogiji Maharaj. Swamishri started talking about Ishwarcharan Swami and mentioning great characteristics in his personality.

The discourse had ended, but no one knew what was to come. Swamishri was going to recite a page from the life of almost every sadhu in the Sanstha.

Swamishri started praising one sadhu after another...Balmukund Swami, Doctor Swami, Mahant Swami, Tyagvallabh Swami, Kothari

After performing devotional rituals Swamishri praises his guru Yogiji Maharaj
and then the sadhus of BAPS, New York, August 1998.

Swami, Viveksagar Swami, and many others. When Swamishri had
finished praising all the senior sadhus. He then started praising every
sadhu that came to mind. They weren't mentioned in any particular
order, but they all had one thing in common. Swamishri saw a positive
quality in all of them.

Many of the sadhus and devotees present had tears welling up
from the corner of their eyes. Swamishri was singing the praises and
glory of his disciples. Since the discourse was over, Swamishri had
taken his feet off the footrest to prepare to stand up. At this point,
with his feet still dangling in the air, he was so engrossed in this
smruti session that he forgot to place them on the ground.

Dusk was settling in the northern suburbs of New York City and the
park was almost empty, but Swamishri had lost all track of time. It was
starting to get dark and Swamishri was showing no signs of stopping
from recalling the virtues of his sadhus. He continued to sing the glory
of these sadhus patiently and devoutly. He had mentioned over 60
sadhus by now. Swamishri was remembering sadhus serving as *pujari*,
kothari, in children's activities, youth activities, satsang activities, in the
kitchen, in the farms and those advanced in particular fields, i.e. music,
academia, oration, art, architecture, administration, public relations,
writing and even housekeeping. He praised sadhus for their humility,
simplicity, honesty, patience, tolerance, stability and sacrifices.

These sadhus, who were probably travelling in a corner of Gujarat,

Eternal Virtues

had no clue that their guru was appreciating and praising them.

It was really dark now. The sadhus and devotees could barely see Swamishri's face, but Swamishri was nowhere near finished.

The assembly had lasted 70 minutes! It was 7.50 p.m. and the darkness was forcing Swamishri to get up. Still, Swamishri continued to mention names as he stood up and finally placed his airborne foot on the ground.

At one point the sadhus interrupted and said, "Swami! You've talked about a lot of sadhus and their qualities, but all of this is only possible because of you. We are sadhus because of you." Swamishri refused to take any credit, "This is Yogiji Maharaj's grace. He was able to inspire all of you."

Swamishri started walking towards the parking area, continuing the praises. He stopped for only one moment to say, "We should always see the good in others. We have to unite and learn to get along with each other. That is the only way to inner peace."

Swamishri was breathing very hard now because he was walking and constantly talking. He continued to mention more sadhus.

The sadhus told him that while reading the Bhaktachintamani today, they came across a similar list of devotees Bhagwan Swaminarayan had spoken of.

Swamishri added, "Bhagwan Swaminarayan has revealed the importance of always seeing the good in God and his devotees. Singing their praises helps us to progress spiritually."

Swamishri continued to breathe heavily and remember more sadhus. He sat in the car and still carried on. Swamishri continued throughout the entire return journey to Dr Mahendrabhai's house. After entering the house he still didn't stop. He continued for another 15 minutes. Then, even after laying down on his bed to rest, Swamishri called Aksharvatsal Swami and mentioned and recounted the qualities of seven more sadhus.

Everyone was overwhelmed. This was an evening that none would forget. The sadhus left the room with the hope that Swamishri would rest. He had been speaking continuously for over 90 minutes!

Yes, that is the peak of Swamishri's *smruti*. It is capped with love and compassion.

This isn't an account of his sharp intellect or memory; it's a saga of his affection and appreciation for his devotees.

Swamishri's constant communion with Bhagwan Swaminarayan and close bond with his devotees across the world is something that everyone, including those mentioned in this chapter and those reading it will always remember.   ◆

Swaminarayan Akshardham, New Delhi, was inspired and created through the blessings of Pramukh Swami Maharaj.

Kaushalam
कौशलम्

*Kaushalam is efficiency, excellence and perfection.
The ancient shastras describe God as being the
source of all knowledge, skills and talents.
God is proficient in everything he does,
similarly the Gunatit Sadhu has this divine attribute.
Though a sadhu's virtue is his constant rapport
with God and has no need for worldly proficiency or
excellence, his* kaushalam *attracts people and
leads them towards God.
Pramukh Swami Maharaj has a peaceful,
patient, simple and loving persona,
but his all-round efficiency should
never be underestimated.*

Swamishri is proficient across the board. His architectural genius, interest in art and music, organizational skills, administrative proficiency and human relations skills are just a few of his strengths. There are many more that can only be experienced and witnessed in his presence.

Swamishri has show this versatility since childhood, his excellence seeping out of his simple childhood activities.

Swamishri was one of the best swimmers in the village. Young Shantilal hardly ever lost a swimming competition at the village lake.

He was also the brightest student in his class. Swamishri was especially fond of mathematics and history. He ranked number one in his class.

Swamishri was also an adept cricketer. He was the captain of the village cricket team and was always the first to be picked. About Rs. 500 had been collected to purchase new cricket equipment for the village team. Shantilal, then only a teenager, was entrusted with what for that era was a relatively large sum of money.

Many visitors are astonished to learn that Swamishri built Swaminarayan Akshardham in just five years, despite the many difficulties.

On the very day he was going to buy the cricketing gear , he received a letter from guru Shastriji Maharaj. That was the end of his cricketing career. The day marked a new beginning in his life. There were to be no more swimming competitions to win or maths tests to ace, Shantilal was going to rise to a new level of proficiency and perfection.

Shantilal's excellence was now going to lead thousands on the path to spirituality and *moksha*. Shastriji Maharaj groomed him to become a great sadhu.

Pleased by the young Narayanswarupdasji's proficiency and efficiency, Shastriji Maharaj involved him in the Sanstha's management and decision-making meetings. Shastriji Maharaj gave him prominence in the assemblies. In 1945, when Swamishri was just 23 years old, Shastriji Maharaj included Swamishri on the Sanstha's Board, entrusting him with major responsibilities. At the age of 24 he was made Kothari of Sarangpur mandir. On 21 May 1950, Shastriji Maharaj, having thoroughly tested and groomed him, appointed 28-year-old Swamishri as the Pramukh (President) of BAPS Swaminarayan Sanstha.

Swamishri at first declined the post. He disliked having authority and a designation. He wanted to be a mere *sevak*. Eventually, due to the insistence of his guru, he accepted the responsibility. Even after becoming president of the Sanstha, he never demanded respect or asserted his authority. He worked silently under Yogiji Maharaj's guidance. Swamishri's *kaushalyam* had the Sanstha soaring to unimaginable heights. A careful study of the Sanstha's growth since 1950 reveals this. The last 60 years of success and growth bear Pramukh Swami Maharaj's stamp.

Since 1971, after Yogiji Maharaj passed away to Akshardham and

Swamishri became the spiritual guru of BAPS, the Sanstha's scope of work has considerably broadened. The following facts and figures provide a glimpse of Swamishri's *kaushalyam*:

BAPS is serving mankind in many nations

It has 3,700 satsang centres worldwide

More than 900 mandirs in over 15 countries

Sixteen hospitals and mobile clinics serving over 365,000 patients annually

Thirty-one educational institutions and schools train 12,000 students morally and academically each year

The Sanstha provides scholarships to more than 5,000 students every year

It has rebuilt 21 villages and colonies in Gujarat, Maharashtra, Orissa and Tamil Nadu following natural disasters like famines, floods, earthquakes and tsunamis

It spiritually nurtures and morally moulds thousands of children through 6,700 special weekly assemblies

Providing spiritual and moral direction to hundreds of thousands of people through over 815,000 satsang assemblies annually

Providing a wholesome experience of Indian culture to over 34,000,000 individuals through international cultural festivals in India, UK, USA and Africa

Instilling values in over 6,300,000 people annually through cultural monuments such as Swaminarayan Akshardham in Gandhinagar and New Delhi.

How does Pramukh Swami Maharaj manage such an enormous organization? He has no personal or monetary gains. The organization runs on the service and dedication of selfless volunteers. The organization runs on the financial contributions and offerings of its humble, mainly middle class devotees.

It is near impossible to describe how Swamishri is able to motivate and inspire these volunteers, how he is able to get them to dedicate their lives and livelihoods to better society, and how he is able to satisfy and manage all of them. There is only one word that describes this unachievable task: *kaushalam*.

Experienced community leaders and management experts don't understand how Swamishri does it. A visit to a BAPS Mandir or Swaminarayan Akshardham, New Delhi, inspires a series of questions in their minds:

"How was Swamishri able to construct Swaminarayan Akshardham in just five years?"

Swamishri's expertise in planning mandir complexes in India and abroad have amazed even experienced architects.

"How can you create majestic traditional mandirs in London, Toronto, Atlanta, Houston and Chicago in 17 to 23 months?"

"The Cultural Festivals of India attracted tens of thousands of people in Europe and North America. How do you plan and execute them to such perfection?"

"How do you start, organize, and maintain thousands of satsang assemblies across the globe?"

"The children's activities at BAPS are awe-inspiring. How do you coordinate them across so many countries, sub-cultures and languages?"

"How do you maintain such consistency across all of your centres?"

"Along with hundreds of mandirs, BAPS and BAPS Charities have set up scores of medical facilities, schools and hostels. How do you operate them?"

"How do you activate your forces to respond so promptly and effectively at times like the Gujarat Earthquake, the South Asian Tsunami, and Hurricanes Katrina and Rita?"

"How do you motivate your volunteers to dedicate and sacrifice so much of their time and resources to help the community?"

There is a common answer to all these questions: Swamishri's spiritual *kaushalyam*.

The greatest skill or quality of a true leader is his ability to train others. Swamishri has fostered this *kaushalyam* in thousands of his

Eternal Virtues

sadhus and devotees, to help them take the Sanstha to new heights with each passing day.

His capacity to motivate others and build their self-confidence is unequivocal. He places responsibility on their shoulders and gives them the trust to help bear its weight. Swamishri has moulded ordinary men to perform not-so ordinary tasks.

The following incidents will inspire you as well…

Swamishri has built marvellous mandirs and entrusted their administrative responsibilities to young sadhus. He has trained them to deal with such tasks and to tackle the social dilemmas facing devotees. Swamishri has placed enormous trust in them. He has set an example that will revolutionize religious organizations across India.

The mandirs created by him conform to the ancient *Shilpashastras*, thus reviving a lost art. Not only has he used his discerning eye and skill for maintaining symmetry in the traditional carvings, but he has taught many of the sadhus and dedicated volunteers. Swamishri is involved from the start: picking the land, finalizing the plans, choosing the types of stone and marble to be used, design of the inner shrine and the *sinhasan* for the *murtis*. He is very particular about making sure the assembly halls, dining halls, sadhus' quarters are built to specification. Also, he maintains the spirituality and the traditional touch in each of these contemporary constructions. His *kaushalyam* has revived the traditional art of constructing mandirs.

He has a special skill in the making of *murtis*. He has an expert eye for reviewing *murtis* as they are made and guides the sculptor to obtain the best result: "The ear on the left side of this *murti* is a bit too high…the left shoulder of this particular *murti* is too thin…the cheeks on this *murti* aren't full…"

Swamishri can tell with just one glance. Even the best sculptors

He is constantly aware of what needs to be done, energetically and expertly ensuring that all work is completed.

are stunned by Swamishri's sharp eye. Swamishri's *kaushalyam* has turned some sadhus into some of the best sculptors around today.

Swamishri's mastery in architecture is equally profound. He has made valuable design and construction suggestions throughout various projects, including, Swaminarayan Akshardham and the mandirs in Nairobi, London, Atlanta, Chicago and Houston. His valuable contributions from the structure's height, width, symmetry to the complex's floor plan have amazed some of the world's best architects.

Swaminarayan Akshardham, New Delhi, has brought about a cultural renaissance. It redefines a Hindu mandir. It's breathtaking beauty and colossal presence has earned it a place in the *Guinness World Records* as the world's largest Hindu temple. Swaminarayan Akshardham is a fusion of modern technology, contemporary presentation techniques, spirituality and India's glorious heritage. Swamishri's *kaushalyam* helped the sadhus and youths that were involved in its creation gain confidence and experience, thus creating a cultural renaissance that will be passed on to future generations.

Swamishri has always motivated sadhus and youths to achieve academic excellence. Swamishri promotes the study of Sanskrit, literature, traditional music and art.

Sanskrit, the mother of all languages, is waning with time. Losing Sanskrit would limit access to the Vedas and other ancient shastras. Swamishri has groomed some of the most learned Sanskrit scholars in all of India. Though Sanskrit is not the easiest of languages to learn, Swamishri has personally motivated many sadhus and youths to master the 'language of the *devas*'.

As a result the sadhus have been able to study, analyze and add to the inexhaustible Indian literature and philosophical lore.

Through Swamishri's inspiration, Bhadresh Swami is the first in the Swaminarayan Sampraday, since Sadguru Gopalanand Swami approximately 200 years ago, to write commentaries on the Upanishads, Shrimad Bhagvad Gita and the Brahmasutras.

Swamishri has always supported and promoted publications and literary works. Publications in English, Hindi, Gujarati, Marathi, Sanskrit and other languages are constantly published to help satisfy the spiritual hunger of people from those backgrounds.

He pays close attention to each publication. He goes through every detail; correcting or appreciating them to enhance their content and quality.

Swamishri's creativity and *kaushalyam* have resulted in a wide range of audio, video and print publications for all spiritual aspirants.

He doesn't hold a degree in music, but his appreciation and encouragement are a reflection of his *kaushalyam*. Swamishri provides a platform for sadhus and youths to develop and sustain traditional Indian music through instruments such as the *sarod*, sitar, *bansuri*, *tabla* and others. Swamishri is a patron of devotional music in any shape or form.

Surprisingly, Swamishri has deep knowledge of agriculture and animal husbandry. Thousands of farmers have benefited from his guidance. Many of them have received advice directly from Swamishri. Swamishri's expertise has helped the sadhus and devotees develop the Sanstha's agricultural products and cattle to be among the best in the nation. Many animals from the Sanstha's cattle farms have won national livestock awards. Swamishri's sound practical advice has helped set an ideal standard amongst Gujarat's farmers.

What seems to amaze the common man is the flawless organization and management of the mega festivals.

In 1945 when he was only 23 years old Swamishri had organized Shastriji Maharaj's 80th birthday celebrations in Bochasan. After that there were frequent festivals. The Gadhada Kalash-Jayanti Celebrations in 1961, Shastriji Maharaj's Centenary Celebrations in 1965, Yogiji Maharaj's Diamond Jubilee Celebrations in 1967, the opening of the Yogi Smruti Mandir in 1975, the Bhagwan Swaminarayan Birth Bicentennial Celebrations in 1981, the Gunatitanand Swami Birth Bicentennial Celebrations in 1985, The Cultural Festivals of India in 1985 (London) and 1991 (USA), the innaguration of various traditional mandirs around the world and more recently, the BAPS Centenary Celebrations in 2007. Swamishri has given a new perspective on how to celebrate festivals. They weren't just large gatherings or carnivals, but they gave the participants a message that changed their lives forever.

The festivals included exhibitions, de-addiction programmes and other activities geared at promoting a morally pure society. His inspiration and direct supervision have provided a platform to train younger sadhus and devotees and also provide entertainment and education for families.

Swamishri also responds spontaneously to emergencies. How? In the aftermath of natural disasters, Swamishri lost no time in activating and coordinating a team of sadhus and volunteers so that relief could be provided to the victims. BAPS Charities was among the first to reach the site after the devastating Gujarat Earthquake. Victims in Kenner, Louisiana, noted that BAPS Charities was the first relief operation to provide warm nutritious meals in the wake of Hurricane Katrina. Swamishri's organizational and managerial excellence earned the appreciation and praise of the government for the emergency and longterm relief efforts for victims of the South Asian Tsunami, Maharashtra Earthquake and other disasters.

Hundreds of thousands of individuals have seen Swamishri fix their lives together one piece at a time. They become emotional as they remember Swamishri's unconditional support and precise care in such trying circumstances. Such is the quality of the villages rebuilt by the Sanstha that they have received national awards. Swamishri had taken a great deal of interest in the construction of these villages, analyzing every detail to provide the best possible facilities to the villagers.

Swamishri also has an eye for reviewing financial statements and accounts ledgers. The Charity Commissioners of Gujarat have been amazed by Swamishri's accounting skills. When the Sanstha's accounts department present the annual reports to Swamishri, he always politely asks a question or makes a suggestion that they have overlooked. People that make contributions expect clean and organized accounts that are easy to trace. Swamishri himself insists that every penny be accounted for. He has promoted a set of principles upon which the accounts are prepared. Swamishri has thus trained many volunteers with the same skill set and eye for detail.

The Sanstha's legal advisers are surprised by Swamishri's legal expertise. He has always believed in and enforced the following of legal guidelines set by the local governments before considering any sort of expansion or activity. The BAPS's flawless legal track record is one reason why the Supreme Court in New Delhi approved the construction of the Swaminarayan Akshardham on the banks of the Yamuna river and why the Gujarat High Court ruled in favour of the expansion of the BAPS mandir complex in Gadhada.

There are scores of projects and activities in progress at any point in time, and with them a multitude of problems that require Swamishri's guidance. Swamishri faces each one with a renewed strength and vigour. Each instance shows a different angle of his proficiency. His decision-making skills, his stability and presence of mind, patience and bravery, long-term thinking, simplicity, positive influence and his fair and just attitude are just a few of his numerous strengths.

BAPS works efficiently because of Swamishri's *kaushalam*.

Not only is Swamishri proficient in running a multinational organization, but he also guides devotees, providing solutions to their day-to-day personal, family and business problems. From wealthy entrepreneurs to small-time farmers, he provides guidance to all in their personal dealings.

Swamishri has shown *kaushalam* in so many different aspects of his life. He has helped pass that *kaushalam* on to the younger generation to safeguard the Sanstha's and their personal future.

That *kaushalam* is priceless, but that is not what makes Swamishri different. Ishwarcharan Swami describes Swamishri's true *kaushalam*, "There is a small chance that someone can do all of these things, a very small chance; but to do it without taking any credit, pleasing everyone and making sure no one is offended in the process is impossible. Hundreds of thousands of people are working together, cooperating, not complaining or bickering. To inspire that kind of love and respect in so many different people is impossible. Swamishri is a vast ocean of divine virtues. You can see it, hear it and feel it. Yet, Swamishri always remains immersed in God and is at peace — satisfied and complete."

Dr David Frawley, an esteemed Vedic scholar, was amazed with Swamishri's *kaushalam* at work at the Swaminarayan Akshardham, New Delhi, and commented, "Swamishri is very proficient at motivating other people. He doesn't shout or force; it all comes naturally. In many cases, he doesn't even have to tell them. He is a divine soul that can inspire them to work in this peaceful and selfless environment. He is very polite and is in constant rapport with God, how else can he work tirelessly for others without any expectations for power in return? This sadhu has the strength to move mountains, to change mankind, to change the face of Hinduism."

Robert O. Blake Jr. has been selected as the Best Deputy Chief of Mission worldwide by the US government for his excellent management and administrative skills. Chief Blake has also served as US Ambassador to various nations. Upon seeing Swaminarayan Akshardham in New Delhi, the veteran officer couldn't wait to meet its creator, Pramukh Swami Maharaj. When he got the opportunity, he said, "You are not just an outstanding spiritual leader. You are a great leader. You motivated thousands of people to work together and finish this masterpiece in just five years. The credit goes to you. There is a lot we can learn from you, starting with your superb leadership skills."

Swamishri's response, "All the credit belongs to Bhagwan Swaminarayan and my guru Yogiji Maharaj."

Swamishri always shies away from the credit and separates himself from his expertise and proficiency. That in itself is a great virtue.

On 30 April 2006, Dr Prashant Chhaya, an orthopaedic surgeon, came to Junagadh for Swamishri's darshan. He revealed, "I can barely manage the five employees in my clinic. How do you manage this gigantic Sanstha?"

"God manages everything," Swamishri replied in one sentence. Dr Chhaya was persistent, "I understand that, but he works through you. How do you manage them?"

"God is the all-doer. If you believe in that divine concept, you can inspire everyone. God works through all of us. If we understand everyone's greatness, cooperate with them and work to please God, everything falls into place."

President and owner of Torrent Pharmaceuticals, U.N. Mehta, came for Swamishri's darshan in Ahmedabad on 26 December 1994.

"There is a lot I have to learn from you. Akshardham (in Gandhinagar) is a masterpiece. It's a great idea," he praised.

"It was Bhagwan Swaminarayan's inspiration and the sadhus' hard work," Swamishri replied in brief.

"All of your devotees have this sense of energy and zeal. They never quit or tire. There is a divine force working in them. Your sadhus are educated and work professionally. You get everything done. It is amazing. Please give me a few words of advice," he requested.

"God has given us this human body. We should always use it to help others. The goal of this body is to attain *moksha* for our *atma*.

Spirituality is the key. Satsang helps us to realize the difference between right and wrong. Satsang also helps us to realize that one day you are going to leave all this behind. You must work to liberate your *atma*."

Swamishri lives that advice in his own life. That is why he is able to work proficiently and never desires credit.

Former Professor of Religion and Dean at Wabash College, Dr Raymond Williams, asked Swamishri a few questions:

"Technically, you have no experience when it comes to living a social life. You are a sadhu. How are you able to guide your devotees in that aspect of their lives?"

"God gives me the answers. God has experienced everything."

"Do you ever hesitate before answering or after answering? Have there been times when you wish you had answered differently?"

"No, I have never felt it that way."

"For example, what if one of your devotees asks you about buying a small business. You tell him to buy it, and it fails miserably. He loses everything. Don't you feel like you made a mistake? Don't you feel like you should have told him not to buy it?"

"No, of course not. God gives me the answers. God knows your past, present and future. He does everything for a reason. Some good will always come of it."

God is at the core of all his decisions and reasoning.

God is the source of his energy.

God is the source of his skill and proficiency.

God is the reason behind his accomplishments.

That is why Swamishri is relaxed, at ease and in a state of constant stability.

This is his true proficiency and what the Shrimad Bhagvad Gita calls, *"Yoga karmasu kaushalam..."*, meaning, "Working with proficiency is Yoga..."

To work with efficiency without expecting anything in return and remembering God in each activity is *kaushalam*. That is Yoga.

Swamishri's worldly and spiritual *kaushalam* and proficiency illustrates that he is what the Shrimad Bhagvad Gita calls, a true *kaushalya* yogi. ◆

Dhairyam धैर्यम्

Sthairyam Pragalbhyam Sahaha
स्थैर्यम् प्रागल्भ्यम् सहः

Dhairyam is patience.
Sthairyam is stability of mind, even in disturbing situations.
Saha is to tolerate difficulties for God's devotees.
Pragalbhyam is maturity – one free of irresponsible behaviour.
These qualities add to God's greatness and in turn,
the Gunatit Sadhu's greatness.

Pramukh Swami Maharaj's greatness is that he can cover both ends of the spectrum.

He is powerful yet patient.

He is courageous yet calm.

He is able yet understanding.

He doesn't get frustrated or nervous.

He is composed amid crises.

He is at ease in chaos and grief.

Throughout his life Swamishri has maintained these qualities, even in the most testing situations. The terrorist attack on Swaminarayan Akshardham, Gandhinagar, and his quintuplet bypass surgery are just two of many such instances.

Swamishri's true identity is his stable and serene state of mind amid the chaos and excitement of the innumerable activities that he oversees.

Usually, people's patience and stability aren't put to the test everyday. They are only put under the microscope on certain occasions. Yet, in Swamishri's life, every single day, if not moment, tests his patience. His life is an ideal example of unflinching serenity and patience. He doesn't have to instruct or lecture, his life itself is a practical demonstration.

The greatest tests of his patience are the daily sessions of personal consultations with devotees. It has been a part of his routine for decades. Swamishri meets hundreds of people everyday whether he

Prayer assembly for people killed in the terrorist attack on Akshardham, Gandhinagar, in 2002.

Daily, Swamishri meets so many people, listens to so many problems and gives so many decisions, yet his interest in others' welfare never wanes.

is in a small village or a huge metropolis. Devotees explain their problems and issues, trivial or serious. Swamishri listens to each one of them with enthusiasm and dedication. They leave satisfied with a decision and blessings. The problems change, the people change and time passes, but Swamishri is the constant factor. Swamishri meets people while he is eating, walking, during assemblies and even while he is getting ready to go to sleep.

It doesn't end there. Swamishri counsels devotees and sadhus even while he is in bed. At night, while everyone thinks he is sleeping, he is, in fact, on the phone talking to sadhus and devotees around the world, adjusting to their time zones.

Swamishri listens to numerous problems everyday. He pays attention to detail, makes decisions and consoles devotees day in and day out. Such a routine can get frustrating, but not for Swamishri.

Swamishri was in Dhari and had temporarily left the assembly to use the bathroom. He came out of the shower and a devotee approached him with a personal matter. He expressed his wish to talk to him immediately. Swamishri had to get back to the assembly to address the audience, but Swamishri heard the pain in his voice. So, he sat down.

Swamishri sat there on the stairs right outside the bathroom.

There was barely any room, fresh air or even light, but that didn't bother him. He sat there and listened to the devotee empty his heart out for 15 minutes, before giving him a satisfying solution.

The sheer number of devotees would intimidate others, yet Swamishri is undaunted. He continues to meet each devotee, answer each phone call and read each letter as if it is his first.

He has been doing this for the past 40 years. There are no vacations. Swamishri meets devotees seven days a week, 365 days a year. It doesn't stop even when he is ill.

Swamishri had woken up from the anaesthesia. Robert, one of the attendants, expressed his wish to receive Swamishri's blessing, "I want to explain my situation to him. I am sure my marriage plans will work out if he gives me his blessings." Swamishri blessed him just hours after his bypass surgery.

No two consultations are ever alike, yet the often trivial nature of the problems would irritate anyone. But Swamishri deals patiently with each.

Swamishri meets international dignitaries and tribal villagers with the same ease and earnestness. Swamishri's ability to deal with diverse issues and individuals without being overwhelmed further testifies to his patience. There is no such thing as the 'right mood' or 'right mindset' for him. He is always in the mood to listen, advise and bless.

Swamishri counsels individuals through many ways. The most time consuming and taxing of them all is letter writing. In the past 40 years, Swamishri has read and answered over 700,000 letters. Replying to letters can be tedious, cumbersome and frustrating. However, he has refused to add these words to his vocabulary.

On 5 March 2006, Swamishri was in Ahmedabad when Amrutnayan Swami called from London.

"Swami! What are you doing?"

"I was reading and writing a few letters and you called..."

"You've spent your whole life writing letters."

"Helping devotees is bhakti. It is part of my devotion to Bhagwan Swaminarayan."

"I would be bored of reading the same problems over and over again."

"There is nothing to be bored of. It is our *seva*!"

"I would go crazy if I had to read all those letters."

"Don't go crazy! In happiness or sorrow, you must patiently get through any situation. We must do our *seva*..."

Swamishri never tires or gives up. He patiently surmounts any difficulty.

In March 2006, Swamishri was in Sarangpur. He had an eye infection. His eyes were swollen and he was experiencing a throbbing pain. The doctors had put a pad on the infected eye to protect the other eye. They had also advised him to wear shades for protection. Still, Swamishri didn't take a single day off.

He was meeting devotees and writing letters all day. He would read and write letters in between meeting devotees. The minute he would pick up a letter, someone would come in to meet him. Swamishri patiently met all of them. After they were all finished, Swamishri read the letter for half an hour before another devotee came to meet him.

Swamishri sat with him until 8.30 p.m. and then had dinner. After dinner about a hundred devotees had come from nearby Botad for his darshan. He met them all.

After meeting them, Swamishri asked Dharmacharan Swami to bring more letters. Narayancharan Swami interjected, "Your eyes are giving trouble, yet you do not stop reading letters."

"If I take a break now, they will all pile up. It's better to read them daily."

Swamishri again requested Dharmacharan Swami to bring the letters. He decided to give a summary of the letters to Swamishri so that he wouldn't have to strain his eyes by reading them.

Swamishri wasn't satisfied, "You can give me a brief summary, but give me the letter as well so that I can read it."

Swamishri continued reading and writing until it was time to go to bed.

The next day was no different. Swamishri was trying to get through a long and poorly written letter. Swamishri could barely make out the handwriting. Brahmavihari Swami couldn't hold back, "Your eyes are troubling you and you are still reading letters."

"I have only been able to get through one letter today. Every time I pick up the letter someone else comes to meet me."

"You shouldn't have bothered reading it. There's no need to."

"Of course there is! That devotee must be suffering so much. It must have taken him a long time to write the letter. He must be in so much pain. The least we should do is to read it."

"He is in pain? What about you? We are all in pain just seeing you reading that long letter!"

Swamishri laughed it off and replied, "You try to help and it still seems to trouble others!"

The long, difficult to decipher letters often have very little substance. Swamishri reads them and replies to them respecting the feelings and effort put in by his devotees.

Personal consultations are no different. Swamishri may be in the middle of an important meeting or a spiritual discourse and a devotee may interrupt the moment with a very trivial question or problem. Others try to hurry the person, but Swamishri patiently gives him his undivided attention.

On 24 April 1995, Swamishri was in Surat meeting hundreds of devotees. A 78-year-old devotee grabbed everyone's attention.

"I want to file a complaint!" he said.

"What's the matter?"

"Why did God take my wife before me?"

"Isn't it a good thing that she is in Akshardham? Plus, she didn't have to live a single day without you. It is a great fortune."

"When she was in the hospital on her deathbed, she wanted to see me for the last time, but she passed away before I got there. It's your fault. You should have let her live for just a bit longer."

The senior's voice was climbing the decibel chart. He continued, "They even delay an execution for a final death wish. This is your fault. You should have granted her this one wish."

"She was a true devotee. All her wishes have been granted and now she is in Akshardham…"

Swamishri responds to devotees and pleases them, Sarangpur.

"I am going to go, too."

"Perfect. Then you will meet her there."

"Not really. I am not going to be able to recognize her there. Why did you take her early?"

Everyone standing around was getting agitated, but Swamishri patiently consoled him.

"It is better that your wife went to Akshardham first. She didn't have to see a single day as a widow…It would have been harder on your wife if it was the other way around…"

Swamishri was calm and relaxed. The elderly man was accusing Swamishri and didn't want to understand. Nevertheless, Swamishri lovingly blessed him.

Swamishri has met some of the world's most influential people. He runs an international organization and more importantly is at a spiritual height that is incomprehensible to most. How does he maintain his composure to listen to such questions and answer them?

Thousands of people put Swamishri's patience and stability to the test. He always comes off with flying colours.

In Ahmedabad, Ishwarcharan Swami observed Swamishri's hectic meeting schedule for a month and noticed that Swamishri met thousands of people. He suggested, "You have had a hectic month. It must have been strenuous."

Swamishri remained silent. Ishwarcharan Swami continued, "The new assembly hall is very suitable for all. Devotees can listen to your blessings and have your darshan properly. Swami! There is no end to these personal consultations. I think it's best to stop them. You have to listen to everyone's questions and give them answers. Anyone else would go crazy in a week! Maharshi Aurobindo did not give personal consultations. Most spiritual gurus do not give personal consultations."

Swamishri answered, "Many of their questions aren't real questions. If they just thought about it for a few minutes, they would have realized the right thing to do. I listen to their questions so that they are satisfied. I have no problem with that."

Swamishri's patience and state of equilibrium maintain his joy even in trying situations.

Swamishri's patience and stability are shown through his ability to understand others. Many times he has spent hours talking about the same thing to the same person on different occasions.

Swamishri's ears are bombarded by people with all sorts of problems – domestic troubles, depression, physical ailments, social strife, administrative issues and spiritual confusion. While most people in his situation would look for a way out or an escape, Swamishri listens attentively.

As one community leader said, "Swamishri has to have more than two ears." How else can one person listen to thousands of other people for several hours at a stretch?

On 18 August 1998, Swamishri was in Westchester, New York, recovering from his bypass operation. Viveksagar Swami was asking him a few questions.

"Ninety percent of our energy is used in removing people's misconceptions and making them understand. Only ten percent is left for productive work. Why do you think that happens?"

"The only reason you achieve ten percent productivity is because you have used the other ninety percent to understand each other," Swamishri reasoned.

"Don't you ever feel like leaving all these activities to just sit in a corner and turn the *mala*?"

"No. Once you are at that spiritual level, it won't bother you."

Though he is very particular with his work and teaches other to do the same, Swamishri is extremely patient with careless and inexperienced people. He patiently teaches them the same things over and over again. He may reprimand them from time to time, but never does he lose patience or give up hope. He motivates them, encourages them and guides them. He patiently forgives them time after time, knowing that they will eventually learn not to err.

Another facet of his patience is tested when he is insulted and criticized for no justifiable reason.

Swamishri has given his life for the betterment of mankind. Yet, there are times when he is insulted by individuals that are green with envy. Devotees and even others wonder why Swamishri never says anything in return. How can he be so patient? Why does someone that is truthful, helpful and selfless have to suffer so much?

But Swamishri is at peace. His tempered nerves have stood the test of time.

In 1980, Vishwavihari Swami asked Swamishri a similar question in Kunkavav, "How long will you have to suffer like this?"

Swamishri was optimistic, "Devkiji and Vasudevji were Bhagwan Krishna's parents and they had to suffer until the very end. It happens to everyone…"

Swamishri often says, "There is an ancient Indian proverb, 'A good deed faces one hundred obstacles.' This is a sign that we are doing the right thing. You are bound to face hurdles and suffer, but you should never give up."

He always remembers his gurus Shastriji Maharaj and Yogiji Maharaj.

On 25 July 2006, Swamishri was speaking to Dr B.R. Patel on a similar topic, "Shastriji Maharaj had a lot of will power. He would always accomplish what he had planned to. He never quit. There was a Sanskrit verse that he used to recite: 'Many people quit before they even start, they are the lowest. Then there are those that quit after they face a few obstacles, they are mediocre. The best are those that never quit, come what may.' Shastriji Maharaj faced many hurdles, but he never quit. Even when you are doing good for the society and country, some people will try to stop you or cause problems because they are jealous. They don't want you to get the credit for it. Shastriji Maharaj had a lot of opposition. They would try to beat his sadhus and kick him out of villages. Shastriji Maharaj was patient, saying, 'God is with us, so everything will turn out fine.' Due to this faith, the mandir in Bochasan was possible."

Swamishri has lived those same ideals; he always maintains his composure.

A few years ago, an individual tried to get in the way of Swamishri's humanitarian activities. He spread a lot of propaganda and started false rumours. A devotee who had been following the events became restless and questioned Swamishri, "Why are you letting that person be an obstruction? He is worthless. Why don't you use your powers?"

Swamishri smiled and calmly replied, "Haste makes waste.

Swamishri prays by chanting 'Swaminarayan, Swaminarayan'.

Dhairyam • Sthairyam • Pragalbhyam • Sahaha

Bhartruhari Rishi states, "The patience of such a great person is never exhausted."

Patience is highly rewarded. God and his Sadhu are very patient and understanding. They are forgiving and are very kind."

The devotee was not convinced, "The shastras say that one who has offended God and his Sadhu lose all their merit. However, it seems as if these people are getting by just fine."

"They are getting by, but they are not at peace. Bhagwan Swaminarayan, Shastriji Maharaj, Yogiji Maharaj and the 500 *paramhansas* have always been very patient. We have to learn to be patient too. Yogiji Maharaj used to tell us to turn the *mala* when we got frustrated. We have to learn to turn the *mala* in these situations. God will get everything done. We have to learn to be patient, just as our gurus were."

Swamishri was in New York in July 1998. The devotees and sadhus had gathered around him. Jashbhai Patel from London asked Swamishri a question, "Why are God's devotees always suffering?"

"The righteous always have to suffer, but God gives them the strength to succeed. Yogiji Maharaj suffered from those around him and those against him. Even those around him were jealous. He suffered a lot, but God always gave him the strength to succeed. When Yogiji Maharaj was in Tanzania some individuals mailed derogatory propaganda flyers spreading false information. Yogiji Maharaj said, 'We do not need to respond.'"

This led to the discussion of a few incidents in which Swamishri had been unfairly insulted.

C.P. Patel called out impatiently, "Sometimes I get really worked up. I want to set them straight…"

Swamishri interrupted him, "There are a lot of people like you that want to set them straight, but Yogiji Maharaj wouldn't let them do anything. There is no reason for us to get excited."

C.P. Patel continued, "But Swamishri, you are so pure and

innocent. I can't stand it when they insult you like that."

"Let me give you an example. Imagine an elephant walking down a path and a dog starts barking. The elephant isn't going to stop, he continues walking as if he doesn't hear anything. He is confident and unperturbed. That is exactly how a true sadhu works."

Swamishri continued, "This Satsang has grown because of tolerance and patience. Satsang will grow if we tolerate."

The devotees were surprised by Swamishri's statement. This understanding was beyond human comprehension.

Explaining, Swamishri said, "Not even a dry leaf can move without God's will. Everything happens by God's will. When you respond to such things, they reply as well. We should never do anything to hurt others. God sees everything."

Sarvamangal Swami had asked Swamishri a similar question, "You always tolerate insults. You patiently listen to what people have to say. When someone insults you, I don't even feel like eating for a few days. Don't you ever get frustrated or annoyed by all these people? Don't you ever lose your temper?"

"Never. I never lose my temper. It has never bothered me." This is Swamishri's maturity and patience at its finest.

Swamishri is also patient when it comes to dealing with people and their imperfections. It takes years to change people. He patiently and persistently works at it. He encourages them, corrects them and makes it a point not to offend them. Swamishri works to perfect the moral, social and spiritual lives of thousands of individuals.

Just witnessing a single conversation between Swamishri and young Bharat will prove the point. Bharat is a youth who serves at the BAPS mandir in Bhadra.

Swamishri had just arrived in Bhadra and was going to his room after doing Thakorji's darshan. Swamishri met Bharat on the way.

"Bhar...aaat! How are you?" Swamishri asked.

Bharat sniffled long and hard before he answered, "Now that you've reminded me, I have a cold."

Swamishri lovingly asked him again and Bharat responded with a long and hard sniffle. Everyone that witnessed the incident started to laugh hysterically. They were probably entertained by the youth's foolish and childish ways, but Bharat knew that Swamishri cared about him more than anyone else around.

Bharat is mentally challenged. He stutters when he talks and has a lisp that you can't miss. Yet, his *seva* in Bhadra is unparalleled.

Swamishri recognizes this and always sits with him when he visits Bhadra. He teaches him how to act in public, talk to others and be polite.

Bhadra is the birthplace of Aksharbrahman Gunatitanand Swami. In a conversation with Bharat, Swamishri tests his satsang knowledge.

"Bharat! Who was born in this town?"

"Bhadra was born here."

Swamishri smiled and said, "No, Bharat. Gunatitanand Swami was born here. Bhadra wasn't born in Bhadra!" Swamishri made him repeat the answer five times, just as a caring mother would do to her child.

Swamishri asked him another question, "Whose *murtis* are there in our mandir?"

"The birthplace."

The nonsensical reply made everyone laugh.

Bharat was starting to get confused. Swamishri put his hand on his head lovingly and told him to repeat after him, "The first *murti* is Gunatitanand Swami. The second is Bhagwan Swaminarayan and the third is Gopalanand Swami. Now, repeat this."

Bharat repeated and Swamishri asked him again.

"Who is that first *murti* of?"

"That is Gunatitanand Swami."

Bharat was starting to pick up the names.

None of the other sadhus or devotees had ever thought of teaching Bharat the names of the *murtis*, but Swamishri believed in him. He patiently took the time out to teach him.

Swamishri instructed the local sadhus to teach Bharat the names of all the *murtis*. The rest of them thought that Bharat was mentally challenged, but Swamishri thought he was quite capable.

"At least he is willing to learn everything we teach him." Bharat experiences his mother's patience in Swamishri.

There are times when someone that is always comforting others loses his cool and patience when dealing with his own mental or physical problems. Swamishri's patience remains unrivalled.

In 1966, the *murti-pratishtha* of the mandir in Sardargadh, in the Sorath region, had been organized. There was a small group in the town that opposed, and fearing some trouble senior devotees advised Yogiji Maharaj to postpone the ceremony. Yet Yogiji Maharaj was touched by the love of the village devotees and decided to go.

Eternal Virtues

Swamishri made the necessary arrangements out of respect for Yogiji Maharaj's wishes. The *murti-pratishtha* was completed without trouble and all the devotees were overjoyed. Yogiji Maharaj and the sadhus then left the town, but a few devotees left a little later. The troublemakers decided to take advantage of the situation and started throwing stones and bricks at their cars. The devotees managed to escape and no one was seriously hurt.

When the senior devotees came to hear of the incident, they blamed Swamishri for going ahead with the plans. They rebuked him. Swamishri folded his hands and said, "I apologize. It was my fault." Swamishri didn't even mention that it was Yogiji Maharaj's decision.

This incident only became known 23 years later when Gunvant-bhai Dani wrote about it in the *Swaminarayan Prakash*. He had witnessed this incident and was extremely touched by Swamishri's ability to patiently tolerate the criticism and not say a word in return. He reminded Swamishri of the incident in Gondal.

He said, "I wrote an article on the Sardargadh *pratishtha* incident. I was just amazed by your tolerance and patience." Before Gunvant-bhai could further narrate the incident, Swamishri stopped him in mid-sentence, "I have been rebuked many times by the seniors. My only goal was to please Yogiji Maharaj. As long as he was pleased, I didn't mind tolerating anyone's criticisms."

As you can probably imagine, running a global organization requires its share of patience, stability and presence of mind. Swamishri has demonstrated all three on numerous occasions, making effective and timely decisions with a tender smile on his face.

Swamishri has often told the sadhus and devotees to pray in difficult times, "Prayer will provide peace of mind and stability. It will give us patience and show us the way."

Prayer is Swamishri's source for stability and patience. He demonstrated this following the horrific terrorist attack on Akshardham on 24 September 2002. Swamishri, then 82 years of age, was seated in a meeting in Sarangpur discussing the BAPS Charities rehabilitation work in Bhuj after the Gujarat Earthquake.

It was around 4.50 p.m. Swamishri was given the phone and told that the call was from Gandhinagar. Swamishri spoke to the sadhu on the phone and listened attentively. The sadhus gathered around Swamishri couldn't seem to understand what they were talking about. Swamishri was calm and relaxed. The phone call ended and Swamishri spoke to everyone in the room, "There has been a terrorist attack on Akshardham. There has been a lot of carnage and the terrorists are inside. Let us pray to Bhagwan Swaminarayan so that there is no more loss of life and that the terrorists are caught."

Swamishri closed his eyes and started praying to Bhagwan Swaminarayan. He started chanting the Swaminarayan mantra. The sadhus joined in.

At that time around 2,000 devotees and 250 sadhus had gathered in Sarangpur to celebrate Shastriji Maharaj's *shraddh*. Swamishri requested all of them to gather in the assembly hall and pray to Bhagwan Swaminarayan. Thousands of devotees joined in the 'pray-a-thon' in hundreds of mandirs across the world.

What is worth mentioning at this point is Swamishri's demeanour. His attitude, facial expressions and the tone of his voice were a picture of calm. At the age of 82, Swamishri was probably the most relaxed person in that room. Swamishri prayed and then engaged in a strategic conversation to discuss the next steps. His mental stability and patience helped the organization take a course of action that the whole world would appreciate.

Political and spiritual leaders from around the world called to express their condolences. Even the President of India, Dr APJ Abdul Kalam, called. Swamishri was constantly on the phone with the administrators in Gandhinagar, receiving updates and providing sound advice.

At 9.00 p.m., almost all of the tourists inside the Akshardham complex had been evacuated, though there were a few people still inside the multimedia theatre. The theatre was locked and the authorities decided to keep the victims secured inside it until dawn. The terrorists had started shooting stray bullets in the grounds outside and the authorities did not want to risk any more lives.

There was more to be done. Swamishri had an important task before him. His response would determine the future of Gujarat, if not India. Even while lying in bed Swamishri maintained his composure, praying and receiving updates from Gandhinagar.

At around 12.35 a.m., Swamishri was told that Parmeshwar Swami had fallen victim to the gunmen's bullets. Swamishri talked of his sterling *seva* for the organization and plunged into deep thought.

He knew that if the people of Gujarat were to learn that a sadhu had been killed by the Muslim terrorists, the state would flare up in riots. The simmering Hindu-Muslim sentiments would burn with redoubled fury.

Swamishri immediately made an appeal for peace. The following morning and the day after, as people turned on their television sets, flipped the dials on their radios and opened their morning papers, they noticed that Pramukh Swami Maharaj had made a very sincere appeal for peace. The result? A quiet and serene Gujarat and India.

Out of respect for the victims of the attack, India was closed for two days. Even Mumbai, which is regarded as a 'city that never sleeps' had its lights out.

Political leaders around the world closely monitored India and its western state of Gujarat. To their surprise, Pramukh Swami Maharaj's appeal for peace calmed the minds and hearts of millions of Hindus.

Analysts around the world credited Pramukh Swami Maharaj's timely and effective appeal. It wasn't that easy. Hundreds of people were boiling with anti-Muslim sentiments. Many devout Hindus were outraged by the attack on innocent pilgrims at a Hindu mandir. In response, Swamishri's soothing voice played on the airwaves and in the hearts of millions of Hindus, "Now is the time for peace and solidarity. Let us pray that such an attack is never repeated..."

A leader of a renowned organization assessed the importance of Swamishri's words, "Swamiji! This is one of those times that just a slight expression of anger on your face or even just a snap of your fingers would have set Gujarat and India on fire. I must say that your peace appeal saved Gujarat and India. The power of your spirituality and the result of your patient and stable thought process should be rewarded."

Another community activist also congratulated Swamishri, "You saved Gujarat from all out carnage and devastation..."

A reputed Kshatriya citizen from a town in the Saurashtra region disclosed his plans of a prayer assembly in his own town. Swamishri had only one piece of advice, "Make sure you speak of peace. Don't let anyone instigate or promote violence..."

A famous television news producer was also amazed at Swamishri's appeal for peace and its effect, "Pramukh Swami Maharaj's peace appeal has left most of us thinking. It was very timely and extremely effective. If someone attacks your house, you're bound to flex your muscles and try to be a 'hero'. Pramukh Swami Maharaj and his sadhus didn't mention violence or retaliation. They just spoke of peace. They weren't shocked or inactive. They produced results and touched millions of Indians around the country. It's a notable achievement."

Hundreds of letters, phone calls and emails poured in from all parts of the world, appreciating and honouring Swamishri's patient and peaceful response.

At an international Anti-Terrorism Conference in Germany,

Pramukh Swami Maharaj's pacifying and dynamic response was appreciated and used as an example. Coining it 'The Akshardham Response', strategists and political analysts acknowledged it as the most effective and efficient response to any terrorist attack.

Indian ambasador to America, Ronen Sen, was in London at the time of the attack. He recalls his initial discussion with Swamishri, "I was amazed. Your appeal for peace will never be forgotten. Everyone in Britain was worried about the repercussions, but your response was ideal. It will serve as a prototype."

Swamishri commented, "No amount of violence or bloodshed would have brought those departed souls back to life. So then why lose more innocent lives? The Sanstha has suffered a great deal too, but we had to maintain peace and be patient. Leave the rest of it to God. We are not supposed to retaliate or punish people. That is in God's hands."

New York Senator Michael Balboni is the State's Homeland Security Chief and has a lot of experience with counterterrorism initiatives. On 15 May 2004, he addressed a large public gathering at the Hofstra Arena on Long Island, "I have a lot of experience dealing with terrorism. I have learnt something from Swamishri's unique response to the terrorism in Gandhinagar, India. I have learnt that peace and tolerance are effective counterterrorism initiatives. Swamishri's response in the aftermath of the terrorist attack on Akshardham halted a cycle of violence and revenge. Swamishri gifted the state with peace and stability."

On 8 October 2002, a letter from Kaushik Joshi to the editor was published in *The Times of India* describing Swamishri's mental stability:

"In the wake of the attack on Akshardham, Pramukh Swami has shown magnanimity by not indulging in any blame game and imputing motives. Akshardham is his most priceless, splendid and wonderful creation. Yet, he has been calm. His saintliness is very touching. His heart bleeds for the helpless victims of the barbaric act..."

Shri Raghuvir Chaudhry is the President of the Gujarati Literary Association. He offered reverence at Pramukh Swami Maharaj's feet, "The attack was meant to stir communal riots and tear apart the fabric of society. The terrorists didn't succeed. Pramukh Swami Maharaj's disciples look at him with the utmost reverence. A single word of hatred or violence would have left Gujarat in a state of unimaginable devastation. I didn't see a hint of anger in his eyes. He saved hundreds of lives. He encouraged the state to pray, not punish.

Akshardham was thrown open to the public in less than a week. He revived the ancient Hindu principles of tolerance and patience. Pramukh Swami Maharaj is responsible for carrying forth our morals and values. Centuries ago, the famous poet Morarsaheb had said, 'Shānti pamāde tene to sant kahiye...' or 'A true sadhu is one that brings peace..."

A renowned Jain acharya, Pujya Shri Chandrashekharvijayji, wrote a letter to Swamishri, "My heart is intensely shocked at the terrible turmoil that was inflicted on Akshardham. To ask you what pain must have afflicted you is improper because you are a saint who lives on a *sthitpragna* level. You console devotees who come in tears to offer their condolences. This is the high level of saintliness you have."

In the Shrimad Bhagvad Gita, Arjun enquires of Shri Krishna as to how a person with a steady mind *(sthitpragna)* speaks, behaves, etc. Shri Krishna replies, *"Sukhe-dukhe same krutvā lābhālābhau jayājayau..."* A *sthitpragna* person is one who is undisturbed in happiness and misery, in gain and loss and in victory and defeat.

Pramukh Swami Maharaj's unwavering steadiness and calmness in the midst of the carnage at Akshardham and his appeal for peace thereafter is a living proof in our contemporary times of the highest Hindu wisdom prescribed in our shastras and of the great souls that lived in the past. As long as we have *sthitpragna* souls like Pramukh Swami Maharaj there will be sanity, peace and redemption in our world.

Bhagwan Shri Krishna describes a *stithapragna* or a mentally stable person to Arjun in the Shrimad Bhagvad Gita:

"One who maintains his equilibrium in happiness and sorrow, in victory and failures, in loss or gain is truly *stithapragna*..."

Swamishri's every step leaves an imprint of his *sthitpragna* ways. It inspires the ethos of a beautiful, borderless world.   ◆

कान्ति:
Kantihi
Ojaha
ओज:

Kanti is almighty God's divine beauty and splendour.
Oja is the divine glow that radiates from his face.
Devotees have described God's attractive form and
beauty in thousands of kirtans and verses.
Sadguru Premanand Swami and other sadhus
in Bhagwan Swaminarayan's time captured
his divine beauty in their verses.
The Gunatit Sadhu who beholds God also
emanates that same beauty and lustre.
This divine beauty and lustre attracts and
mystifies thousands of individuals,
leaving them with an experience beyond description.

Anyone that has had Pramukh Swami Maharaj's darshan will have experienced that divine radiance. His innocent face and sparkling eyes have pacified the hearts of millions. That beauty and lustre is beyond comparison and beyond description.

It is divine – a reflection of God.

The enlightened and elderly Sadguru Sant Swami described that divine sparkle in Swamishri's eyes on various occasions, each time as if it was the first. The following excerpt is from a taped video interview in 1985, "Shastriji Maharaj's personality and aura reminded one of Bhagwan Swaminarayan. There wasn't the slightest difference. As I look at Pramukh Swami Maharaj, I notice that his persona and aura are identical to that of Shastriji Maharaj. Shastriji Maharaj's eyes were very powerful. No one could look into his eyes with confidence. They would always lower their eyes. Even his opponents would praise his work. Pramukh Swami Maharaj is exactly the same.

"The chieftain of Gadhada brought eight government officers to meet Shastriji Maharaj. Shastriji Maharaj was 85 years old at the time. After meeting him, one of the officers confided in the chieftain,

'Look at the lustre and sparkle in his eyes. It is enchanting.'"

Pramukh Swami Maharaj has that same sparkle in his eyes. It is Godly; how else would an 87-year-old sadhu attract hundreds of thousands of children, youths and grownups alike.

His divine aura and splendour have attracted spiritual giants like Sant Swami and some of the world's brightest and most successful individuals; neither are the type to be influenced or attracted by anyone.

Professor Jaroslav Fric, known as the 'Multimedia Man' of Europe experienced Swamishri's divine *kanti*. Professor Fric lived in the Czech Republic and was known throughout the world for his pioneering work in the realm of directing and cinematography. He directed and produced the 14-screen multimedia show that was shown in the exhibitions at Swaminarayan Akshardham, Gandhinagar from 1992 to 2006.

On 19 November 1992, he was asked in an interview about his most memorable moments with Swamishri. Professor Fric's eyes welled up with tears, as he fought to regain his composure, "It is very difficult to answer this question because now the work is over and whatever that remains is spiritual connection and friendship. I can say for myself that Prof. Fric is such a man who has met scholars, kings, queens, prime ministers and presidents of many countries but never in my life have I met a dignitary like Pramukh Swami before.

Eternal Virtues

"In meeting him you feel that he is a part of the great infinity. I cannot describe him in words. He impresses not only me, but my team members too.

"While taking photographs of him, I was trying to capture his thoughts and the depth in his eyes. In all his photographs I find nothing but absolute purity, divine peace and love. This is my life's greatest experience.

"I have taken photos of Kings and great men but seventy percent I had to reject because they were not right due to tension or worry. On the other hand I had taken 600 photographs of Pramukh Swami and I could not reject any of them. Not one! It was very difficult to choose which one to use. Whenever we have met Swamiji his selfless love makes us feel that he is a great power. Forgive me, that love cannot be described in words, there's simply no definition for it."

Swamishri's *kanti* and *oja* have left many people searching for the right words. At the age of 89, Swamishri's face radiates with energy and beauty. Swamishri has never considered enhancing his natural appearance to appear photogenic or younger. His divine glow and splendour is enough to leave many individuals transfixed in his divine *murti*.

Famous Indian scientist and a notable contributor to the super computer, Dr Raghunath Mashelkar, expressed his inner feelings after his first darshan of Swamishri in New Delhi, "I touched Swamishri's feet and felt great peace. There is a tremendous divine glow that radiates from his face. I was so rejuvenated by his darshan, I felt as if someone had just added another hundred years to my lifespan."

On 27 July 2007, Swamishri flew into Morris County Airport in New Jersey following a two-hour flight from Toronto. Carl, the immigration and customs officer, had a few formalities to complete before he could let everyone disembark from the plane.

While waiting at the airport for Swamishri's arrival, the receiving sadhus had told Carl that Swamishri was an 86-year-old sadhu, and so he had expected to see a weary old man on board. But, as soon as he boarded the plane, his eyes fell on an elderly but dynamic sadhu. He had a sparkle in his eyes that was hard to comprehend. There was a glow that radiated peace and tranquillity. Carl was stunned, "He looks at ease. There is something extraordinarily different about his face. He doesn't look 86."

Swamishri's observance of eight-fold celibacy is the cause of this effervescent glow that continues to startle thousands even at this advanced age.

On 17 May 2007, the Ugandan Minister of Internal Affairs, Dr Ruhakana Rugunda came for Swamishri's darshan in Kampala. He observed, "Swamishri doesn't look 86. He looks a lot younger. It's unimaginable."

When Vijaykumar Chopra, the owner and chief editor of the *Punjab Kesari*, a respected newspaper of north India, met Swamishri in 2007 he felt a similar experience, "I would never have guessed that he is 86."

On 22 June 2007, the Board Chairperson of Dupage County, Illinois, was equally amazed by Swamishri's energetic ways and lustrous eyes. He couldn't believe that Swamishri was 86 years old.

Swamishri was addressing a satsang assembly in Singapore on 30 October 1996. John, a Chinese Christian describes his experience during that assembly, "Swamishri was turning the *mala* when I noticed how calm and relaxed his face was. It was a reflection of his mind and soul. I saw a divine aura emanating from him. I couldn't believe my eyes."

Most people that have witnessed this aura can't believe their eyes. They have trouble describing it. The only way to understand is to experience it for yourself.

Yet, when these incidents are reiterated in front of Swamishri, he radiates with a different type of glow — a glow of humility and servitude. He radiates with devotion for Bhagwan Swaminarayan.

On 3 July 2005, Swamishri was in Jamnagar, when Dr V.M. Shah, an orthopaedic surgeon, came for Swamishri's darshan.

"Your face radiates with energy and splendour even at this age. And your eyes are so powerful that I feel attracted to them."

"It is all God's grace. Everything you see is because of God."

"It is your effort that makes 'everything' possible."

"That effort is Bhagwan Swaminarayan's blessings and my guru's grace."

Swamishri's humility is his true magnificence and beauty.

In Vachanamrut, Panchala 5, Bhagwan Swaminarayan says: "Moreover, the beauty of God is such that it cannot be compared to any other object in this world – including everything from Brahman to the smallest blade of grass."

It is only natural for that same splendour and beauty to emanate from the Gunatit Sadhu. After all, God is forever present through him. ◆

Mardavam मार्दवम्

Prashrayaha प्रशयः

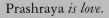

Prashraya is love.
Mardavam means a tender and affectionate intellect.
God's mardavam *and* prashraya *touch the*
lives of millions through his Gunatit Sadhu.
Pramukh Swami Maharaj's love and affection
have brought a smile to many a face.

Pramukh Swami Maharaj is pure, divine love.

He speaks with affection; he deals with affection; he walks with affection, simply put; he is affection incarnate.

He is considerate about other people's emotions and feelings. He is careful to never hurt anyone. He always notices and cares for those that everyone seems to forget.

He is very gentle and tender.

Swamishri runs a global organization, motivates thousands of volunteers, coordinates the BAPS Sanstha's activities and spiritually guides the lives of over 800 sadhus; yet, he does all this with gentle affection. He negates the Machiavellian ideology that grips most leaders: "It is better to be feared than loved…" and the common belief that leaders should be 'tough, harsh and outspoken'.

But, he is not an ordinary leader. Swamishri is a Gunatit Sadhu who guides and nourishes his devotees through his unconditional love, inspiration and encouragement. His unconditional love steers millions on the path to spirituality.

It is not in Swamishri's nature to be harsh. Even when Swamishri has to tell off someone for their own good, he feels uneasy. In certain situations, he has to be very direct and firm, but even while doing so he is careful not to hurt the other person's feelings.

"I hope I didn't hurt his feelings…" is the first thought on his mind.

Even young children are attracted by Swamishri's motherly love.

Moments later, he apologizes. He has never hesitated in apologizing to a sadhu or even a five-year-old child. He has apologized privately and sometimes in front of thousands. Swamishri respects everyone's feelings.

In 1994, Swamishri was at a spiritual camp in Karjat and spoke to the participants about discipline and living a moral and spiritual life. Swamishri was very direct and to the point. He said everything he had to. A few sadhus noticed that he was feeling uneasy, as he was not used to talking like this.

On the last day, Swamishri addressed the camp, "Please forgive me for being very direct the other day. I apologize if I have said anything to offend or hurt you..." He couldn't finish the sentence. He was moved to tears. Everyone was forever touched by his tender heart.

Swamishri's birthday celebration assembly is one of the best times to witness his heart melt in front of thousands of devotees. Swamishri asks for blessings from his devotees! He lovingly calls them and meets them as if it were their birthday.

The Amrut Mahotsav, Swamishri's 75th Birthday Celebration, in Mumbai was a prime example.

Thousands of devotees had gathered in Sion, Mumbai. For almost three hours, sadhus and devotees had narrated incidents from their lives praising Swamishri, but he was more concerned about his devotees, "You have come from different corners of the world. You have travelled a lot and must have been inconvenienced. I regret that

Eternal Virtues

I haven't been able to meet all of you personally. I know that all of you want to meet me and I want to meet you too…I am sorry." Swamishri tried hard to hold back his tears, but he couldn't any longer.

Tears filled the eyes of thousands of devotees as they watched their beloved guru fighting back tears. Swamishri continued, "It is difficult to meet everyone because there are so many people here. Don't feel left out. Though you are far from me physically, you are in my heart! God will bless all of you for your selfless services. Again, I apologize for not being able to meet you. I am sorry. I ask all of you to bless me so that I am able to please all of the sadhus and devotees. Pray to Bhagwan Swaminarayan so that I can please all of you…"

Everyone in that assembly remembers those moments. Swamishri's genuine love filled the void of not being able to meet the devotees personally.

There is one very important reason he is able to equally love all his devotees. He sees Bhagwan Swaminarayan in their hearts. He believes that hurting their feelings would cause pain to Bhagwan Swaminarayan. That is the spiritual source for his love and tenderness.

Many people ask: What is it about Pramukh Swami Maharaj that attracts educated youths to follow his commands and dedicate their lives to serving society?

What is it about his smile and voice that attracts thousands of children?

What is it about his personality that makes people from all walks of life love him more than life itself?

Toddlers, teenagers, labourers, tribal villagers, farmers, established businessmen, executives, political leaders and spiritual leaders all feel a sense of belonging and attraction to him. Why?

The answer: Pramukh Swami Maharaj's unconditional love.

The BAPS National Youth Convention 2007 at the Hyatt Regency in Jacksonville, Florida, was one such experience. During the convention 8,000 children, teenagers and youths experienced Swamishri's unconditional love. The experience ended with thousands of moist eyes.

"That's it? We have to leave you? When will we see you again?"

Thousands of voices echoed the same questions as Swamishri departed for Toronto.

Yagnesh Devani, a successful young entrepreneur, experienced the same heartbreak when Swamishri left his house in Mombasa, "Why don't you stay here forever? When will I experience these moments of unconditional love again?"

Swamishri was leaving Bochasan. All the devotees gathered around Swamishri for his last darshan. All except for one. Manibhai of Thasra was sitting in the corner. He hadn't moved. Swamishri walked towards him and put his hand on his head. Manibhai was blind. Manibhai asked who it was and he heard the familiar soothing voice, "It's me. Pramukh Swami."

Manibhai was in tears. He was lost for words. He cried his heart out as Swamishri lovingly caressed his head.

The elderly gentleman would always remember this day.

Swamishri was travelling in the tribal village of Chuli, on the banks of the River Narmada. Neemabhai had been waiting for Swamishri for years. He wanted Swamishri to grace his hut.

In 1998, Swamishri walked into his hut. The hut had a straw roof and the walls and floors were made of cow dung. Swamishri ducked through the main door and called out, "Neemabhai. I am here. Come, let me bless your hut."

Neemabhai had prepared some *adadna vada* and offered them to Swamishri. Swamishri offered them to Harikrishna Maharaj and ate a small piece. Neemabhai was in tears, overjoyed. He said, "How will I ever be able to repay your kindness? Your love is beyond all social barriers."

When US President Bill Clinton first met Swamishri in October 2000, he forgot the cup of coffee in his hand as

"The first time Pramukh Swami met me in Miami, I saw in his eyes that he is a man who has not come ahead by eclipsing others. He has come forward by always placing others before him. And that is why I had a deep desire to meet him again."

- Bill Clinton
former US President

Eternal Virtues

his eyes locked with Swamishri's eyes. He could feel the love and affection in Swamishri's voice. The experience left a lasting impact.

Then, on 4 April 2001, he visited Swaminarayan Akshardham, Gandhinagar, in Swamishri's presence. After a tour of the complex, President Clinton was coming down the stairs at the front of the monument with Swamishri. He was overcome with a sudden urge to speak. Just two or three steps left, President Clinton started talking to a few of the sadhus, "Ever since I met him in Miami, I was moved. When I look into his eyes, they are filled with integrity," he said.

The president sat on a nearby seat to put his shoes on. Swamishri was standing in front of him as President Clinton continued, "See, there are too many leaders, religious groups and people in this world who believe that by pulling others down, you can bring yourself up. And by discounting others, isolating or segregating them... but (pointing to Swamishri) he is different! Swamiji connects. He connects with others and everyone around him. He works through connectivity. That is why he has been able to bring peace and harmony and so many people together."

President Clinton continued to speak, "The first time Pramukh Swami met me in Miami, I saw in his eyes that he is a man who has not come ahead by eclipsing others. He has come forward by always placing others before him. And that is why I had a deep desire to meet him again."

He looked at Swamishri, patted the empty seat next to him and requested Swamishri to join him. Swamishri smiled and sat next to him. President Clinton leaned back on the sofa and made himself comfortable. The scorching afternoon sun was shining down on them, but President Clinton was in no rush to leave. He said, "In order to embrace what they believe they have to reject other people and their convictions. And he (Swamishri) is the person I have met who is trying to go beyond all that. And I believe that the great challenge of the world is to find that sort of integrity; to be able to celebrate your own religion, celebrate your own race or ethnic group, but still embrace our common humanity and our common connection to God is more important."

The sadhus asked him if he had experienced something special when he met Swamishri in Miami.

"Most definitely. I have read about him as well. I am sure all of you have experienced what I just described on numerous occasions."

The Secret Service agents accompanying the President were surprised that he chose to sit on the couch in the hot afternoon sun.

Affection more tender than a flower...

They were falling behind on their schedule too. They tried to hint the time restraint to President Clinton, but he was busy praising Swamishri.

President Clinton placed his hands in Swamishri's hands and experienced his affection. He didn't remove his hand until he was reminded to get up by his staff. The plain sofas, the crowd of people, the ignored security protocol and the blistering sun went unnoticed as President Clinton continued to speak of Swamishri.

Finally, George, the Chief of the Secret Service Detail, reminded the President that they had other engagements. President Clinton didn't mind the heat and the traditional setting; it seemed as if he was trying to squeeze out every extra second of Swamishri's affectionate presence. President Clinton wanted to stay, "Just when you are starting to have the time of your life, you have to leave."

Swamishri's loving persona has worked wonders.

In 1991, Ron Patel, the Sunday Editor of the *Philadelphia Inquirer* came to meet Swamishri. He was skeptical and cynical at first, but was impressed by Swamishri's love and affection.

In 1992, he accepted Swamishri's invitation and visited the land of his father for the first time. Swamishri organized his trip around India. Swamishri had looked after him like a father. He helped him strengthen his ties with his ancestral roots. He published a feature story about his trip to India in the *Philadelphia Inquirer*.

Eternal Virtues

In 1998, after Swamishri's bypass surgery, he sent a 'get-well soon' card, "You have given me the love of a father and a mother. You are my father and you are my mother. You are my family. May you live forever."

Swamishri's unconditional love changed the life of an atheist. For Ron Patel, Swamishri's love was the ultimate in divinity.

Meet Chatur! He was born deaf and mute and serves in the printing department at Swaminarayan Aksharpith in Ahmedabad. Swamishri's love for him is beyond description. Chatur will never be able to explain it to us, but the smiles and tears on his face say it all.

Surprisingly, Chatur understands everything Swamishri says and Swamishri understands Chatur's grunts and sighs. They speak the language of love. Sadhus and devotees gather to see the amiable exchanges between the two. It has brought tears to many eyes.

As the wintry cold sets in on London, hundreds of children and youths gather in the assembly hall for Swamishri's darshan. They have been serving in various departments all day and haven't been able to have his darshan. At around 10.00 p.m., Swamishri would enter the hall for five minutes or so and everyone's hearts would race with joy.

The next five minutes would fly by in a flash as Swamishri would walk back towards his room. But that was enough. Five minutes of his unconditional love was enough to keep the youths going until the next night. A popular community leader witnessed the scene one night and said, "No wonder, thousands of youths are attracted to him. He loves them unconditionally."

Little toddlers and children are also attracted to Swamishri's motherly love. They run up to him and hug him. Swamishri tends to their emotions.

Abhay Jaiswal had come for Swamishri's darshan with his uncle. The six-year-old boy chatted freely with Swamishri. Somewhere in the middle of that conversation, he asked Swamishri to grace his home, "Why don't you come to Karvan? We can have so much fun together."

On 3 March 1997, Swamishri was in Por in Vadodara district. He had finalized his programme for the two days, but the next two days after that remained a mystery. He kept it a secret even from his attendant sadhus.

On the morning of departure from Por, Swamishri told the sadhus that he wanted to go to Karvan. He arrived in the town and went to Abhay's house. No one had remembered the boy's invitation, except of course, Swamishri. Swamishri dedicated those two days for young Abhay Jaiswal.

In 1990, Swamishri was travelling in the tribal district of Panchmahal. Five-year-old Shambhu requested him to grace his hut.

Shambu was overjoyed to see Swamishri come to his hut and teach him how to perform Harikrishna Maharaj's *arti*. Shambhu would relive that day with each passing moment in his life.

Swamishri's love and care for all takes a variety of forms. Bhaskar Mehta had lost his father as an infant. Swamishri walked him through life, leading him in the right direction. Bhaskar was bent on becoming a sadhu, but Swamishri instructed him not to, reasoning, "Who will take care of your mother?"

Swamishri convinced him to get married and Swamishri asked a few devotees to start looking for a compatible match. Swamishri spoke to the bride's family, arranging the dates and logistics as any father would.

There was only one small problem. Bhaskar couldn't afford to pay for the wedding. Swamishri called him, "Don't worry about the wedding. I am coming to Bharuch soon. I will take care of everything. I will arrange your wedding while I am there. We will set up the ceremony in an assembly hall and we will feed all the guests along with the devotees. It will work out perfectly."

Swamishri also spoke to the bride's family, but her brother, Samir, was a bit hesitant in letting the Sanstha take up the cost of the wedding, "We can't take the Sanstha's money like this."

Swamishri explained, "Don't worry about all that. Your father and uncle have done so much for this Sanstha, it is my duty to look after your family. Don't worry about the cost right now. Think of it as a gift from God."

Swamishri instructed the local sadhus and devotees to help organize the wedding. It was celebrated with grandeur. Bhaskar's father had left him when he could barely walk and the bride's father had died in an accident. Swamishri filled their fathers' void – his care and concern would grace them for eternity.

Sadhus that have given their lives for Swamishri's humanitarian and spiritual activities have experienced his unconditional love too. There are enough stories to fill several books. Swamishri has guided and nourished them time and again. They will never forget.

Swamishri is especially caring when a sadhu is not well. Swamishri is the first to jump at a chance to serve, everything from arranging for medical care to preparing his meals.

Swamishri had looked after Sarvamangal Swami's needs for two years as he was recovering from a serious illness.

Yogamuni Swami, when he was a young and newly-initiated sadhu, hurt his leg while doing *seva* and had developed a serious infection. While he was in Sarangpur, Swamishri would make it a point to go and see him twice-daily in his medical room.

Balmukund Swami and Tyagvallabh Swami also experienced Swamishri's loving care when they fell ill. Recalling that experience, Tyagvallabh Swami writes about it with a feeling of great gratitude, "I realized how much Swamishri loves me. He thinks of me more than I can ever think of him. He loves me an infinite times more than I will ever be able to love him. This helped me realize that Swamishri has given me more than I have earned. I do not want anything else. He has given me everything with his unconditional love."

Swamishri's love for sadhus shows from the attention he pays to the smallest details in their lives.

In 1980, a large assembly had been organized at Kenyatta Hall in Nairobi. Narayanmuni Swami and another sadhu had come to the venue a few hours before Swamishri to help prepare for the event. As soon as the assembly ended, Swamishri called Narayanmuni Swami and the other sadhu near the stage. He instructed them to go back to the devotee's house and have their dinner, "Tomorrow is Ekadashi. Make sure you go early and have your meal."

Swamishri made arrangements for a car to take them to the devotee's house. He had already set aside food for them.

His love is aptly described by this verse: "*Het to kare che evu anant janani jevu...*", meaning, "His love is equal to that of infinite mothers..."

Devotees suffering from a serious illness in hospital, usually have one wish – Swamishri's darshan. When Swamishri hears about a devotee's illness, he makes changes in his travel plans to visit the hospital.

Ratansinh from Radhu was suffering from a terrible skin disorder and had been admitted to a hospital in Nadiad. His whole body was paining from the illness. Doctors refused to touch his pus-filled body and even his wife had trouble coming near him.

A few days later, Ratansinh received word that Swamishri was coming to see him. He was overjoyed. As he was struggling to sit up in his bed, Swamishri arrived and sat on the bed. He soothed him and prayed for his recovery.

From the very young to the elderly, Swamishri showers his love unconditionally

"Everything is going to be fine. Bhagwan Swaminarayan will completely cure you," he said passing his hand over his body.

Ratansinh sat in his bed speechless and in tears. Swamishri cared for him more than he could imagine. In a matter of days, Ratansinh began to recover. The doctors were amazed at the rate of progress. In a few weeks, no one would have guessed that he had had such a severe illness. Ratansinh didn't understand if that skin disorder was a severe disease or a blessing in disguise.

Dahyabhai was suffering from terminal cancer. Imagine his surprise when Swamishri suddenly came to his house in Limbasi one night at 9 o'clock.

Returning to Bochasan from a newly opened cattle camp in Bhavanpura, Swamishri instructed his long-time driver, Indravadan, to turn the car at an unfamiliar crossing. Indravadan knew that this wasn't the road to Bochasan, but he complied. After a few kilometres, Swamishri's car pulled up in Limbasi. Weaving through the narrow streets of the town, Swamishri finally found Dahyabhai's house and he knocked on his door. Dahyabhai was startled to see Swamishri standing at the door.

"Swamishri! What are you doing in Limbasi this late at night?"

Swamishri smiled and walked into the house. Swamishri put his hand on his head and blessed him. After talking to him for a while, Swamishri took his leave and left for Bochasan.

Dahyabhai stood on his porch with tears in his eyes as he watched Swamishri's car drive away.

Swamishri's unconditional love had made those moments of Dahyabhai's life eternal.

Swamishri doesn't stop there. His love follows you to Akshar-dham. In Jaykrishnabhai Patel's case, that sentence has a literal meaning.

In 1990, Swamishri was in Colchester, England's oldest town. From there, he was scheduled to do a *padhramani* at P.N. Morjariya's house in London. Before leaving, he made a few unusual arrangements. He made arrangements for two separate cars; one for Harikrishna Maharaj and the other sadhus and the second for himself and an attendant. He also instructed the sadhus to put Harikrishna Maharaj's water jug and his *pagh* in the other car.

The sadhus were confused, but they carried out the instructions. Swamishri completed the visit to Morjariya's house. Then he asked the driver of the other car with Harikrishna Maharaj to return to the mandir, and told his driver, Arun Kumar, to take the car towards south London; he needed to get there on time.

Arun Kumar's car sped through the streets of London, arriving at a particular destination. Arun Kumar's eyes widened as he noticed that they had come to a funeral home in the middle of a cemetery. The parking lot was empty, as was the funeral home. Swamishri got out of the car and sat on a bench in the cemetery. He waited for 45 minutes, reading the names on the tombstones.

The attendant sadhu and Arun Kumar were still trying to figure out what they were doing here. Soon it became obvious.

A small group of family members arrived for Jaykrishnabhai's final rites. They were surprised to see Swamishri there.

"When did you get here? I didn't even know you were coming!" cried Jaykrishnabhai's son.

A few days ago, Jaykrishnabhai had called Swamishri while he was in Crawley, "Please take me to Akshardham. Come bless me at my cremation rites." Swamishri had given him his word.

Jaykrishnabhai was from Bhadran. When Swamishri was just 21 and studying Sanskrit in Bhadran, Jaykrishnabhai's father, Ishwarbhai, had served Swamishri. Jaykrishnabhai was in Africa at the time, but Swamishri had continued to shower the family with his affection.

That is why Swamishri arrived unannounced at Jaykrishnabhai's funeral. Swamishri is a true friend. Swamishri performed the final rites for Jaykrishnabhai's mortal body and also offered his final respects. He helped push the coffin into the crematorium and cremated Jaykrishnabhai.

Jaykrishnabhai's body was reduced to ashes in a matter of minutes, but Swamishri's affection would live forever in his soul.

Such is Swamishri's unconditional and everlasting love.

Such is Swamishri's flower-like tenderness.

He loves everyone and that is why everyone loves him.　◆

Swamishri addresses the Peace Summit at the UN assembly hall, August 2000, New York

Kirtihi Manaha
कीर्तिः   मानः

Kirti *is fame.*
Mana *is being worthy of worship and reverence.*
God is adored, respected and
worshipped throughout the universe.
The same is true for the Gunatit Sadhu.
He does not work for it nor does he desire it.
It is his oneness with God that earns him fame,
reverence and praise.
He is respected and adored by all.
From the United Nations to the smallest
tribal villages of Gujarat, Swamishri has been
showered with praises and respect.
The true reason behind his fame is his pure, divine character.
Countless world, spiritual and community leaders
have expressed their admiration for Swamishri.
The following is a selection of just a few...

People around the world are starting to realize that power and material objects do not yield peace. They are turning to spirituality and religion to fill a void in their lives. Religion and spirituality is the key. Your sadhus are setting an example of content, co-existence and selfless service. There is an ideal for all of mankind. His name is Pramukh Swami Maharaj.

- The Dalai Lama

Pramukh Swami Maharaj is always considerate, simple and humble. He leads a multinational organization, yet is always relaxed. He is as light as a flower. He is able to do so because he has surrendered himself to

With Pujya Swami Chidanandji,
Divya Jivan Sangh

With Pujya Swami Chinmayanandji,
Chinmaya Mission

With Pujya Ranganathanandji,
Ramakrishna Mission

With Jain Acharya Pujya Muni Shri
Shushilkumarji

With The Dalai Lama, 1985

With Pujya Vishveshtirthji,
Madhvacharya, Pejavar Math

With sadhus of the Akhil Bharat Sadhu Samaj, 1981

With the Late Pope John Paul II, 1984

With Dr Firoze Kotwal, Parsi Religious
Leader

With Dr Y. Nizamuddin, Daoudi Vohra
Religious Leader

With Chief Rabbi Baksi Doron

Bhagwan Swaminarayan. He continues to serve society with the aim to please God. He thinks nothing of himself. He is just a means. God works through him.

- Pujya Swami Shri Chidanand Saraswatiji
Divya Jivan Sangh, Rishikesh

Spiritual progress and liberation can only be attained in the company of a God-realized sadhu. Pramukh Swami Maharaj is a God-realized sadhu. His presence rids people of their materialistic desires.

-Pujya Swami Chinmayanandji
Chinmaya Mission

Pramukh Swami Maharaj's life is an extraordinary example of love and harmony. If the entire nation were to take a cue from him and live by those standards, it would solve all of our problems. He has sacrificed in the true sense.

- Acharya Mahapragnaji
Jain Acharya, Terapanth

Pramukh Swami Maharaj's life is an example of spiritual beauty. That beauty shines throughout India and the world as he continues to guide mankind on the path to spirituality. He loves unconditionally and forgives. Revenge and vengeance are never to be seen in his life. This is illustrated in his credo: "In the joy of others lies our own…"

- Dr Rowan Williams
Archbishop of Canterbury

Pramukh Swami Maharaj's humility and selfless love have touched my heart.

- HRH Prince Charles
The Prince of Wales

When I look into his eyes, they are filled with integrity. I saw in his eyes that he is a man who has not come ahead by eclipsing others. He has come forward by always placing others before him.

- President Bill Clinton
Former President,
United States of America

With HRH Prince Charles,
The Prince of Wales

With Former US President Bill Clinton, 2000

With Former Prime Minister of
UK Tony Blair

With HRH Prince Phillip,
The Duke of Edinburgh, 1997

With President of Israel Shimon Peres

With Former Secretary-General of the United Nations Kofi Annan, 2000

With The Right Honourable Stephen J.
Harper, Prime Minister of Canada, 2007

With HH Sheikh Isa Bin Salaam al
Khalifa, Bahrain, 1997

With Saiyad Saif Bin Hamad, Diwan of
the Sultanate of Oman

With HH Sheikh Khalifa Bin Salman al
Khalifa, Prime Minister of Bahrain

Eternal Virtues

I feel a very strong and divine aura in his presence. I feel at peace in his presence. I forget about all my worries and difficulties. He truly loves people unconditionally. That is why he is able to counsel and take part in their difficulties and problems. Their problems become his problems. I can see it in him.

- **Dr A.P.J. Abdul Kalam**
Former President of India

You are safeguarding Indian culture. I have heard and read a great deal about you. Today, I realize that it is all true. You are culturally, morally and socially changing our country. You have inspired some of the nation's greatest engineers, technologists, scientists and philosophers to give back to the community. Only God can inspire them. He inspires them through you.

- **Giani Zail Singh**
Former President of India

I had the fortune to meet Pramukh Swami Maharaj ten years ago. I was impressed then and I am impressed now. I experience spirituality like never before. It is unique. Bhagwan Swaminarayan's spirit of social reform is living through Pramukh Swami Maharaj.

- **Tony Blair**
Former Prime Minister,
United Kingdom

Ancient India was known for its sadhus, sages and sadgurus. Out of all the sadhus in India, Pramukh Swami Maharaj is different. There is no doubt about his work. It rises above the rest. This is not specific to India; it is known all over the world. He is the walking and talking form of India's spirituality and morality.

- **Lal Krishna Advani**
Former Deputy Prime Minister of India

Swamishri's pure heart never ceases to amaze me. I have interviewed many celebrities and figureheads throughout my career as a journalist, but there is something different about Pramukh Swami Maharaj. It's his simplicity and transparency. There is no mal-intent in his answers. It is pure. He is selfless and humble.

- **Ron Patel**
Sunday Editor,
Philadelphia Inquirer

With Dr A.P.J. Abdul Kalam, former President of India

With Prime Minister Manmohan Singh and Lal Krishna Advani, Leader of the Opposition Party, 2005

With Jomo Kenyatta, founding Father and President of Kenya, 1974

With Giani Zail Singh, former President of India, 1985

Honoured at the Canadian Parliament, 1988

Honoured at the House of Commons in the British Parliament, 1988

With Julius Nyerere, former President of Tanzania, 1977

With Yoweri Museveni, former President of Uganda, 1997

With Vasudev Pandey, former Prime Minister of Trinidad, 1988

Eternal Virtues

Pramukh Swami Maharaj has given so much to mankind. It is indescribable. I have gained so much from his darshan, his blessings and that simple dialogue with him. Meeting such a God-realized sadhu gives meaning to one's life.

Bhagwan Shri Krishna says in the Shrimad Bhagvad Gita that he always manifests in the different ages. He is present today through Swamishri. His personality is as pure as the waters of the Ganga. Every time I meet him, I feel like I am bathing in the holy waters of the Ganga.

- **L. M. Singhvi**
Former Indian High Commissioner in the
United Kingdom

Despite being the President of BAPS, I have seen Swamishri perform menial *seva* in Sarangpur. 'I am the President of this organization. I cannot perform such ordinary tasks.' This kind of pride doesn't exist even in the deepest corner of his mind. He doesn't have the slightest trace of ego. He sees God in all.

- **Justice B.J. Diwan**
Chief Justice,
Gujarat High Court

Swaminarayan Akshardham, New Delhi, is one of the contemporary Seven Wonders of the World. In fact, it is the best! It is beyond my imagination. This is one of Pramukh Swami Maharaj's miracles. No emperor, king, government or international organization can create such a marvel. Every company, organization and government can learn a lot from this creation.

- **D.R. Karthikeyan**
Director General,
National Human Rights Commission

Pramukh Swami Maharaj is a great spiritual leader. I have met him quite a few times and each time I experience peace. Very few people's presence gives you that feeling. It is a feeling of spiritual elevation. Swamishri's presence has a mesmerizing effect. What surprises me the most is his ability to motivate and inspire so many people. It is always a pleasure and fortune to have his darshan.

- **Dr R. Chidambaram**
Chairman,
Atomic Energy Commission, India

Creating a moral society is at the foundation of building a successful nation. Pramukh Swami Maharaj is doing this through BAPS. He is working to build a society with strong values and a pure character. He is doing an extraordinary job instilling those values in children and youths. I call that developing the nation. Moulding the character of one youth is equivalent to shaping a nation.

- Nani Palkhivala
Prominent Indian Jurist and Economist

Pramukh Swami Maharaj is ultimate divinity.

- Sudarshan Birla
Industrialist,
Birla Industries

Along with his spiritual activities, Pramukh Swami Maharaj has contributed a lot to society through his social initiatives. His work is immeasurable. I bow my head in reverence to his contributions to society and mankind.

- Ramakrishna Bajaj
Industrialist,
Bajaj Group of Industries

◆

Pramukh Swami Maharaj consecrates the murti of Bhagwan Swaminarayan in Swaminarayan Akshardham, 6 November 2005, New Delhi

आस्तिक्यम् *Astikyam*

Astikta is the belief that God exists.
God infuses astikta *in the hearts of his devotees.*
God is the source from which an aspirant develops
true conviction in God.
You cannot form a sentence without a subject.
Similarly, God is the sole basis of spirituality.

With that said, *astikta* has many meanings.

God is the all-doer. Even when the entire creation is destroyed a devotee should remember that God still exists and has a divine form.

God is present in the eight types of *murtis*. He blesses the devotees and fulfils their wishes.

Also, *astikta* includes faith in the word of God, the Vedas and other spiritual texts.

These are all aspects of *astikta*.

The Gunatit Sadhu is nearest to God. Therefore, he is the ideal *astik* devotee. He has experienced and realized God; he lives *astikta*. Swamishri sees God in everyone and everything. Swamishri has immeasurable faith and conviction in God's *murtis*. He knows that they are not merely a symbol or form of God. In fact, he knows that God is present in the *murtis*!

The *murti* of Shri Harikrishna Maharaj he worships and serves daily is dearer to him than life.

In 1988 in Zimbabwe a TV reporter, Moses Fisi, pointed at the *murti* of Harikrishna Maharaj and asked, "What is that a symbol of?"

Swamishri replied, "This is not a symbol. This is Bhagwan Swaminarayan. He inspires us and guides us in everything that we do. We worship him. He fulfils the devotees' wishes and looks after their wellbeing. God is omnipresent, but he is always present in this *murti*. We offer everything to him before we use it."

Swamishri's faith in *murtis* is evident through this dialogue.

Just observing Swamishri serve and worship Bhagwan Swaminarayan instills *astikta* in others.

Harikrishna Maharaj is the small metallic *murti* of Bhagwan Swaminarayan that Swamishri keeps with him wherever he travels. Also referred to as 'Thakorji', the *murti* was initially from Junagadh. Aksharbrahman Gunatitanand Swami used to worship the same *murti*. When Yogiji Maharaj left Junagadh, he was granted permission to take the *murti* with him. Yogiji Maharaj served the *murti* until he passed away to Akshardham on 23 January 1971. Since then, Swamishri has served the *murti* with the conviction that God is manifest within.

Thakorji is Swamishri's life. His existence is centred around Thakorji. He offers everything to him before he eats, drinks or uses it.

Swamishri keeps Thakorji in the forefront when he is honoured, or when he is inaugurating something. Grand celebrations and even *padhramanis* are performed with Thakorji as the centre of attention. Everything in this world is Thakorji's. Swamishri believes that everything is due to his grace and blessings.

In 1988, Swamishri was getting ready to go to a satsang assembly at a local community centre in Atlanta. A devotee walked up to Swamishri and demanded to meet him. He was building a motel and wanted Swamishri's blessings. He had brought some soil from his property in a cloth. He wanted Swamishri to step on it and consecrate it.

Swamishri called Brahmatirth Swami and told him to bring Thakorji. Before the attendant sadhus could figure out what was going on, Swamishri sat down on the floor, took Thakorji into his hands and placed him on the soil. He chanted the *dhun* and placed flower petals on the soil. He told the devotee that the motel would turn out perfect because Thakorji had consecrated it.

The devotee was overjoyed, but more importantly, this incident showed Swamishri's unflinching devotion to and faith in Bhagwan Swaminarayan.

Once, Swamishri was in Ahmedabad after Diwali to celebrate the Prabhodini Ekadashi. Prabhashankar Pandya got up to make an announcement in the assembly, "The devotees of Ahmedabad offer this *seva* to Swamishri today..."

Swamishri interrupted him, "The *seva* is not for 'Swamishri', it is for Thakorji. Please announce that the *seva* is being offered to Thakorji. I am nobody. All of this is Thakorji's. It exists because of

Swamishri meditates upon Shri Harikrishna Maharaj and his gurus during his morning puja

his grace. I am a servant; you cannot offer anything to me. You can only offer it to God."

The Canadian Parliament had decided to honour Swamishri in 1988. Swamishri arrived at the Parliament with Thakorji. The Speaker of the Parliament announced Swamishri's presence to the MPs and requested him to stand, "With us today is a great Hindu sadhu. Please join me in welcoming His Divine Holiness Pramukh Swami Maharaj."

The MPs applauded, but to everyone's surprise, Swamishri did not stand. Swamishri told Nirbhayswarup Swami to stand up first with Thakorji in his hands. Swamishri then stood up for a brief moment, folded his hands and then resumed his seat

Why didn't Swamishri stand up first? The answer was obvious to everyone around him. In Swamishri's mind he wasn't being honoured. The Parliament was honouring his beloved Thakorji.

The Mayor of Nairobi had come to present Swamishri the Key to the City. As he walked to Swamishri to present him with the Key, Swamishri led him by the hand and brought him to Thakorji. He told the Mayor to offer it to Thakorji first and then accepted it.

Similar incidents occurred at the British Parliament, the United Nations Millennium World Peace Summit, and the Suvarna Tula Celebrations at Alexandra Palace in London. In fact, there have been countless such incidents.

Swamishri offers abhishek to Shri Harikrishna Maharaj, Mombasa

On 5 June 1977, Swamishri was leaving Mumbai for London. He was flying aboard the Air India jumbo 'Samrat Ashok'. Hundreds of people had gathered at the airport for the last darshan of their guru before he left.

At around 1.25 a.m., the Airport Manager and the Captain requested Swamishri to board the flight. They escorted him to the plane and asked him to board first. Swamishri hesitated and looked around. Once again, the Captain requested Swamishri to board first. Swamishri waited for a few more moments and Thakorji arrived. Swamishri told the attendant sadhu with Thakorji to board first.

Swamishri smiled at the officers and then boarded the plane. Though they were treating Swamishri like a celebrity, in Swamishri's eyes, Thakorji was the only celebrity.

Swamishri believes that God is manifest in the *murti* of Harikrishna Maharaj. Why else would he always introduce him to the likes of Indian President Kalam, American President Bill Clinton, Prince Charles, Sheikh Isa Bin Salman of Bahrain, the late Pope John Paul II and the Dalai Lama.

In 1978, the second Kenyan President, Daniel Arap Moi came to meet Swamishri at a satsang assembly in Kenyatta Hall. The concert of devotional songs ended and President Moi came to receive Swamishri's blessings before leaving. As he was walking away, Swamishri called out to him and led him to Harikrishna Maharaj. He introduced President Moi to Harikrishna Maharaj and taught him how to do darshan.

One can only wonder what President Moi was thinking, but one thing was for sure – Swamishri's faith in Bhagwan Swaminarayan was unquestionable.

Swamishri always shows his reverence for Thakorji. If at times Thakorji's seat is lower than his, Swamishri immediately instructs, "This isn't right! God is almighty. We are his servants, so make sure his seat is higher than mine."

Swamishri was doing *padhramanis* in Vadadala. He arrived at a devotee's house, where there was only one seat. Swamishri immediately instructed the sadhus to seat Thakorji on the chair, while he sat on the floor with the sadhus.

Swamishri was inaugurating the newly built air-conditioned J.J. Market in Surat. He arrived on the stage and noticed that there was a lavish seat for him and a very simple one for Thakorji. Swamishri told the attendant sadhu to place Thakorji on the seat originally meant for him while he sat on the plain one. It was only after the devotees decorated Thakorji's seat that Swamishri took his seat.

His reverence for Thakorji is obvious at photo sessions too. He always ensures that Thakorji is clearly visible in the picture.

Swamishri was in Kunpad in Vadodara district. All the devotees wanted to take a group picture with Swamishri. They were so excited that they gathered around Swamishri and accidentally covered Thakorji. Swamishri told them, "Make sure you get Thakorji in the picture. Everyone is so worried about how they will look in the picture that they forget Thakorji. All of our success and achievements are due to him. Don't forget that."

When devotees or sadhus make a special food dish for Swamishri and say that it is specially made for him, Swamishri dissuades them, "Don't make anything special for me. Make it for Thakorji."

Swamishri never accepts anything that hasn't been offered to Thakorji first, even if it is only a glass of water. He often tells sadhus, "If you eat something without offering it to Thakorji, it is as good as eating dirt."

Swamishri circumbulates the memorial shrine of Yogiji Maharaj, Gondal

Once, Swamishri was exhausted from travelling all day. He arrived in Mahelav at about 8.00 p.m. The devotees had organized a procession around the village. Though Swamishri was extremely tired, he got onto the tractor and pleased the many devotees who were present. Nearing the end of the procession, a devotee extended his hands to garland Swamishri. Swamishri grabbed his hand and said, "Offer it to Thakorji first and then to me."

Swamishri remembers Thakorji even amidst chaos.

On Sunday 17 April 1988, the youths in London had something special in mind for Swamishri's entry into their assembly.

"We want you to sit in a *palkhi* and come to our assembly."

Swamishri refused, "It's not right for me to sit in a *palkhi* in front of Thakorji. Place Harikrishna Maharaj in the *palkhi*, I will walk…"

C.M. Patel, President of the London Satsang Mandal, requested Swamishri on behalf of the youths, "Swamishri! These youths have worked really hard to organize everything. It would really please them."

Swamishri would not budge. When they persisted, he said, "You can carry me out from here to the door, but not into the assembly. Is that okay?"

The youths were not satisfied, "The point is to welcome you into our assembly, not just upto the door."

C.M. Patel tried to convince Swamishri. The discussion continued for quite a while. Eventually, Swamishri relented, but laid down the terms, "I will sit with Harikrishna Maharaj, and you have to promise me that you will not lift the *palkhi* more than one foot off the ground."

The youths quickly agreed before Swamishri changed his mind.

Swamishri was skeptical, "What if you do raise it up to your shoulders?"

"You have a lot of strength. Weigh down the *palkhi*, so that we cannot lift it," the youths joked.

"You lose all your strength once you start flying too high. We should always show our reverence to Thakorji and the mandir," Swamishri replied.

Swamishri agreed to enter the assembly in a *palkhi*, but only very reluctantly.

The next day, he was carried into the assembly seated in a *palkhi*, holding Harikrishna Maharaj in his lap. He looked down and was uneasy the whole time. He breathed better after the youths put the *palkhi* down at the side of the stage. Swamishri could be seen praying to Thakorji for forgiveness, for what he believed was a grave mistake.

Swamishri is very particular about performing Thakorji's *seva* on time. He becomes concerned whenever sadhus are late in offering *thal*, putting Thakorji to bed or even offering him water. Swamishri takes care of Thakorji as he would serve Bhagwan Swaminarayan himself.

If anyone tries to commend him on his devotion towards Thakorji, he says, "I don't do anything for Thakorji. He provides for us. Who are we to take care of him? He takes care of us."

Swamishri cares for Thakorji even when his own health is not too good.

In 1980, after his cataract surgery, Swamishri was being wheeled out of the operating theatre on a stretcher. His first words, "Have you put Thakorji to rest? It is already time."

In 1978, Swamishri was extremely ill at Vyara. He had a high fever and was sleeping because of the effect of the medication. At around 12.30 p.m. he got up and asked the sadhus, "Have you offered *thal* to Thakorji? It is time."

In 1998, Dr Jeffrey Moses and Dr William Schwarz completed Swamishri's angiography at the Lenox Hill Hospital in New York. They urged for an emergency bypass operation. Dr Subramanium was

Swamishri absorbed in darshan of Shri Harikrishna Maharaj and his gurus while doing mala in his morning puja

called and he prepared himself for the operation. In the meantime, Swamishri had been fully examined and prepared for the major surgery. The time was 11.30 a.m. Swamishri decided to go in for surgery at 3.00 p.m. The physicians explained that it was not a good idea to delay. They should perform the bypass as soon as possible. Still, Swamishri insisted to wait till 3.00 p.m. The doctors accepted Swamishri's wish. So, Swamishri waited in his ICU room as sadhus read the *Haricharitramrut Sagar* and sang bhajans.

At exactly 3.00 p.m., Swamishri entered the operation theatre with Thakorji at his side. Arrangements had been made for Thakorji to be seated near him. It was a major operation, but everyone breathed a sigh of relief after it was completed successfully.

After two weeks, while Swamishri was recovering at Dr Mahendrabhai's house in Westchester, the sadhus asked why he had insisted on waiting until 3.00 p.m. to begin the operation.

Swamishri explained, "If we went in at three o'clock, we would be able to serve Thakorji *thal* and let him rest for a while before waking him up. We would be able to work according to his schedule and not inconvenience him."

Swamishri's focus has always been on Thakorji and his *seva*. He has never thought of himself.

On 28 February 1990, Swamishri was on the outskirts of Bochasan inaugurating the premises of Shriji Cold Storage.

Bhagvatcharan Swami was walking with Thakorji in his hand. Swamishri performed *pujan* rituals at the main door and then untied the *nadachhadi* with Thakorji at his side. Swamishri and Bhagvatcharan Swami entered the storage factory.

The flooring was very peculiar. It was made of wooden planks so that sacks of potatoes placed on them would cool evenly. Swamishri walked into the factory and consecrated the machinery and rooms with flowers.

All of a sudden, there was a loud thud. Swamishri turned around and noticed that Bhagvatcharan Swami had fallen through a weak plank. He had tried to maintain his balance and save Thakorji but had failed. Harikrishna Maharaj had fallen out of his hands.

Swamishri rushed over to Harikrishna Maharaj and picked him up. He started massaging his whole body with his fingers. Tears welled up in Swamishri's eyes as he started apologizing to his beloved Thakorji.

Swamishri finished the *padhramani* at the factory and got back to the car. He turned Harikrishna Maharaj towards him and kept apologizing, "Bhagwan Swaminarayan…O…Harikrishna Maharaj… My Lord…Forgive me…I am sorry…." Swamishri's voice was barely a murmur as he conversed with Harikrishna Maharaj.

Swamishri arrived in the assembly and sat quietly as Viveksagar Swami finished his speech. Then, Swamishri was given the microphone to speak.

He attempted to speak and got through about three minutes when his eyes again welled with tears and his voice choked with emotion. The pain of Thakoriji's fall was still hurting Swamishri. He pushed the microphone away and concluded the assembly.

In 1980, the same had happened when Thakorji had fallen from the top tier of a caravan while Swamishri and the sadhus were travelling in America. It was nobody's fault, yet Swamishri performed 25 *dandvats* in the caravan and offered *thal* to Thakorji, repeatedly saying, "Please forgive me. It was my fault. Please forgive me…"

Swamishri was quiet the rest of the way – apologizing to Harikrishna Maharaj.

Swamishri's feelings towards Harikrishna Maharaj's *murti* is not mere devotion. It is *astikta* – the ultimate level of faith and spirituality.

Another symbol of his *astikta* is mandirs. Swamishri has built traditional mandirs around the world that are alive with spiritual and cultural activities. These mandirs are not just marvels of ancient Indian architecture. They are a symbol of Swamishri's faith in Bhagwan Swaminarayan. Worldwide, he has inspired over 800 mandirs.

These mandirs are a haven for spiritual and religious activities that infuse *astikta* in those that visit them. Swaminarayan Akshardham in New Delhi, and traditional mandirs in London, Nairobi, Chicago, Houston, Atlanta and Toronto inspire hundreds of thousands of individuals to live morally pure and spiritually enriched lives.

Hundreds of people leave the campuses of these magnificent mandirs with a revived sense of faith and belief in God.

Mahendrabhai Jamnadas Amin would always house sadhus when they visited Nadiad. In fact, he had been doing so since Yogiji Maharaj's time. His wife, Bhanuben, had always been a firm believer in community service.

One afternoon, Mahendrabhai came home after talking to Swamishri about the plans for the new mandir in Vaso. He started telling his wife about it, but she wasn't too impressed, "Building mandirs is like piling stones on top of each other. Your Swami should build hospitals and community centres to help the needy." Mahendrabhai decided it was best not to argue.

That evening, Swamishri came to Mahendrabhai's house. Swamishri started talking to Mahendrabhai and his male relatives about the Vaso mandir, "The mandir will be fabulous. It's a shame that some people do not understand the importance of a mandir. They think that these mandirs are just lifeless stone structures. They are a source of spirituality and values. There is a time in everyone's life when they need solace and comfort. These mandirs provide that comfort and peace. That is why we build mandirs."

Bhanuben was sitting in a nearby room and heard Swamishri's discourse. She immediately realized her mistake. She felt a surge of devotion overflow in her heart. Swamishri's talks had breathed a sense of faith and conviction in her. She was convinced that Swamishri's mandirs breathed spirituality.

Swamishri's intense faith in God has inspired many atheists and agnostics to believe in the existence of God.

On 10 November 2005, successful entrepreneur Bipinbhai Kotak came to visit Swaminarayan Akshardham in New Delhi. After being overwhelmed by his complete tour of the complex, the biggest surprise for Bipinbhai was when he came for Swamishri's darshan. His atheistic son fell at Swamishri's feet!

His son explained, "I am an atheist and I have never bowed to anyone before, but I feel different around Pramukh Swami Maharaj.

I felt a spiritual current jolt my body when he touched me. I think Pramukh Swami Maharaj is God. I have never felt anything like this before."

Ron Patel, the Sunday Editor of the *Philadelphia Inquirer,* was also touched by Swamishri's faith in God. On 13 September 1998, Ron Patel interviewed Swamishri for about 30 minutes. He asked many questions regarding God's existence and free will.

Swamishri answered all of them very clearly and consistently. He expressed his faith in God and his powers. Swamishri said that God is the all-doer and that whatever he does is right. Swamishri's conviction was so firm that at one point during the interview Ron Patel's emotions got the better of him and his eyes became moist. He said, "I have never met anyone that has so much faith in God." Swamishri's conviction and resolute faith changed the sharp news editor forever.

A famous entrepreneur from Dubai, Bharatbhai Shah, had a similar experience. One glimpse of Swamishri and he felt a sudden spark of faith.

Satish Gujral is a renowned architect and the brother of former Indian Prime Minister Indrakumar Gujral. He has never believed in God! He had never visited mandirs or bowed to *murtis*.

After hearing a lot about Swaminarayan Akshardham, New Delhi, Satish Gujral came to visit it with his wife in November 2005. The atmosphere was different. He was feeling spiritually inclined. He couldn't seem to figure out why, but he couldn't resist going to meet Pramukh Swami Maharaj. The rest is best described in his own words, "I am an atheist, but this monument has the power to make an atheist believe in God! The atmosphere here is beyond logic and reason. There is a divine power behind all of this. I can feel it. I feel that it is still with me. Don't get me wrong, I have seen the world. I have seen plenty of monuments, but I have never seen anything like this before. It is mind boggling. I am an architect myself and I have seen plenty of architectural wonders, but this is different. Given the limitations in India, this project should have taken about 50 years. Swamishri completed it in five! What they have made is truly remarkable. Monuments like these cannot be explained with logic. This monument is different to all others. It will attract many more people."

In New Delhi on 3 March 1994, Swamishri had told the Russian Ambassador Anatoli Drukol, "If you have faith in God, you can experience his existence."

Ambassador Drukol was very impressed by his visit to

Swamishri absorbed in darshan of and prayer to Shastriji Maharaj, Yagnapurush Smruti Mandir, Sarangpur.

Swaminarayan Akshardham, Gandhinagar, "The monument is amazing. Actually, I am an atheist, but I believe there is a lot of power in faith."

Swamishri often says, "Faith is the key to success. Faith is the key to a happy life."

Thousands of devotees across the world have the firm faith that God is always present on earth. The reason behind that faith is Swamishri's presence. He has nourished that faith on various occasions.

On 23 January 2006, Swamishri was in Mumbai paying a special tribute to Yogiji Maharaj. A youth stated his confusion, "Today, when they were singing Yogiji Maharaj's bhajans I thought of Brahmanand Swami. He was devastated when Bhagwan Swaminarayan left his mortal body for Akshardham. I am worried about what will happen to us in the future…"

Swamishri replied, "Always remember that Bhagwan Swaminarayan never left and is never going to leave. He will be present through the Gunatit Sadhu forever. He may change forms and be present through different mortal bodies, but he is always present. You will love and become attached to the other form too. Never even think that Bhagwan Swaminarayan has left this world."

On 7 November 1997, Swamishri was to leave London to fly to Mumbai. A few hundred teenagers had gathered for a special assembly in Swamishri's presence. One of the teenagers said that he would dearly miss Swamishri and asked, "After you leave, who is going to look after us?"

Swamishri didn't say anything. The teenager continued, "Today, all the *kishores* will receive a *mala* from you. We will turn it every night and think of you. Will you give us strength through the *mala*? You will, right? Promise?"

Swamishri spoke very confidently, "Bhagwan Swaminarayan has already promised all of his devotees that. You should never say things like 'Who will take care of us?' and 'What are we going to do without you?' Bhagwan Swaminarayan, Gunatitanand Swami, Bhagatji Maharaj, Shastriji Maharaj and Yogiji Maharaj are with you! Yogiji Maharaj had written a letter to a devotee in the town of Vyara. In it he said that we are never alone. God, the Gunatit Sadhu and all the *akshar muktas* are always with us. We must keep that firm in our minds. They are with us while we eat, sleep, talk and perform any other activity. If we don't have that understanding then we will always feel lonely. With that understanding you will be comfortable wherever you go. Remember that God is always with us."

Then Swamishri said, "Faith is the source of strength in life; the faith that God is always manifest. That he is always with us."

Bhagwan Swaminarayan describes the importance of understanding God as always present on earth in Vachanamrut, Gadhada I 37:

"There is a person who has bhakti for God in his heart. He understands that the manner in which the incarnate form of God resides on this earth, and the manner in which the devotees of God remain in the vicinity of God is exactly how they remain when *atyantik pralay* occurs. He also understands that God and his devotees possess a form; but never does he understand them to be formless...A sadhu with such conviction is so highly respected by me that even I place the dust of his feet on my head. In my mind, I am afraid of harming him, and I also long to have his darshan...In fact, the darshan of such a true Bhakta of God is equivalent to the darshan of God himself. He is so great that his darshan alone can liberate countless wretched *jivas*."

This is ultimate proof of *astikta* and the Gunatit Sadhu. Swamishri lives that *astikta*.

In Vachanamrut, Kariyani 11, Bhagwan Swaminarayan goes on to say: "Moreover, just as that devotee cannot remain without God, in exactly the same way, God also cannot remain without that devotee. In fact, he does not leave the heart of that devotee even for a fraction of a second."

This is the acme of Swamishri's faith and conviction. He cannot live without God and God cannot live without him.　　　　◆

Anahamkrutihi
अनहंकृतिः

Anahamkruti is the total absence of ego.
Anahamkruti incorporates all of God's liberating qualities...
that is probably why Veda Vyas mentions it last.
God is the all-doer and Supreme Being, yet he doesn't
have the slightest hint of arrogance.
That is the greatest evidence of his divine power.
The Gunatit Sadhu possesses the virtue of anahamkruti
through his constant communion with God.
It is the true definition of a sadhu.
The social norms of society encourage and
at times require modesty and kindness.
Anahamkruti is beyond that.
The Gunatit Sadhu is synonymous with
anahamkruti *because he has no*
'I', 'Me' and 'Mine'...

Pramukh Swami Maharaj is at such a spiritual level where no feelings of his own self remain. He exists to serve God.

Swamishri has lived for the betterment of society. He has worked tirelessly to help others. His work has impressed and humbled some of the world's greatest spiritual leaders and social reformers.

His practical knowledge has helped hundreds of thousands of individuals live by the teachings of the Vedas and Upanishads.

He has made more than 15,500 village, town and city visits to revive the traditions of Hinduism and spirituality.

He has created mandirs and monuments around the globe that will carry forth Indian culture for generations to come.

He has reformed society through anti-addiction campaigns, tribal care programmes, women's activities and disaster relief operations.

Swamishri has visited the homes and huts of thousands, paving a passage into their hearts and transforming their lives.

He has cared for millions through his educational, healthcare and environmental initiatives.

His unconditional love has set a standard for world peace and religious harmony.

His dedication has helped BAPS Swaminarayan Sanstha grow from a small local organization into an international organization that has positively influenced the lives of millions.

Analyzing the seven decades of his pure and spotless sadhu life often raises a question: which is the most overpowering of all the divine virutes of Pramukh Swami Maharaj?

The answer is Swamishri's humble persona.

He is polite and simple; natural and transparent.

He never craves or expects recognition or praise.

Swamishri has been honoured and felicitated every day of the week for the past 40 years! He has been welcomed and received at the United Nations, the British Parliament and by the likes of President Clinton, Ted Turner and the Sheikh of Bahrain; however, it doesn't seem to faze him.

He is untouched by all his awards, accomplishments and fame. It is like a waterproof coating; he remains unaffected by it all. Swamishri doesn't accept or recognize the credit he receives because of one simple reason. He believes that he hasn't accomplished anything; it is all God's grace.

His answer to any compliment or reward is always: "It is all due to the grace of Bhagwan Swaminarayan and our gurus." This is his thought even in deep sleep.

The following incidents illustrate his profound humility.

The 1985 Suvarna Tula Celebrations at the QPR Stadium in London, England had attracted thousands of people from across Europe. Shri C.K. Pithawala, an industrialist from Gujarat, was mesmerized by watching a video of Swamishri's humble blessings at the end of the occasion. He came to meet Swamishri and became a devotee. An excerpt from Swamishri's blessings at the time of the Suvarna Tula reveals his humility:

"First, I bow at the feet of Bhagwan Swaminarayan who has given me this human body. I also bow at the feet of my gurus Shastriji Maharaj and Yogiji Maharaj for blessing me and accepting me as their disciple. They are the reason for my standing before you here today. They gave me the opportunity to serve you. My existence is solely dependent on them. I am fortunate enough to have been given the opportunity to serve BAPS and spread their principles and teachings. This *seva* is beyond my capabilities, but the only reason I have been able to do it is because of my gurus' blessings...Nothing is possible without God's grace..."

After visiting Swaminarayan Akshardham, Gandhinagar, the Police Superintendent of Bihar State, Ajay Verma, came for Swamishri's darshan. He said, "I have been longing to meet the creator of Swaminarayan Akshardham..."

Swamishri replied, "God is the creator. He inspires all of us."

On 3 January 1994, Kantibhai Kamdar, a leading builder and Jain community leader, visited Swamishri in Madras. He said, "Just

as Mahavir Swami had come in the fifth century, God has sent you to liberate us. Your work is amongst the best in India and the world."

Swamishri responded, "I am only a servant. God is almighty and the all-doer."

Deepak Jhaveri, a reporter for the *India Post* in the United States, interviewed Swamishri. He asked, "Don't you ever tire from the constant travel and your organization's growth?"

Swamishri replied, "It is God's work. I don't believe that I am doing anything. It is all due to the guru's blessings and God's inspiration. You only feel the burden on your head if you try to carry a pot of water. If you swim in the ocean, thousands of gallons of water are above your head but you don't feel a thing. Similarly, you should always pray to God saying, 'You are doing everything through me.' He will guide us through success and failure. You can work in a way that pleases him and produces results that please everyone."

Dipak asked, "Humility is at the foundation of your organization. This I have realized on my first visit today."

Swamishri added, "None of us believe that we have done anything. Bhagwan Swaminarayan does everything. God is the all-doer. It is that principle that lets everyone share the credit. There is no jealousy or hatred."

On 11 January 2006, Justice J.G. Joshi, a district judge of Surat, had come for Swamishri's darshan in Sultanabad. He said, "A few weeks ago, I attended the opening of the new court in Mangrol. The Gujarat State Chief Justice Bhavanisinh spoke to me about a conference for State Chief Justices he attended in New Delhi. President Abdul Kalam addressed them and said that Pramukh Swami Maharaj can succeed where technology and contemporary science have failed. Swaminarayan Akshardham is a prime example."

Swamishri was quick to reply, "No one except God can succeed. God is the source of energy for everyone and everything. He enables us to raise our hand and put it down. He inspires us all. He can achieve the impossible. Always believe in God. He is the all-doer. If he wants us to succeed, we will. If we do not succeed, there must be a reason. If we keep that understanding, we can always be happy. We have to understand that God knows what's best for us."

Swaminarayan Akshardham is something anyone would be proud of. People even brag about how many times they have visited it.

Whenever Swamishri is praised for creating Akshardham he lowers his head and gives the credit to others, "No, no, I haven't done anything. This is all because of Shastriji Maharaj and Yogiji Maharaj's blessings, Bhagwan Swaminarayan's grace, and the efforts that all the sadhus and devotees have put into it."

When the sadhus and devotees try to credit Swamishri and praise him, Swamishri immediately interjects, "You have got it all wrong. I haven't done anything. Bhagwan Swaminarayan and Yogiji Maharaj have done everything. Praise them. Praise the sadhus and devotees that have contributed to the complex. I am just a servant."

No one has been able to get Swamishri to take credit for building Swaminarayan Akshardham. They have tried in meetings, personal discussions and even satsang assemblies, but Swamishri always points to Bhagwan Swaminarayan and his gurus.

Scores of community leaders and politicians have praised Swamishri for building the cultural and spiritual complex. The sadhus and devotees have archived everything they have said. They have also noticed that Swamishri is unaffected by their praises.

Swamishri had just finished meeting a political leader when Brahmavihari Swami asked him a question, "Everyone that comes here can't stop talking about Akshardham and its creator. You, on the other hand, don't even notice that they are complimenting you."

Swamishri added, "Of course not. Why should I take credit for it? I haven't done anything. Bhagwan Swaminarayan has created it."

Brahmavihari Swami jokingly remarked, "I hope you can hear all of them complimenting you. We might have to get your ears checked!"

"No, no, I can hear everything," said Swamishri.

"If you aren't going deaf, why don't you respond or react to their comments?"

"I hear that they are praising my guru Yogiji Maharaj and Bhagwan Swaminarayan. It is their greatness, not mine."

The reason Swamishri is able to be so humble is his love and devotion for God.

A devotee once asked, "If God does everything, what do you do?"

"I am his humble servant," Swamishri replied.

Swamishri is God's servant and doesn't like to be compared with him.

If someone gets too excited and compares him to God or his guru, calls him God or calls him greater than God, Swamishri feels as if he has committed a grave mistake.

He instantly replies, "I am nowhere near God. I am his servant!"

The BAPS Youth Activity Coordinator in London, Krishnamurti Pattni, decided to get some edible treats for the youths. He asked Swamishri, "What should I get for everyone? Ice cream or Indian sweets?"

Swamishri replied, "Whatever you want to offer to Harikrishna Maharaj…"

"You are our God. God works through you…"

Swamishri stopped him and clarified, "Bhagwan Swaminarayan is God. I am his servant. I am a devotee."

"But doesn't God reside in you?"

"God resides in one who becomes his servant!"

Manubhai Madhvani, an industrialist in England, had organized a spiritual discourse. BAPS volunteers helped organize the event. He thanked Swamishri, "You deserve the credit for this event. We offer all our merits from this *katha* at your feet…"

Swamishri immediately said, "Offer the merits at the feet of God."

Impressed by Swaminarayan Akshardham, the chairman of Stock Holding India, R. Jayramanji, told Swamishri, "Akshardham is beyond my imagination. You have to be God to create such a monument."

"No. I am his servant. Man can never be God."

On 8 January 2006, Arvindbhai had come from Nairobi for

Swamishri's darshan in Surat, "Just as the soul breathes life into our body, you breathe life into Satsang."

Swamishri disagreed, "God breathes life into everything."

Shantibhai, an established businessman from Jamnagar, had brought special garments for Harikrishna Maharaj. The day he offered the garments, sales in his company started booming. He fell at Swamishri's feet and said, "Everything comes from your feet..."

Swamishri stopped him from bending down and said, "Everything comes from God's feet. I am his servant."

Swamishri arrived in London after his bypass surgery. He spoke to the youths, "We are God's servants. And that's the way it should be. Becoming God's servant is the greatest accomplishment. If you can't be a true servant and become arrogant, then you are bound to face miseries. Yogiji Maharaj was an ideal servant. He was never arrogant. He never said things like: 'This is mine...' or 'I did this...' He encouraged people to pray. He was always humble..."

An American youth came to meet Swamishri in Dallas, Texas, "I was born a Christian. We believe that God was present through Jesus. If that is true, who are you? Are you God or human?"

"There is only one God. I am God's servant. A sadhu helps spread God's message. No one can become God. There is only one God and I am his servant!"

Swamishri has never passed the chance to mention that he is a servant of God.

Swamishri humbly greets the devotees on his way to Thakorji's darshan.

Another aspect of Swamishri's humility is his bhakti for his gurus. On 12 October 1993, Swamishri met Muni Chandrashekharvijayji in Surendranagar. While talking to Swamishri, Muniji mentioned, "You have surpassed all of the previous gurus."

Swamishri looked down as if he had insulted or offended his gurus, "There is no way I can surpass them. I cannot surpass my gurus. If they hadn't laid the foundations, I wouldn't have been able to do anything. They have done all this."

Muniji realized that in Pramukh Swami Maharaj's eyes, guru bhakti was his greatest accomplishment.

Many people wonder what goes on in Swamishri's mind when he is honoured and felicitated in the presence of thousands.

A youth in London spoke his mind and asked Swamishri, "What are you thinking when they honour you in front of thousands of people?"

"They are honouring God. I am not capable of anything! They honour us because of God. They honour and worship the God in us. Why would they honour or worship me? I am a servant. We must remember to follow Bhagwan Swaminarayan's wishes and commands and try to please him. That is true honour."

In Houston, Pravinbhai asked Swamishri a question, "All these sadhus praise you in your presence, yet you remain humble. How is it so?"

"They are praising us because of God. If we don't remember that then we would become arrogant."

Eternal Virtues

"How often do you think that?"

"That thought never goes away."

If the first person singular, 'I', doesn't exist in his vocabulary, how can the possessive pronoun, 'mine' exist?

Swamishri is never jealous or competitive. He never tries to surpass others or try to stay in the lead. Swamishri is always content. He is always at ease with himself and with others.

That is why he can bow to everyone, even his disciples...

That is why he can respect others, even those that hate him...

That is why he can care for everyone – children, teenagers, youths and elders...

That is why he can laugh at himself, even in public...

That is why he can comply and apologize, even to a toddler...

That is why he is always happy, even amidst insults and stressful circumstances...

That is why he can be humble, even though he possesses God's liberating qualities...

That is his *anahamkruti* – his humility!

Sadguru Muktanand Swami says in a bhajan:

> "*Hu tale Hari dhukadā, te talāy dāse re;*
>
> *Muktānand mahā sant ne, Prabhu pragat pāse re...*"

meaning, "God resides in the great sadhu who is humble..."

These words by Muktanand Swami evidently refer to a sadhu like Swamishri.

Swamishri has no ego. He derives his strength from his faith in God...

That's why God works through him.

That's why God resides in him. ◆

Glossary

A

adadna vada	a fried delicacy made of crushed black grams
adivasi	tribal villager
agna	instruction, order, command
ajatshatru	one who has no enemies
akaran daya	extreme compassion; compassion with no cause
akshar muktas	liberated souls in Akshardham
amli	tamarind
aparoksh jnana	knowledge of the manifest form of God
arti	worship ritual of waving lighted wicks before the *murtis* of God
atma	soul
atmarup	one who has realized one's true self as *atma*
atyantik daya	ultimate compassion; God's compassion to liberate his devotees
atyantik pralay	final dissolution

B

bansuri	flute
bhagwati diksha	initiation into the sadhu-fold
bhandari	chief cook
brahmacharya	celibacy
brahmarup	possessing qualities similar to Brahman
brahmaswarup satpurush	God-realized Sadhu

C

chana	a type of gram, similar to dried chickpeas
chaturmas	four months of the monsoon season

D

dal	spicy soup of dissolved pulses
dandvat	prostration
datan	thin, soft stick cut from certain trees used for cleaning teeth
dehbhav	body-consciousness
dhabbaas	patting people on the back to bless them
dharna-parna	a fast in which one is allowed to eat only once every two days
dhun	chanting of God's name

F

farali	a special diet of fruits and certain foods sanctioned for Ekadashi fasts

G

galka na bhajiya	a fried savoury delicacy
garbhagruha	the inner shrine of a mandir where the *murtis* are installed
ghughro	a sweet delicacy

H

hari na jan	people of God

harijan	a member of the community traditionally engaged in cleaning public places

I

indriya	sense, through which one can 'know' and perform actions

J

jalebi	a sweet delicacy
jay nad	calling out loud the names of God and gurus in praise
jiva	the soul
jnani	one who is spiritually realized with the knowledge of God

K

kadhi	soup made of buttermilk, gram flour and spices for eating with various rice dishes
kanthi	double-threaded necklace, usually made of small tulsi beads, received by *satsangis* upon initiation into the Satsang Fellowship, and worn as a sign of their affiliation to Bhagwan Swaminarayan
karyakar	volunteer
kat vadi javu	to oblige instantly
katha	spiritual discourse
khakhro	toasted chapatti
khichdi	spiced, boiled rice
kishore	teenager
kothari	chief administrator of a mandir

M

mahant	the head sadhu of a mandir
mala	rosary
mathiya	a thin, fried savoury delicacy
maya	anything that deviates one from the worship of God. One of the five eternal realities or power of God used as the fundamental 'substance' of creation
mayik	pertaining to *maya*, opposite of divine
murti	an image of God
murti-pratishtha	consecration of *murtis* in a mandir

N

nadachhadi	a special sanctified string tied around the right wrist during rituals
nirvikalp samadhi	highest state of realization in which one sees only God
nishkam dharma	*brahmacharya*, celibacy
niyam	moral and spiritual disciplines, and religious codes of conduct prescribed by God, the Satpurush, or the shastras. Bhagwan Swaminarayan has outlined the basic *niyams* for all of his followers in the Shikshapatri

P

padhramani	visit by sadhus to sanctify homes or other premises
pagh	traditional head gear
palkhi	a palanquin for carrying a person
paneer	a cheese-like derivative from milk
papad	thin crispy savoury wafer-like delicacy
param hitkari	one who wishes for the best for others
paramhansa	'supreme swan'. A male sadhu of the highest order
parna	breaking of a fast

paroksh	non-manifest
parshad	a renunciant in white clothes
potlu	a piece of cloth used as a bag
pradakshina	circumambulation
pralay	destruction
prasad	sanctified food, blessed and consecrated by having been offered to God
puja	morning personal worship ritual
pujan	the act of worshipping
pujari	the priest of a mandir who performs the necessary rites and rituals
puri	small, flat and round fried pieces of wheat dough

S

sadhuta	saintliness
samuh lagna	mass marriage ceremony
sanskruti	traditions
sarod	a stringed musical instrument
sarvopari	supreme
satsangi	member of the Satsang fellowship. One who practises *satsang*
satyam	truth, honesty
seva	service
sevak	one who serves
shabdatit	beyond description
Shilpashastras	shastras which give details on the art and architecture of building mandirs
shiro	a sweet delicacy, usually of wheat flour, ghee and sugar
shraddh	rituals in memory of one's ancestors
sinhasan	throne for God
stithapragna	a stable state of the mind; one who is calm and controlled in any situation or circumstance
sud	bright half of lunar month
sukhdi	a sweet delicacy of wheat flour, ghee and gur
suran	a vegetable

T

tabla	Indian percussion instrument
thal	food devotionally offered to God as a form of bhakti
tilak-chandlo	'U' shaped mark made with sandalwood paste and a round mark of *kumkum* in its centre; denotes one's allegiance to the Swaminarayan Sampraday
tyagi	an ascetic, a sadhu

U

upasana	philosophical understanding of the nature of God as well as the mode of worship of God

V

vicharan	spiritual touring
vishay	worldly pleasure
vrat	a spiritual observance

Appendix

Pronunciation Guide

The diacritic ā is used to indicate the long 'a', which is pronounced as in st*a*r, c*a*r, f*a*r.

The transliteration of the root Sanskrit word for each virtue reflects the fact that in Sanskrit the final vowel at the end of the word is also pronounced. A Sanskrit word ending without a vowel is indicated by the oblique mark '᷂' at the end of the final letter.

सत्यम्	Satyam	भगः	Bhagaha
शौचम्	Shaucham	स्वातंत्र्यम्	Svatantryam
दया	Dayā	शौर्यम्	Shauryam
क्षान्तिः	Kshāntihi	तेजः	Tejaha
त्यागः	Tyāgaha	स्मृतिः	Smrutihi
संतोषः	Santoshaha	कौशलम्	Kaushalam
आर्जवम्	Ārjavam	स्थैर्यम्	Sthairyam
साम्यम्	Shamaha	प्रागल्ल्यम्	Prāgalbhyam
तितिक्षा	Titikshā	सहः	Sahaha
उपरतिः	Uparatihi	धैर्यम्	Dhairyam
विरक्तिः	Viraktihi	कान्तिः	Kāntihi
श्रुतम्	Shrutam	ओजः	Ojaha
ज्ञानम्	Jnānam	मार्दवम्	Mārdavam
शीलम	Shilam	प्रश्रयः	Prashrayaha
शमः	Sāmyam	कीर्तिः	Kirtihi
दमः	Damaha	मानः	Mānaha
तपः	Tapaha	आस्तिक्यम्	Āstikayam
ऐश्वर्यम्	Aishvaryam	अनहंकृतिः	Anahamkrutihi
बलम्	Balam	गाम्भीर्य	Gāmbhiryam

Acknowledgements

Bhagwan Swaminarayan, Aksharbrahman Gunatitanand Swami, Brahmaswarup Bhagatji Maharaj, Brahmaswarup Shastriji Maharaj, Brahmaswarup Yogiji Maharaj and Guruhari Pramukh Swami Maharaj for exemplifying these divine qualities and liberating innumerable souls in the process...

Pujya Ishwarcharan Swami for inspiring and guiding me from start to finish...without whom this publication would never have materialized...

Pujya Viveksagar Swami, Pujya Priyadarshan Swami, Pujya Parmanand Swami and the other sadhus who have helped in the compilation of thousands of incidents from Swamishri's life...

Pujya Yogicharan Swami and the BAPS Photography Team in London for the splendid photographs that have added to the quality of this publication...

Pujya Shrijiswarup Swami for the beautiful layout and design...
Pujya Anandswarup Swami, Pujya Vivekjivan Swami, Pujya Amrutvijay Swami, Pujya Amrutnandan Swami, Krupesh Patel, Akhil Patel and the Editorial Team for editing and refining the content of this publication...

Pujya Jnanpriya Swami, Pujya Shantmurti Swami and the BAPS Shri Swaminarayan Mandirs in Toronto and Atlanta for providing a serene, homely and productive environment to translate this publication...